TRAVELS WITH BOBBY

Hiking in the
Mountains of the
American West

BROOKS EASON

ISBN: 978-1-4834-2799-7 (sc)
ISBN: 978-1-4834-2800-0 (e)

Library of Congress Control Number: 2015905741

Lulu Publishing Services rev. date: 9/11/2015

To my daddy, for teaching me to love camping, and to Bobby, for going camping with me.

Climb the mountains and get their good tidings. Nature's peace will flow into you as sunshine flows into trees. The winds will blow their own freshness into you and the storms their energy, while cares will drop off like autumn leaves.

– John Muir

And so from the hills we return refreshed in body, in mind and in spirit, to grapple anew with life's problems. For a while we have lived simply, wisely and happily; we have made good friends; we have adventured well.

– Frank Smythe

My dad would often talk about wanting to go to Alaska or the Rocky Mountains, but there was always something holding him back. I never was able to figure out why he didn't do it. I guess he was in the same old societal rut—putting it off until one day you wake up and realize you're just too damn old to do it the way you feel it should be done. We can't ever let that happen.

– Bobby Ariatti

CHAPTER 1

Attack in the Night

Shook-a. Shook-a. Shook-a. Shook-a.

It was three in the morning. I was fast asleep.

Shook-a. Shook-a. Shook-a. Shook-a.

I started to wake up. Something was dripping on me.

Shook-a. Shook-a. Shook-a. Shook-a.

I sat up. Something was wrong. Bobby was gone; so was his sleeping bag.

Shook-a. Shook-a. Shook-a. Shook-a.

The noise grew louder. Then something struck my right shoulder. I raised my hands to protect myself, but it was too late. The attacker hit me in the face.

* * *

Bobby and I had started the day at work in Pascagoula, Mississippi. After lunch, we drove west along the gulf to Bobby's house and then to New Orleans, where we caught a flight to Salt Lake City. From there we flew to Reno, where we landed at 10:30 p.m. Our plan was to rent a car, drive south to Carson City, and find a motel room. The next morning, we would drive the rest of the way to Yosemite. Because of good weather and a misleading sign, however, we changed our plans.

The weather in Nevada was perfect—fifty degrees, no humidity, not a cloud in the sky. We headed south in our Hertz Thunderbird, the moon roof open, singing along with Bob Seger to "Roll Me Away." Then we saw the sign—Washoe Lake State Park. Underneath the words was an image of a tent. We had a tent—we were going to camp the next two nights in Yosemite—and it was an ideal night to sleep outside. I glanced over at Bobby; he shrugged. I took the off-ramp, and we headed for Washoe Lake.

It was midnight when we turned into the park entrance. A mule deer in the parking lot stared at us. We searched for a sign pointing the way to the campground but couldn't find one. Roads went to the left and right. We took the road to the left, along the shoreline of the lake. At the end, we came to a beautiful grassy meadow. Bobby and I studied the meadow. It was no doubt for picnics and Frisbees, not tents and campfires. We returned to the entrance and took the road to the right but found only rocky strips for RVs.

So we had two options—we could leave the park, continue to Carson City, and find a motel, or we could pitch our tent in the meadow along the lake. It was now after midnight. Wherever we stayed, our plan was to rise before dawn to get to Yosemite as early as possible. Bobby and I chose the meadow beside Washoe Lake. We would leave no trace, and we would not get caught.

The roof of my tent was mesh, with a detachable rain fly. The fly was needed only if there was a chance of rain or heavy dew or the night was cold. We pitched the tent without the fly and crawled into our sleeping bags. As we stared up through the mesh at the stars, Bobby and I talked of our plans for the weekend. Soon I was asleep.

I was still asleep—sound asleep in fact—when the strange sound began, when something started dripping on me, when Bobby disappeared without a trace. And I was just waking up when I was struck on the shoulder, then in the face.

The attacker, as you may have guessed, was the Washoe Lake State Park sprinkler system. After all, without sprinklers, there are no grassy meadows in western Nevada. Bobby, who is a light sleeper, woke at the first sound. He realized our predicament immediately, grabbed his sleeping bag and air mattress, and fled.

Next to my wife Carrie, Bobby is my best friend. If I really need him, I know I can count on him. Faced with a crisis, and with time to think, Bobby would never let me down. But at Washoe Lake, with no time to think, Bobby saved only himself. He escaped from the tent and left me lying there. And Bobby not only abandoned me, he also left the front flap of the tent wide open, with nothing between me and the nearest sprinkler head. When it made its next revolution, I was defenseless.

The blast of water brought me to my senses. I climbed out of my wet sleeping bag, grabbed it and my air mattress, and hauled them to dry land. I then returned for the tent, which was getting wetter by the second. Fortunately we had not staked down the corners. I was able to lift the tent and carry it to safety.

The emergency over, I turned my attention to Bobby. From the instant the sprinklers had started until now, he had not said a word. He had not helped, or even offered to help. I spotted him, standing near the lake, holding his barely damp sleeping bag and air mattress. He was taking it all in, absorbed by the drama. He was grinning.

I demanded an explanation: "Why did you leave me? Why didn't you wake me up?" Bobby mumbled something, but it was drowned out by the sound of the sprinklers.

We assessed our options. On the inside, my sleeping bag was dry enough to make it through the night, and our air mattresses would keep us off the wet floor of the tent. We returned to the tent, which was now on what Nevada without sprinklers looks like: rocky, dusty, and dry. Just before I fell back to sleep, the sprinklers stopped.

The next morning, my anger had passed. With less irritation, I repeated the questions I had asked the night before. But Bobby still couldn't say why he left me, why he didn't wake me up. He couldn't explain why he chose to stand by the lake, peering at the tent, wondering when I would emerge. All he could say was that he didn't understand why I'd stayed in the tent. I was asleep, I reminded him. He pointed out that it's not like he left a wounded comrade behind to be taken by the enemy or eaten by wolves. He asked why he and his sleeping bag should have gotten soaked while trying to wake me up and said there was no sense both of us getting wet. I responded that he didn't have to get soaked, that he could have kicked me and said something on his way out the door. Bobby knew I was right, but he claimed I would have been pissed if he'd kicked me.

We speculated about the cause of the attack in the night. The sprinkler was undoubtedly on an automatic timer, but we chose a better story. We imagined we were victims of a sadistic park ranger, a vigilant protector of the sanctity of the park, a Western Barney Fife. The imaginary ranger, a stickler for the rules, had spotted our tent pitched illegally on his meadow. He had flipped the sprinkler switch and watched with delight as we—first Bobby, then I—scrambled to safety. As we drove south toward Yosemite, I closed my eyes, trying to get a fix on the imaginary ranger with his evil grin. But all I could see was Bobby's grin from the night before.

Thus began the first of my travels with Bobby.

CHAPTER
2

About Bobby and Daddy and Me

I have been west. I camped in Yellowstone with my parents and sister on my eighth birthday, July 3, 1965. It snowed that day and was so cold my sister and I slept in the same sleeping bag. I also went on two wonderful raft trips with my daddy in the early nineties—on the Colorado through the Grand Canyon and on the Middle Fork of the Salmon in Idaho. I did not go on a real hiking trip to the West, however, until September 1996, when my friend Bobby Ariatti and I traveled to Yosemite via Washoe Lake. Since then, Bobby and I have returned to the mountains of the West nearly every year. In the years after our trip to Yosemite, we went to Glacier National Park, Grand Teton National Park, the Cascades in Washington, the Wind River Range in Wyoming, and back to Glacier. On two of the trips—to Yosemite and the Cascades—Bobby and I went alone. On the others, we had company. My travels with Bobby have been among the great joys of my life. This is the story of our first six trips together, but we have been on many more since then.

Bobby and I are both lawyers. When we started our travels, he was forty-three and I was thirty-nine. He worked as a corporate lawyer at a shipyard in Pascagoula that builds warships for the Navy, and I worked at a law firm in Jackson, Mississippi. My firm and I represented the shipyard. Nearly two decades have now passed since the sprinkler attack in Nevada. We're both still working as lawyers, but Bobby will soon retire and spend more time doing what we both love to do. I'm still in Jackson. I've changed law firms twice, but I still represent the shipyard.

* * *

Bobby spent his early years in New Orleans. There is still a trace of southern Louisiana in his speech. When Bobby was ten, his father, who was fifty, suffered a massive heart attack. He survived only because a doctor friend was having dinner with the Ariattis at the time. The physician revived Bobby's dad, bringing him back from the dead. The doctor later attributed the heart attack to stress from Mr. Ariatti's work as a tile contractor, a business he inherited from his father and always despised. A diet of pasta, no exercise, and three packs a day of unfiltered cigarettes didn't help.

Mr. Ariatti decided to slow down, to enjoy whatever time he had left. He looked for some land for a weekend retreat in Mississippi and found a spot in the woods on a ridge alongside the Wolf River near the Gulf of Mexico. He spent his spare time in the fall of 1964 and the winter and spring that followed building a log home. The Ariattis moved into the log house on the river in the summer of 1965, the same summer I camped with my family in Yellowstone. Bobby, who turned twelve that July, immediately took to the woods and the water, returning to the cabin just to eat and sleep. The plan was to go back to New Orleans at the end of the summer so Bobby could attend seventh grade at Christian Brothers School. The tuition had already been paid. After his summer of freedom on the river, however, Bobby balked. On the day they were to return to the city, he sat on the porch and cried. Bobby's dad, who didn't want to go back either, couldn't have scripted it any better. Watching her baby cry was all it took to pry Bobby's mother away from New Orleans for good. They enrolled Bobby in a school on the coast and never went back to the Crescent City.

Life along the river restored Mr. Ariatti's health. After nearly dying in early 1964, he lived nearly thirty more years. The election of 1992, however, finally did him in. Bobby's dad despised Bill Clinton as much as he did the tile business and couldn't bring himself to live in a country over which Clinton presided. On January 20, 1993, the day of Clinton's inauguration, Mr. Ariatti suffered his final heart attack.

In the early nineties, when Mr. Ariatti was still alive, Bobby built a house for his own family beside his parents', using lumber from the pine trees he cut to clear the site. The log home and Bobby's house are on Bob's Road, named for his dad. Throughout his life, Bobby's dad refused to install air-conditioning in their log home, preferring to leave the windows open through the hot Mississippi summers. He had escaped the city and believed there was no point in living in the woods if you couldn't hear the birds and the frogs. Bobby remembers lying in bed as a teenager, sweating, thinking his dad was crazy.

Bobby and I often send books we've read to each other. After reading *Winter* by Rick Bass, which I had sent him, Bobby emailed me a note about his dad.

> One part of the book really turned on a light. That was the part about how we tend to become our fathers. My dad was a big outdoorsman. He had a camp in the marshes of Louisiana with two other guys (one was named Connick, the grandfather of Harry Connick, Jr.) They would spend three-day weekends down there either fishing or duck hunting. Dad was a rabid duck hunter.
>
> We used to watch Marlin Perkins together religiously. Dad would tell me stories of a friend of his who went to Canada every year to tag geese. Dad would try to describe the scenery related to him. Although he never had the chance to travel and experience Canada or the West himself, it was amazing the way that he could relate those second-hand descriptions with such zeal and credibility. He would often talk about wanting to go to Alaska or the Rocky Mountains, but there was always something holding him back. I never was able to figure out why he didn't do it. I guess he was in the same old societal rut—putting it off

until one day you wake up and realize you're just too damn old to do it the way you feel it should be done.

We can't ever let that happen.

* * *

On our trips to the West, on the trail and beside the campfire, Bobby has told me stories from his teenage years on the Wolf River. One was about an alligator and a goat. Bobby's dad raised goats. One year, some of them began to disappear. Bobby and his dad suspected an alligator; they could see a trail leading from the water to the goat pen. Mr. Ariatti's favorite goat bore a striking resemblance to a fawn. When it disappeared, he decided to put a stop to the problem. He went out on the river with his .30-30 rifle in their twelve-foot pirogue, a small canoe with only a few inches of freeboard. He found what was left of the goat and spotted the alligator nearby. Only its eyes were above water. The first thing he noticed was how far apart they were. It was a big one. But that didn't stop Bobby's dad. He pulled alongside, taking aim. Before pulling the trigger, however, he noticed something else—he looked at the front and back of the pirogue and the head and tail of the alligator. The reptile was longer than the boat. He decided to go back for a bigger boat and an assistant. He summoned Bobby, and they got out the longer aluminum pram and returned to the river. They again found the huge alligator, and Bobby's dad shot it right between the eyes. The gator leaped completely out of the water and then sank below the surface.

During the mid-sixties, Marines trained on the Wolf River and in the surrounding forests and swamps before they shipped out to Vietnam. The low wetlands resembled the jungles where they were headed. At night, Bobby and his friends would spot landing craft coming up the river. The boys would climb on top of the Ariattis' boathouse, wait until the Marines were alongside, and then attack with bottle rockets and water balloons. Sometimes the Marines would pull over and give chase, which is exactly what Bobby and his buddies wanted. Like the Viet Cong the Marines would soon confront, Bobby and his pals had the home-field advantage. They knew the woods much better than the Marines did. They would lose the Marines by leading them down trails booby-trapped with holes and trip lines. The Marines would either give up the chase and return to the river or wind up lost in the woods. When the sun came up, the boys would switch sides, becoming the soldiers' friends. They would mount their dirt bikes, ride through the woods until they found the Marines' camp, and sell the soldiers civilian food. The Marines were willing to pay top dollar to keep from eating C rations. Bobby's gang bought more bottle rockets and balloons with the profits.

A few years later, Bobby went to Vietnam himself. He graduated from high school in 1971 and started college that fall at the University of Southern Mississippi. It was late in the war, and the lottery and draft cast a long shadow over the lives of boys Bobby's age. College deferments ended in September '71, the same month Bobby started college. He remembers sitting in front of the television with his roommate, watching the lottery, waiting to see if fate would send either or both of them to Southeast Asia, perhaps to die. Bobby was the unlucky one. He was born on July 27, 1953, the day the armistice bringing a halt to the Korean War was signed. His birthday came up number sixty in the lottery. His roommate drew number 325. Bobby—the peace baby—wanted nothing to do with the war. Before he could be called up, Bobby volunteered for the Navy, relying on friends who said this was a sure way to avoid combat.

While he was in the middle of boot camp, the Nixon administration decided the draft was no longer necessary and cancelled it. Bobby's low lottery number was meaningless; he hadn't needed to volunteer after all. When Bobby heard the news, he came to a conclusion that seemed perfectly logical in his teenage mind. He walked to his locker and started to pack, thinking surely he could now go home. When the drill instructor spotted him and demanded an explanation, Bobby explained his reasoning. He had only volunteered for the Navy to avoid the draft. Now, the draft having been cancelled, Bobby figured he could "unvolunteer." This was only fair. But the drill instructor was both unsympathetic and unpersuaded and made it clear in colorful language that Bobby wasn't going anywhere; his young ass belonged to the United States Navy.

Not only that, but Bobby's friends had been wrong when they said he could avoid combat by joining the Navy. Bobby became the exception to the rule when he earned the distinction of being one of only two members of his basic training class of nearly seventy to be sent to Vietnam. In

September of 1972, just after he turned nineteen, Bobby was dispatched to Charleston, South Carolina, to await orders. He had no idea where he was headed, no notion what lay ahead. After two days of biding his time, Bobby received his orders. He was assigned to the *USS Cone*, an old World War II destroyer that until recently had been scheduled for decommissioning. Bobby had until the next morning to gather his gear and board the ship. At seven a.m., they hoisted anchor and headed for Vietnam.

After steaming south and passing through the Panama Canal, the *Cone* began the long voyage across the Pacific. The sailors soon learned why the ship had been headed for mothballs. Among other problems, the plumbing system was obsolete. To compensate for this deficiency, the ship would stop its engines and come to a halt so the sailors could bathe in the sea. Some of the crew would jump off the ship and bathe. The others would stay on the deck, armed and watching for sharks.

Once in Vietnam, Bobby learned that the ship's mission would be to shell the North Vietnamese shore at night as part of Operation Linebacker. Bobby was the captain's phone talker. Bobby's job was to stand by the captain and relay phone messages and coordinates for targets. Bobby got the job because he was the only one on the crew who could remember what was said and repeat it, perhaps because he was the only one who wasn't stoned. Bobby had gone to Catholic schools his whole life and had never even seen pot, much less smoked it. But he was the exception. According to Bobby, they assigned an expendable crew to the expendable ship.

The crew wore self-inflating life jackets that were affectionately known as Mae Wests because of how the sailors looked when the jackets were filled with air. All a sailor had to do was pull the pin, and the jacket would automatically inflate. Bobby had never done drills at night with live ammunition. When they went on their first mission, he was scared to death.

As they headed up the North Vietnamese coastline, Bobby saw flashes coming from ashore. At first, he thought they were signal lights, but then he realized it was enemy fire. The shells exploded above the *Cone*, and shrapnel rained down. Their range was much longer than that of the *Cone's* five-inch guns. Bobby said they experienced incoming fire for what seemed like forever as the ship snaked its way closer to the shore.

Suddenly there was a huge explosion on the deck to Bobby's right. From the corner of his eye, he saw the giant fireball. He heard the noise and felt the concussion. In the instant that followed, thoughts raced through Bobby's mind. One thought dominated—volunteering for the Navy was unwise. But Bobby's acute hindsight couldn't help him now. Only the Mae West could. He grabbed the pin and pulled and headed for the passageway that would take him from the bridge to a lifeboat.

With his hand on the lever of the watertight steel door, Bobby looked back at the captain to see if he was coming. But the captain was still looking through his binoculars as if nothing was wrong. Then he looked at Bobby, saw his inflated Mae West, and asked what he was doing. Bobby pointed to the deck below, to the site of the explosion, and said they'd been hit. The captain then said, "No, Ariatti, actually that was *us* shooting at *them*."

This news gave Bobby mixed emotions. He was relieved, but he felt like an idiot. He walked back over to the captain and resumed his station. In a minute or two, the captain looked at Bobby again, reached into his pocket, slowly pulled out his pocketknife, opened it, and poked a hole in Bobby's Mae West. Before their next mission, and several after that, the captain asked if Bobby planned to go for a swim. But Bobby never pulled the pin again, and he never went for a swim. In March 1973, shortly after the January ceasefire, he came home to Mississippi.

A year after returning home, Bobby married Stephanie, his high school sweetheart. The wedding was on June 29, 1974. Bobby had fought in Vietnam and was a married man before he turned twenty-one. He and Stephanie have three children: Derek, born in 1980; Kristen, born in 1986; and Allison, a surprise, who came along in 1994 just before Bobby turned forty-one.

When I first wrote this chapter, I spelled Bobby's son's name Derek. I sent the draft to Bobby, and he emailed a correction:

> Derek is spelled "Derrick." (For your information, the reason for the spelling was that I had invested all the money I had saved by 1980 in an oil venture with a guy who had drilled nine holes in the last two years, all successful. We liked the name Derek but superstitiously

figured that spelling it "Derrick" after an oil derrick was good luck. Struck out again. The hole was as dry as a frickin gourd.)

In addition to his career as a lawyer, Bobby spent many years in the Air Force Reserve, retiring in 2012 as a lieutenant colonel. I find it hard to picture Bobby in this role, not because of his failed effort to avoid Vietnam but because I've never heard him give orders to anybody. On our camping trips, Bobby willingly lets me be in charge. I make nearly all the decisions: where to go, where to camp, what trails to hike. Sometimes he'll offer an opinion, but usually he declines to do even that. Whatever I decide is fine with him. He's just happy to be there. When we're hiking, I'm always in the lead, except when we're going uphill and I can't keep up.

Bobby is a great traveling companion for other reasons as well. As we plan our trips, he's like a little boy waiting for Christmas, and when we get there, it's like Christmas morning. He marvels at the beauty of the mountains. His excitement is contagious. Bobby is also great around a campfire. In the Southern tradition, he is a wonderful storyteller. Whether being serious or funny, sober or not, Bobby is always good company. I have loved our travels together, but I think he's loved them even more. Years after the six trips described in this book, he wrote this to me:

> Our trips have always been enjoyable at the time, but they have become even more enjoyable after having the chance to age over the years in the cells that contain my memories. It's like special times you remember with your family. A whole year may pass, but what you remember about it after it has come and gone is the one experience that has become part of your soul—going fishing or duck hunting with your dad or waking up in the wilderness, crawling out of the warmth of your sleeping bag, and watching the sun come up over a mountain with a cup of coffee warming your hands. For a number of years, if it weren't for our trips, I don't think I'd remember anything at all.

* * *

As for me, I grew up in Tupelo, Mississippi, best known as the birthplace of Elvis Presley. I learned my love for camping from my father, Paul Eason, the finest man I've ever known. Three decades before Bobby tried but failed to avoid Vietnam, Daddy tried but failed to fight in World War II.

Daddy grew up in Tupelo and started college at Ole Miss in 1939. After Pearl Harbor, he increased his workload so he could finish early and join the Naval Air Corps. He graduated in December 1942, a semester before the rest of his class. By the time Daddy finished flight school and got his wings, the air war in the Pacific was in high gear. He wanted to go, but the Navy brass had other plans. Daddy had done too well in flight school. He was assigned to be a flight instructor, to teach others who were bound for the Pacific. Daddy protested and made his wishes known, but to no avail. He stayed behind, never leaving the States.

In the summer of 1945, Daddy was stationed in Atlanta, training pilots to fly a large plane called a PBY. By then, the Germans had surrendered, but the Japanese had not. While on a flight in August, an important announcement came over the radio. The United States had just dropped a new weapon—something called an atomic bomb—on the Japanese city of Hiroshima. The young pilot at the controls of the PBY banked into a turn and headed back to the base.

After he was discharged in 1946, Daddy took advantage of the GI Bill and returned to college for one more semester—the one he'd missed—and one more football season. During the week before the game between Ole Miss and archrival Mississippi State, Daddy and several other veterans printed antagonistic leaflets to drop on the Mississippi State campus. Six of them drove the fifty miles to Tupelo, rented three planes, and flew south to Starkville. In their first pass over the school, the three planes complied with FAA altitude requirements. But it was a windy day, and the first drop of leaflets scattered widely. Most did not even land on the campus. For their second pass, the planes swooped low, ignoring the rules. The pilot in the lead plane, who had flown a P-47 over Europe in the war, flew so low his passenger later said he'd looked up and seen the top of the school's flagpole. The leaflets were dropped successfully, and the planes flew back to Tupelo. Daddy and his friends returned to Oxford, their mission accomplished.

Several weeks later, when Daddy was again home in Tupelo, he was confronted by an excited airport official demanding to know where they had gone in the three planes. Unbeknownst to Daddy and his friends, one of the planes had bullet holes in it. There was but one explanation. Veterans of the war were also taking advantage of the GI Bill at Mississippi State. When the enemy planes flew past their dorms, at least one of them opened fire.

After his one semester at Ole Miss, Daddy returned to Tupelo, where he lived a life of unsurpassed civic commitment and community service, spending six decades giving of himself to others. I am not alone in regarding him as one of the greatest members of the Greatest Generation. Daddy contributed in many ways. After retiring from the private sector, he served three terms on the Tupelo City Council and was chosen as Vice Mayor. He also was the longtime Chairman of the Tupelo Parks and Recreation Commission, helped build houses for Habitat for Humanity, and delivered meals to the elderly for Meals on Wheels. But these contributions are insignificant compared to the one for which he is known and loved. Daddy's greatest contribution was the gift of his time—thousands and thousands of hours of his time—to three generations of boys in Tupelo.

When he was a boy himself, growing up in the Depression, Daddy was a member of Boy Scout Troop 12. He earned Scouting's highest rank, the Eagle, in 1939. Shortly after he moved back home after the war, Troop 12 found itself in need of a new Scoutmaster. Daddy was young and single and had time on his hands. In 1947, at the age of twenty-five, he became the leader of the troop. Four decades later, Daddy told me he had thought he would take a turn at the helm for a few years and then hand over the reins to someone new. He had not imagined just how long his turn would be. Daddy served as the head Scoutmaster of Troop 12 for forty-five years, until he turned seventy. For another fifteen years after that, he served as one of the assistant Scoutmasters, continuing to attend meetings and camp with the troop. He enjoyed excellent health. He stayed in the hospital with my mother before she died in September of 1999, but until then had never spent a night in a hospital, not even as an infant. In November of 1921, when he was born, doctors still made house calls. Daddy was born at home.

Daddy married my mother in 1950, three years after he became the troop leader. His Scouts acted as if they had veto rights; they had to give his fiancée their stamp of approval before the wedding could take place. I did not fully appreciate Mama's contribution to Daddy's Scouting—tending to my sister and me while he went to meetings and on camping trips—until I had children of my own.

In 1951, some of the boys in the troop pointed out to Daddy what he already knew: that camping was the very best part of Scouting. Ken Kirk, the troop's senior patrol leader and a future professional football player, suggested the troop should go on a campout every month. Daddy agreed, and during that summer a tradition was born. Troop 12 began going on an overnight camping trip every month, without fail. Since then, in blizzards and thunderstorms, in bitter cold and stifling heat, Troop 12 has never missed a month. Not one, not since Harry Truman was President.

In March of 1993, the troop went on its 500th consecutive monthly campout. Former troop members who lived all over the country returned to celebrate and camp together at Camp Yocona, the Boy Scout camp thirty miles west of Tupelo. Among those present were men and boys who had become Eagle Scouts under Daddy's leadership over the course of six decades—the forties, fifties, sixties, seventies, eighties, and nineties. Daddy seemed to take it all in stride; he never seemed to realize that we had all come to honor him. I did not take it in stride and was far too emotional to say what I felt. After I got back to Jackson, I wrote Daddy a letter to thank him for teaching me to love the outdoors and to love camping, and to tell him that he was my hero. He still is and always will be.

Though accurate records apparently don't exist, it is almost certain that more boys became Eagle Scouts under Daddy's leadership than that of any other Scoutmaster in the history of the Boy Scouts of America. When Daddy earned his Eagle award in 1939, he became only the fifth Troop 12 Eagle Scout. I was the 125th in 1972. There have now been more than 400. Troop 12 went on its 600th consecutive monthly campout—fifty years without a miss—in the summer of 2001 and its 700th in the fall of 2009. Daddy and I camped with the troop at the 600th. We didn't camp at the 700th, which was the weekend after Daddy turned 88, but we went to the banquet honoring the milestone. One of the younger boys in the troop was asked at the campout to identify the Father of Scouting. The correct answer was Lord Baden Powell. The boy's answer was Paul Eason. Two years later, when Daddy turned ninety, he was given the key to the City of Tupelo, and a resolution honoring him was presented on the floor of the United States House of Representatives. Daddy died on July 1, 2013, four months before his ninety-second birthday. On the second weekend of January 2014, Troop 12 went camping for the 750th month in a row. The troop had tee shirts printed with Daddy's picture on the front and back. I got one for everybody in my family and my sister's, and I wear mine often.

Not surprisingly, my first memories of camping are the result of Daddy's involvement in Scouting, but they are of camping trips I was too young to attend. I remember watching Daddy pack his backpack, preparing for a trip to one of the many places around Tupelo where the troop camped. When he came home at the end of the weekend, he would pick me up and rub his whiskers on the back of my neck. I would inhale the wonderful, mysterious smell of campfire smoke, a smell I still love. I couldn't wait until I was old enough to go.

Daddy took our family—my older sister, my mother, and me—on camping trips a number of times even before I became a Scout. Every summer, my sister and I would each get to take a friend to Camp Yocona. We hiked, canoed, and fished. Daddy taught me how to split firewood, build a fire, and pitch a tent.

In 1968, I turned eleven and was finally old enough to join the Scout troop. I didn't miss a single campout for the next four years. We camped and hiked at the Civil War battlefields of Shiloh and Brice's Crossroads, built a rope bridge across the river at Tishomingo State Park, and sat by campfires listening on the radio to Archie Manning's heroics as the quarterback for Ole Miss.

The most memorable campouts were the worst ones. Every spring, the troop went on a canoe trip, usually on Bear Creek in northwest Alabama. Only the older scouts were permitted to go. The first year I was eligible was 1971, when I was 13. That February, a rare snow had fallen in Tupelo, and I had broken my arm in a sledding accident. But I wouldn't let that stop me. When it was time for the canoe trip in March, I persuaded my doctor to let me go with a plastic bag over my cast, and I persuaded two of my friends to let me ride in the canoe with them. I sat in the middle, unable to paddle.

Shortly after the canoes were launched, trouble started. The water was too high and too fast. At least half the canoes, including Daddy's, capsized at some point on the first day of the three-day trip. Gear that had not been tied down either sank or floated away. Sleeping bags and clothes got soaked.

That night, it rained hard, and the river rose several more feet. The next morning, the troop was evenly divided. Those who had stayed dry the first day, including my buddies and me, wanted to continue. Those who had capsized, many of whom had shivered through the night in wet sleeping bags, wanted out. Daddy studied the raging river and decided we had no choice. We spent the morning hauling the canoes and all our gear up a cliff and then across a muddy cow pasture more than a mile to the nearest road. A huge bull stood in the pasture, pawing the earth and shaking his head. We were ready to break and run if he charged, but he never did.

After I got my Eagle, Daddy talked about retiring as Scoutmaster. But that was more than three decades before he finally gave it up in his mid-eighties. A year or two after that, I asked him if he missed camping. He thought a minute and responded, "I think I've camped enough." Over his sixty years as a Scout leader, Daddy spent more than three years' worth of nights sleeping on the ground in a tent.

Even when I was no longer in the troop, I continued camping during high school, either with friends or my Explorer post, the Scouting organization for older boys. One January, I went on a hiking trip to the William Bankhead National Forest in northwest Alabama with our Explorer leader, Mac Heebner, and my best friend, Paul Coggins. The trail required us to cross the Sipsey River, which was swollen from heavy rains. We walked along the bank until we came to a tree that had fallen across the river. Without hesitation, Mac climbed up on the tree and walked across. Paul looked at me, shrugged his shoulders, and followed. The two reached the other side and then peered back at me. I thought they were insane, especially Mac, who was supposed to be an adult. The river sped past in a muddy torrent. The temperature was in the thirties, and my pack was heavy. Falling could very well be fatal. Resisting peer pressure and showing what I like to think was maturity rather than cowardice, I sat down on the tree trunk and slowly inched across. Mac and Paul laughed, but I lived.

I started college at Ole Miss in the fall of 1975, got married the Saturday after my last exam in May of 1979, and moved to North Carolina, where I went to law school at Duke. After graduation, we moved back to Mississippi, and I worked for a judge in Jackson for a year before starting private practice. I have three children: Ann Lowrey, who goes by both names, was born in 1984; Cliff, named for Daddy's father, was born in 1987; and Paul, named for Daddy, was born in 1990. I also have four wonderful grandchildren, all of who were born after Bobby and I began our trips. Like Bobby and me, they love the outdoors and campfires.

I camped very little in my twenties. I made it to Tupelo a few springs and returned to Bear Creek with Daddy and Troop 12, but there was little else. In my early thirties, I realized I missed being in the woods and sitting around a campfire and began camping with friends. When my kids were old enough, I began taking them with me. I also went on canoe trips with a group of lawyer buddies. We paddled the Locust Fork in northern Alabama, the Nantahala in North Carolina, and the Chattooga on the Georgia-South Carolina border. But I still had not met Bobby, and I still had never been on a hiking trip to the mountains of the West.

* * *

It can be interesting to unravel the history of relationships, to consider the confluence of events that bring people together or pull them apart. In *It's a Wonderful Life,* one of my favorite movies, Clarence the guardian angel gives Jimmy Stewart/George Bailey a unique gift: the ability to see the world as it would have been if he had never been born. As history is recreated, and as George sees how others' lives would have been very different without him and all the good he has done—saving his little brother, who later saved a ship full of sailors; marrying Mary and raising a family; saving the Bailey Building and Loan—Clarence observes that each person's life has a profound effect on the lives of many others. Often, as in the case of George Bailey, a person doesn't fully realize the effect he has.

The lesson George Bailey learned applies to Bobby and me. Two persons who don't know it combined to bring Bobby and me together. A third who doesn't know it started us on our camping trips. Bobby and I know each other because of a judge who wouldn't declare a mistrial and a lawyer who wouldn't control his libido. We started camping in the West because of an eccentric airline president who made an offer we couldn't refuse.

First, the judge. In 1990, I had a trial in an age discrimination case before Judge William Barbour, a federal judge in Jackson. The plaintiff had been laid off by a natural gas refinery at the age of sixty-five. I represented the refinery. The plaintiff had a lousy discrimination case, but he was a nice man with a disabled wife. It was hard not to feel sorry for him.

After closing arguments, I talked to the alternate juror, who was not permitted to participate in deliberations and had been excused. She assured me the jury would make short work of the case and rule in my client's favor. I waited through the day, but the jury did not return a verdict. Late that afternoon, Judge Barbour summoned the lawyers to his chambers. He showed us a note from the jury's foreman that said they were hopelessly deadlocked. The judge first proposed declaring a mistrial. Just as he was about to summon the jurors into the courtroom to dismiss them, however, he changed his mind. He told us that a deadlocked jury can sometimes reach a verdict if they have a chance to sleep on the matter and think about it overnight. He sent the jurors home, instructing them to return at 9:00 the next morning. By 9:30, they had reached a verdict. Sympathy trumped the evidence. My client and I lost.

I then filed a motion for judgment notwithstanding the verdict, arguing that the jury's decision was not supported by the evidence—that no reasonable jury could have found as this particular jury did. Judge Barbour agreed and granted my motion. The plaintiff then filed an appeal, but the court of appeals agreed with Judge Barbour and affirmed his ruling. The nice man who was not discriminated against lost the verdict the jury had given him. He got nothing.

In the meantime, the shipyard in Pascagoula had just lost an age discrimination trial to another nice man in his sixties. The shipyard's general counsel read the court of appeals' opinion in my refinery case and found out I was the lawyer who handled it. He called and hired me to handle the appeal of the case the shipyard had lost. The court of appeals again ruled my way, and I was rewarded with a great deal of work. The shipyard has been far and away my biggest client since then. I have handled more than 200 cases in more than two decades for the companies that have owned it, all because Judge Barbour let the jurors sleep on their decision. Had he declared a mistrial instead, there would have been no verdict to set aside, no ruling to appeal, and no opinion for the shipyard's general counsel to read. Had Judge Barbour not changed his mind, the general counsel never would have found out about me. By changing his mind, the judge changed my life.

Now for the lawyer who wouldn't control his libido. I actually started representing the shipyard before Bobby started working there. Bobby had gone back to law school at Mississippi College in Jackson after Derrick was born. He would spend the week in Jackson and go home to Stephanie and Derrick on the weekend. After Bobby graduated, he went back to the coast to work as a law clerk for a federal judge in Gulfport. The judge was semi-retired and had a reduced workload, giving Bobby plenty of time to train and compete in triathlons, his passion at the time. There were two jail cells in the courthouse, but the judge was no longer taking criminal cases. Bobby turned one of the cells into an apartment of sorts, just as Otis Campbell did at the sheriff's office run by Andy and Barney in Mayberry. Every Sunday, Bobby stocked his cell with clothes for the week. Every weekday morning, Bobby rode his bike to the YMCA for a swim and then on to the courthouse, where he changed clothes in time to meet the judge for breakfast. At the end of the day, Bobby rode his bike home and then went for a run. Weekends were for races. It was a perfect setup, but after a few years, one of Bobby's friends convinced him that he was too old to be a law clerk and that he should leave the judge and join a firm. Several years later, the same friend and Bobby decided to leave the firm and start their own practice.

The new two-man firm did well from the outset. Bobby was happy. But then one day, the firm's young receptionist walked into Bobby's office and closed the door behind her. We'll call the receptionist Jasmine. As soon as she sat down, Jasmine started crying. Her tale came pouring out. The story she told, which Bobby told me beside a campfire in the Cascades in August of 2000, led Bobby to the shipyard, to me, and to our travels together.

Jasmine's boyfriend had been arrested for driving under the influence. Bobby's partner was also the City Judge. We'll call him Jake. Jasmine loved her boyfriend. She approached Jake to see if he would fix the ticket. He was immediately sympathetic. He offered to help, to use his power and influence to protect the young man's record. But Jasmine would have to go to the courthouse with Jake. They walked out of the office together. Jake, ever the gentleman, opened the passenger door of his midnight blue Olds 98 to help Jasmine in.

The rest of Jasmine's story was all too predictable. Along the way to the courthouse, Jake said he needed to stop by his apartment, and he insisted that Jasmine go in with him. Once inside, Jake put it to Jasmine directly. If she wanted the DUI taken care of, she would have to return the favor, then and there.

At this point in telling the story to Bobby, Jasmine was crying hysterically. She was having a hard time talking. Bobby assumed nothing had happened—surely Jasmine hadn't succumbed to his partner just to get a traffic ticket fixed. It wasn't even *her* ticket. But Bobby had to know. He waited until Jasmine calmed down, then looked her in the eye and posed the crucial question: "Did you go legs up?" The sobs resumed. Looking down, Jasmine admitted she had.

And that wasn't all. Jasmine said her boyfriend later came by the office to see her and took the opportunity to express his heartfelt thanks to the good judge. But Jake gave credit where credit was due. He coolly replied, "Don't thank me, thank Jasmine." When Jasmine finished her story, Bobby tried to salvage the situation. He said he would talk to Jake, make sure it never happened again. But Jasmine was inconsolable; she quit.

The story of Jasmine didn't end there. A few weeks later, Jake was studying his City Court docket. He spotted Jasmine's name; this time she was the one who had gotten a ticket. He smiled, picked up the phone, and dialed. When Jasmine answered, Jake was again sympathetic. He made an innocuous offer. If Jasmine would come in and help with Bobby's work, she wouldn't have to worry about the ticket. No strings attached. Jasmine, who was not a quick study, agreed.

Once again, predictably, a joint trip to the courthouse was required. As Jake and Jasmine drove away in the blue 98, Bobby shook his head. But this trip was much shorter than the first one. Jasmine returned in a matter of minutes, on foot. This time, Jasmine didn't go into Bobby's office and close the door. Instead, she told her story in front of the whole office staff. They didn't even make it to the apartment this time, she said. Shortly after they left the office, Jake pulled over and stopped. He suggested they "negotiate" concerning Jasmine's ticket. When Jasmine responded "not this time," Jake was miffed. According to Jasmine, he said: "So you'll do it for your boyfriend but not for yourself." This was too much even for her. She jumped from the car and stormed back to the office. Bobby's secretary, who heard it all, said, "That's it, I quit." She grabbed her purse and stormed out. Bobby wondered—what did *I* do? Why *my* secretary? Jake's secretary stared out the window, whistled, and pretended not to hear. She needed the job.

Bobby soon found out that Jasmine was not the only one. Jake was in the National Guard, and female subordinates claimed they had gotten the same treatment. Sexual harassment charges had been filed. Bobby could see nothing but scandal and ruin looming before him. He would close his eyes and picture the headlines. It was like an old movie, with the newspaper spinning before coming into focus. Bobby was weighing his options, considering going into practice by himself, when he got the call that changed *his* life. Another Gulfport lawyer said the shipyard was in the market for an in-house lawyer. Bobby took this as a sign. He interviewed for the job, and the general counsel—the same one who'd hired me—made him an offer. Bobby accepted, even though it meant giving up his private practice and commuting nearly an hour each way to and from Bob's Road. As for Jake, the other shoe never dropped. There were no newspaper articles, he resigned from the Guard, and the charges went away.

And last, the eccentric airline president. Since I've represented the shipyard, my normal practice has been to work with an in-house lawyer on the cases I've handled. I started working with Bobby shortly after he started at the shipyard in 1993. We tried several cases together and became close friends. We learned that we both enjoy the outdoors—camping, hiking, and canoeing. We planned camping trips nearby in '94 and '95 but didn't get to go because of weather or work.

In August 1996, I was at the shipyard interviewing witnesses. Bobby tracked me down and proposed a camping trip. This time, Bobby wanted to go to the West. He had just learned that Southwest Airlines was offering huge discounts as part of its twenty-fifth anniversary celebration. Herb Kelleher, Southwest's president, had decreed that all Southwest flights for a limited time would be twenty-five dollars per leg. Kelleher was something of an oddity among America's corporate elite. He led Southwest to great success by using humor and encouraging its employees to have fun. Flight attendants sang the safety instructions. They were known to hide in overhead compartments before flights, frightening the poor passengers who opened them. One year, Kelleher, who was not a teetotaler, gave away fifths of Wild Turkey to all passengers who flew on Thanksgiving Day. On another occasion, he resolved a dispute with a business rival by arm wrestling. Kelleher had a bout with prostate cancer, but he remained a chain smoker throughout his treatment. When asked how a man with cancer could continue to smoke, he offered a logical explanation: "I don't smoke with my prostate."

The Southwest twenty-fifth anniversary special was extremely popular. The catch was that Bobby didn't find out about it until the last day. To get the special fare, we had to book our flights by midnight. I called my secretary, and she faxed my calendar to me. Then I called home and got approval for a long weekend trip. We started checking Southwest's schedule and picked Yosemite, via Reno. Before the end of the day, Bobby and I had bought our tickets—$106.00 round trip, including tax.

CHAPTER
3

Yosemite - September 1996

With tickets in hand, Bobby and I began planning our trip. We ordered a map and trail guide and began studying them. We met with a young lawyer on the coast who had spent a summer working in Yosemite. He recommended we camp at May Lake, just north of Tioga Road, which bisects the park from east to west. We had to plan carefully. We were only going to be in Yosemite for three days and two nights and wanted to make every minute count.

After our meeting, we obtained a backcountry camping permit to secure a spot at May Lake. On the back of the permit were instructions for handling confrontations with bears and mountain lions. The instructions for the two were very different. When faced with a bear, the permit cautioned the reader to be passive—avoid eye contact, speak softly, back away slowly. With a mountain lion, the recommended strategy was just the opposite—yell loudly, wave your arms, act aggressive. If we faced one or the other on the trail, Bobby and I wondered if we could keep the instructions straight. And what if we met them both at the same time?

* * *

Our departure date was September 19, 1996. I should mark this date on all future calendars and celebrate it: September 19, the first day of the first of my travels with Bobby.

Even before the sprinkler attack that night, we faced a crisis that day. Bobby and I left the shipyard right after lunch and stopped by his house to pick up his gear before heading to the New Orleans airport. Just as we were about to leave his house, the phone rang. It was Stephanie; she was crying. Her grandmother had been gravely ill for weeks and appeared to be slipping away. The family had been summoned. Stephanie told Bobby he needed to stay. Bobby told her he couldn't; this had been scheduled for weeks. But as the conversation progressed, I watched as he weakened. His resolve was dissolving. When they hung up, the issue was very much in doubt. Bobby brought me up to speed. He said the funeral was already planned; he was to be a pallbearer.

So we had a dilemma. We could do the right thing, cancel the trip, and Bobby could stay home. Or we could flee to the airport and hope for the best. I turned selfish and gently cross-examined him: "She's been very sick for a long time, hasn't she? They don't know when she'll die, do they? Y'all have a big family, don't you? They can find another pallbearer, can't they? She wouldn't want you to miss your trip, would she?" Bobby was a compliant witness. He convinced himself it was a false alarm, that she would rally as she had before. We grabbed his stuff and hit the road.

But the doctors were right. When Bobby called home from Salt Lake City, Stephanie gave him the bad news. While we were somewhere over Texas, her grandmother had passed away. But Bobby was committed now. He was vague and made no promises about his return. I listened as he told Stephanie he would try to finish early and get home.

After he hung up, I asked: "Finish what?"

He smiled. "Depositions," he said.

I couldn't believe it. "Your wife thinks we're taking depositions?"

His grin, the same grin I would see later that night beside Washoe Lake, grew wider. "She might," he confessed. He said she knew we were going camping, but he'd used the fictitious depositions to justify going to California in the first place. She thought we were going camping after we finished the depositions.

A few minutes later, we boarded the plane. Bobby, who doesn't like to fly, had sneaked a bottle of vodka onto the plane in New Orleans to calm his nerves. After his call home from Salt Lake, he poured a strong drink on the flight to Reno.

* * *

The next morning, after my baptism at Washoe Lake, we headed south toward Yosemite, a wet tent and two wet sleeping bags—one much wetter than the other—slowly drying in the back seat. Maybe a sadistic park ranger had decided on his own to flip the switch on the sprinkler system. Or maybe it was an act of God, punishing Bobby for skipping the funeral and me for encouraging him.

We crossed into California and continued south past Mono Lake and the surrounding desert moonscape. The desert plain of Nevada stretched away to the east as far as we could see. To the west loomed the High Sierras, the Range of Light. We turned into the mountains and wound our way up toward Yosemite. I was driving.

Bobby's house on the ridge along the Wolf River is less than fifty feet above sea level. The storm surge from Hurricane Katrina flooded his pool and nearly his house. My house in Jackson is only two hundred feet higher than Bobby's. We are flatlanders, accustomed to thick air, but as we climbed toward Yosemite, the air got thinner by the minute. The western entrance of the park is at Tioga Pass, elevation 9,941 feet. As we neared the pass, taking in the magnificent scenery on the eastern slopes, Bobby and I both began feeling strange. The symptoms hit us simultaneously. We became queasy, then lightheaded. After we entered the park, Bobby checked the map and saw that we would head downhill from here. We pressed on, hoping for improvement. As the elevation dropped, our symptoms disappeared. We stopped just east of Tuolumne Meadows, elevation 8,600 feet, and got out for our first hike.

Our destination was Dog Lake. The distance to the lake was less than two miles, with an increase in elevation of only 600 feet. We left our camping gear in the car. With no packs, the only difficulty would be the altitude. Because of the symptoms we'd already felt, we took our time. The trail passed through lodgepole pines and across a shimmering granite slab that had been polished by glacial ice. After nearly an hour, we came to the opening at the edge of the lake. Dog Lake is surrounded by forest on three sides, but on the east end a meadow rises from the shore toward Mt. Dana and Mt. Gibbs in the distance. Unlike most peaks in the Sierras, these two have a distinct reddish hue. The day was beautiful, the mountains magnificent against the blue sky. We strolled along the lakeshore, searching unsuccessfully for trout in the clear water.

On our return from Dog Lake, we took a side trip to Lembert's Dome, a granite outcropping with commanding views of the surrounding peaks and Tuolumne Meadows to the west. The dome is named for prospector-turned-naturalist John Lembert, who homesteaded in the meadow in the late 1800s, building a cabin near a soda spring. Lembert studied entomology and became an expert in native insects. Like the dome, several moths and other insects he first identified bear his name. But Lembert was too trusting for his own good. His practice was to carry a large wad of cash, and he made no secret of it. Friends warned that this was dangerous, but Lembert declared that he trusted all who lived here, white men and Indians alike. But he was wrong about at least one of his neighbors. When several locals noticed he was missing, they went to his cabin to investigate. They found Lembert dead, a bullet in his brain, his pockets empty.

Bobby and I scrambled almost to the top of Lembert's Dome. The slope got steeper, and we stopped to reevaluate. The trail guide gave this warning: "Near the top, the going is steep and the rock is slick and smooth. You'll need good boots with lug soles, and if you're bothered by heights, don't try it. If you have doubts, remember that coming down a steep slope is more difficult than going up." I looked up at the slope and down at my feet. I remembered climbing a steep slope in the Grand Canyon on my raft trip with Daddy and having a terribly difficult time coming down, the descent made treacherous by the lack of thumbs on my feet. Bobby and I decided not to try it. If anyone asked, we would blame our lugless boots.

After climbing down from Lembert's Dome, we returned to the car and Tioga Road. We drove through Tuolumne Meadows and saw the river of the same name winding through on its way to the Hetch-Hetchy Reservoir. In the short summer at this elevation, the meadow is teeming with wildflowers, but we were too late for the show of color. The meadow also serves as a staging area for hikers and climbers heading into the mountains on the east side of the park. The Pacific Crest Trail crosses here, on its long route from Mexico to Canada. Four years later, we would hike a section of this trail in the Cascades in Washington, some 700 miles north of Yosemite as the crow flies and much farther than that as the hiker walks.

Continuing west, we passed sheer granite cliffs with rock climbers clinging to them. I love the mountains, but I am much too acrophobic to be a rock climber. Just watching frightens me. We stopped briefly at mile-long Tenaya Lake, surrounded by huge, glaciated granite domes. This lake is named for an Ahwahneechee Indian Chief. When Chief Tenaya was told he was to be honored in this fashion, he objected because the lake already had a name: Pywiak, which meant Lake of the Shining Rocks. As glaciers moved from east to west, they polished the granite, leaving a spectacular scene behind.

We finally reached the trailhead to May Lake at six o'clock, about an hour before dark, and loaded our backpacks. The tent and sleeping bags were now dry, the sprinkler attack just a good story to tell later. The trail up to the lake was only a little over a mile, so I made no effort to pack light. I took an oversize Teflon skillet and a heavy propane stove. I even packed a small cooler filled with beer, bacon, and eggs. With a mighty heave, I lifted my pack. Straining under the weight, I headed up the trail. We were hiking in what has become our customary order, with Bobby right behind me.

It was the longest mile and a quarter I have ever walked. The trail was steep, or at least it seemed steep, and we still weren't used to the altitude. May Lake at 9,300 feet is nearly as high as Tioga Pass. I soon regretted packing the beer and skillet.

Our walk began in a mixed forest of pine, fir, and hemlock and then passed between granite walls before opening on to a rock slope. The views from the trail back to the south were magnificent, and we stopped often to catch our breath and enjoy the scenery. We could see the huge granite face of Clouds Rest, illuminated by the setting sun. To its west we saw the most recognizable of Yosemite's wonders, Half Dome. In the distance was the jagged peak of Mount Clark.

The views were splendid, but after a time we grew concerned. We had been walking more than an hour and feared we had somehow taken a wrong turn and missed the lake. Surely it couldn't take this long to walk a mile and a quarter. The sky was getting darker by the minute, and there was no flat ground in sight for a tent. Just as we were starting to worry, we topped a rise, and there was May Lake. We could see peaks of the Sierras to the north. Rising from the western shore was Mount Hoffman, its peak at 10,850 feet. South and east of the lakes were groves of mountain hemlock. We picked a spot along the south shore and put up our tent. May Lake is a mile higher than Washoe Lake. It would be much colder this night, so we added the rain fly. We then gathered firewood, built a fire, and cooked dinner. We sat by the fire and drank the precious cargo I had hauled up the trail. The weight of the beer was hard to justify. I love backpacking, and I love beer, but without a pack mule it's hard to enjoy them together.

Our campfire talk bounced from subject to subject. At some point, we turned to dogs. My first dog was an Eskimo Spitz named Frisky. He was my most loyal friend from the time we got him when I was six months old until he met his end on the highway behind our house when I was eleven. Even before then, Frisky had a number of near-death experiences. His death on the highway was the fifth time he was hit by a car. Frisky's most memorable accident involved a grievous groin injury suffered when he hiked his leg to spray the back tire of a neighbor's car just as the neighbor shifted into reverse. As Frisky stood waiting for us to take him to the vet for repairs, he had the most forlorn look on his face I've ever seen, man or beast. Frisky was the best dog of my childhood, a shepherd mix named Heidi the dumbest. I told Bobby how Heidi had chased cars between the births of her eight puppies.

After I told about my dogs, there was a period of silence. Bobby stared at the fire and stirred it with a stick. I could see that he was contemplating a story of his own, wondering if he should tell it. He reached his decision and looked up. "Have I ever told you about Lucky Dog?" he asked.

Lucky Dog was an ugly mutt they got from the humane society when Derrick was four. Bobby let Derrick choose the new family pet. He passed over several handsome Labrador Retrievers and bird dogs before settling on a homely pooch that Bobby said looked like a cross between a swamp rat and a pot-bellied Vietnamese pig. I asked Bobby if Lucky Dog was named for the street vendors in New Orleans. He said it had nothing to do with them; Lucky Dog got her name because he and Derrick adopted her the day before she was scheduled to be euthanized. She was Lucky Dog because she was lucky to be alive. When Bobby finished telling me about her, however, I wasn't so sure.

When Derrick was little, he was a big fan of the rodeo. He watched a show called the Mesquite Rodeo whenever it came on television and wore a cowboy hat and boots every day. Purina Dog Chow ran a promotion shortly after the Ariattis got Lucky Dog. With proof of purchase labels from Purina products, you could get a custom tag engraved with your pet's name and your phone number. Bobby sent off the labels, and Lucky Dog's tag soon arrived in the mail. It came complete with an s-ring to attach it to the dog's collar. Bobby handed Derrick the tag and the s-ring and told him to find Lucky Dog while Bobby went to the workshop to get a pair of pliers to squeeze the s-ring together to secure the tag. Bobby retrieved the pliers and was walking around the house when he heard Lucky Dog yelping. Derrick had on his cowboy hat and boots and had Lucky Dog in a headlock. Derrick was steer wrestling and had bulldogged Lucky Dog to the ground. Bobby came running and saw why Lucky Dog was yelping. Derrick had decided not to wait for Bobby to put on the tag, but he wasn't trying to attach it to Lucky Dog's collar. Instead, he was trying to push it through Lucky Dog's nose. Bobby wondered what on earth Derrick thought he was doing. Then it dawned on him. Derrick had seen rings in the bulls' noses in the rodeos on television and at his grandfather's farm and figured that was how you do it. Bobby stopped him before he managed to push the tip of the s-ring all the way through.

The s-ring wasn't the end of Lucky Dog's troubles. About a year later, Bobby noticed that something was wrong with Lucky Dog. She scratched her neck and whimpered. When Bobby checked, he discovered the problem. Derrick was the perpetrator again; he had put a rubber band over Lucky Dog's head. Because it was under her collar and hidden by her thick fur, nobody saw it. By the time Bobby found it, the rubber band was buried under Lucky Dog's skin. Bobby took Lucky Dog to the vet and tried to explain, but the vet just stared at him. The vet anesthetized Lucky Dog, shaved her neck, and cut the rubber band out. He then sewed the wound shut. The next day, a friend came over, saw Lucky Dog with her shaved neck and her collar of stitches, and asked if she'd gotten a head transplant. For a time, she had a new name: Frankendog.

When I asked if Lucky Dog was still alive, Bobby smiled and said that was another story. Lucky Dog recovered just fine from her faux head transplant, but finally, posthumously, she suffered one last indignity.

One Sunday morning, Bobby found Lucky Dog lying on the edge of Bob's Road. Her life of pain was over. The family was already dressed for church, so Bobby put Lucky Dog in a wheelbarrow and covered her with newspaper to hide her from the kids. After church, Bobby changed clothes and began to dig a grave. He made it sound like an impossible task.

It was mid-summer, ninety-five degrees, and hadn't rained in weeks. Bobby said he would jump up and land with both feet on the shovel and it wouldn't go in more than half an inch. He stayed at it for an hour. He was sweating and panting but still didn't have much of a hole. He looked at Lucky Dog and decided to try to make her fit. He picked her up by the legs and lowered her into the hole on her back. But she was bigger than the hole; her legs stuck up above the ground. Bobby tried to bend Lucky Dog's legs at the joints to fold them down into the hole. But they sprung back to attention. Rigor mortis had set in; Lucky Dog would never be limber again.

So Bobby resumed digging, but he still wasn't getting anywhere. He was thinking to himself that he never even liked the dog. She was the kids' dog. And where were they? They'd disappeared at the first hint of work. As he stared down at the dog and the hole, the solution came to him. He looked around; Derrick and Kristen were still nowhere in sight. He sneaked down to the workshop and came back with the solution—his Stihl chainsaw.

Bobby said he checked to make sure the coast was still clear and then cranked the saw. He looked down at Lucky Dog. Her legs were sticking up like four branches, and Bobby sawed them off. When the job was complete, Bobby rolled Lucky Dog's body into the shallow grave and stacked her legs atop her body. He covered up all five pieces of Lucky Dog with dirt and returned the chainsaw to the workshop. Bobby said he was pleased with his problem-solving skills, that the only time he felt bad was when the kids came to see the grave. "They were talking about what a good dog she was. I decided not to tell them how I buried her. I never have." Poor Lucky Dog. May she rest in peace, if not in one piece.

After our dog tales, we shifted to stories about practicing law. I told about a case I had defended in which the plaintiff had secretly taped phone conversations with my client's employees. After my client fired one of them, he became the plaintiff's star witness. When we found out about the tapes, we asked the plaintiff to turn them over, and he and his lawyers agreed to provide them. As it turned out, they gave us the tapes without first listening to them, at least not carefully. Had they done so, as my partner and I did, they would have discovered that the plaintiff had taped himself bribing the employee who became his star witness. On one of the tapes, we heard the employee ask for money in exchange for his testimony. The plaintiff eagerly agreed but repeatedly cautioned: "No matter what happens, if anybody ever asks, this conversation ain't taking place." The plaintiff had a great case that was worth millions, but the judge dismissed it after hearing the tape.

Bobby responded with a story of his own. During his time in private practice, Bobby handled repossessions and foreclosures for a flat fee, traveling the state and foreclosing on mobile homes. He made good money, but it wasn't exactly the Lord's work. By the fire in Yosemite, he described a particularly heartless repossession.

One December, a client had asked him to help repossess a mobile home near the coast. The owner of the trailer got wind of the plans and outsmarted them. Before the repo crew got there, he opened the faucet on his well and flooded the yard. The crew didn't have a chance. If they'd pulled into the yard in their heavy truck, it would have gotten stuck for sure. Bobby's client was irate. He didn't just want the trailer; he wanted blood.

He called Bobby again, two weeks later. It was Christmas Eve; Bobby was just shutting things down. His client was in a festive mood and had an update on the mobile home. He'd just sent his crew back to the site. They got there after dark. The owner must have figured he was safe until after the holidays, had let his yard dry up, and he wasn't home to try to stop it. Bobby's client wondered if the owner and his family had gone to church. With nobody there, the crew was in and out in minutes. They hooked up the trailer and hauled it away.

The scene ran through my mind—the unsuspecting family at church, celebrating the birth of baby Jesus, while the repo crew did their dirty deed.

"What about what was inside the trailer?" I asked.

"It got hauled away too," Bobby said, "perfectly legal."

"The Christmas presents?" I asked.

"Yep," Bobby responded.

"Even the tree?" He nodded. The law required personal belongings to be returned, but they wouldn't make it back in time for Christmas.

I closed my eyes and imagined the scene—the generator still running, the trailer rolling away into the night, the lights on the Christmas tree burning, the unopened presents spread beneath it.

When Bobby told me this tale, I was reminded of other Christmas villains. But they weren't as evil as Bobby's client. The Grinch may have been cruel, but he was just a fictional character. And Dr. Seuss's tale didn't end with the theft of Christmas. The Grinch's heart started out two sizes too small, but in the end it grew. The Grinch returned the presents and trees he stole from the good citizens of Whoville. Ebenezer Scrooge was also no match for Bobby's client. Maybe he was a greedy miser, but he too experienced redemption, though it took three ghosts to bring him around. He sent a plump turkey to Bob Cratchit's house on Christmas Day, raised Bob's salary, and became a second father to Tiny Tim.

The true story Bobby told me, however, had no happy ending. Unlike Scrooge and the Grinch, Bobby's unforgiving client did nothing for the hapless couple who lost their home on Christmas Eve. He returned no presents; he sent no turkey. He even made off with the tree. When I think of Bobby's mobile home practice, I wonder: In the grand scheme of things, on the pecking order of housing options, when you lose your trailer, where do you go? And where did this family go? Bobby didn't know. When the family returned home from church, the joy of Christmas in their hearts, the children excited with the anticipation of a visit by Santa, no one was there to greet them. When they stood and stared at their empty lot, their hearts broken, the repo crew and the trailer were long gone. The couple were a latter day Mary and Joseph: they had no place to stay.

Bobby had a different view. When I suggested the comparison, he responded: "Mary and Joseph, my ass. You know good and damn well they spent the mortgage money on Old Milwaukee and Salem Menthols." I couldn't top the Christmas Eve trailer foreclosure, so we turned in for the night.

After reading my description of the trailer repossession in my draft of this chapter, Bobby insisted I had greatly embellished the story. He pointed out that the law does not authorize such a night-time raid, that notice and a hearing are required, and that a judge would never permit it. Bobby claimed, with his lifetime of ingrained Catholic guilt, that he wouldn't permit it either. He also said that mobile homes don't have generators. Well, maybe I took literary license in recounting the story, but maybe, just maybe, Bobby took campfire license in telling it.

* * *

On the drive down from Washoe Lake, we had reviewed the warnings on our permit about bears and mountain lions. That first night in Yosemite, I dreamed of bears: huge, fierce grizzlies with powerful jaws and three-inch claws. In my dream, I was surrounded; I had no place to hide. Just before they got me, however, I woke up. I checked my watch; it was three in the morning, exactly twenty-four hours after the sprinkler attack. I lay there wondering what had awakened me. My heart was racing, my senses alive. Then I heard it: a strange rustling noise. I held my breath, listening, and heard it again. A bear, one of the bears from my dream, was outside the tent.

John Muir, the father of Yosemite, wrote that "bears are made of the same dust we are, breathe the same winds and drink of the same waters. A bear's days are warmed by the same sun, his dwellings are overdomed by the same blue sky, and his life turns and ebbs with heart-pulsings like ours." Maybe so, but as I lay perfectly still and listened to the rustling noise, my heart was pulsing more like a hummingbird's. I nudged Bobby and broke the news to him in a whisper:

"There's a bear outside the tent." We listened intently. "Don't panic," I added.

"You sure it's a bear?" Bobby sounded skeptical.

"Pretty sure. I've been hearing him for a while. Listen, did we remember to hang the bacon and eggs from the bear pole?"

"What? You were supposed to hang the frickin food from the bear pole, *all* the frickin food."

"Shhh. I think I did. You think we should go check?"

"*We?*" His whispering was getting louder. "I don't even eat bacon and eggs. I knew they were bad for you, but I never thought they'd get my ass eaten by a bear."

We stopped talking and listened. Slowly I realized that the noise was not a bear at all, but the wind blowing the rain fly against the tent. Bobby realized it too. He spoke again, and this time he didn't whisper: "Is that what you've been hearing? Is that what you thought was a bear?"

I flipped on the flashlight. Like the night before, Bobby was grinning. And like Bobby on his first mission on the *Cone*, I was embarrassed but relieved. Bobby didn't say another word, and I didn't try to explain.

The next morning, we rose early, ate a quick breakfast, and headed back down the trail, leaving our tent standing. Bear dream notwithstanding, we would spend another night here. It took twenty-five minutes to walk down the same trail it had taken more than an hour to climb the previous evening. We had big plans for the day and, in hindsight, spent far too much time in the car. On this day, we were Yosemite tourists, not the backcountry hikers we liked to think we were.

Our first scheduled stop was the west end of Yosemite Valley. To get there, we continued west on Tioga Road, dropping thousands of feet. As the elevation changed, so did the trees. We passed from mountain hemlock to lodgepole pine, then through red fir, Douglas fir, and ponderosa pine. Along the way, we crossed over Yosemite Creek en route from its origin on the north slope of Mt. Hoffman to the north rim of Yosemite Valley, from which it plunges more than 2,000 feet to the valley floor. Near the western border of the park, we turned south and crossed the Merced River. After we passed through the Wawona Tunnel, we stopped to view the valley.

I had been to this same spot once before, when I spent two days and nights in Yosemite in April of 1989. On that April day, the valley was wrapped in clouds. I could see Bridalveil Falls but little beyond it. This day, however, was different. It was clear and cloudless, and the majesty of the valley opened before us. The view was framed in the foreground by Cathedral Rocks and Bridalveil Falls on the south and the massive brow of El Capitan in profile on the north. In the center, on the east end of the valley, stood Half Dome.

* * *

No words, least of all mine, can adequately describe Yosemite Valley. In the century and a half since the first white man set foot in the valley, however, many writers have tried. As author Freeman Tilden observed fifty years ago, "the national parks, insofar as they may lack anything, do not want for rhapsodies." Yosemite has probably been the subject of more rhapsodies than any other.

John Muir, the foremost advocate and protector of Yosemite, described the valley as "the Sanctum Sanctorum of the Sierra—the grandest of all the special temples of Nature." He wrote that "every rock in its walls seems to glow with life . . . as if into this one mountain mansion Nature had gathered her choicest treasures." Art historian David Robertson described Yosemite as the "global masterpiece" of nature's artists—"Volcano, Earthquake, Glacier, Wind and Water." During his one and only visit to Yosemite, Ralph Waldo Emerson recorded the following words in his journal: "In Yosemite, grandeur of these mountains perhaps unmatched on the globe; for here they strip themselves like athletes for exhibition and stand perpendicular granite walls, showing their entire height and wearing a liberty cap of snow on the head." Joseph LeConte described his feelings on seeing the valley for the first time: "I sit in a kind of delicious dream, the scenery unconsciously mingling with my dream. I have heard and read much of this wonderful valley, but I can truly say I have never imagined the grandeur of the reality." Horace Greeley wrote that Yosemite was "the greatest marvel of the continent." Tilden described Yosemite as having a "gem-like luster, a sort of fulfilling completeness, which makes its devotees cling to it as a first and last affection. They are lovesick swains and proud of it; and they will fight a duel with you over their superlatives."

Having been to Yosemite Valley, I say that all the superlatives are understatements and that exaggeration is impossible. As Emerson wrote after his trip west in 1871, "this valley is the only place that comes up to the brag about it, and exceeds it."

The reasons for the brag about Yosemite are countless. To start with, there are the cliffs and spires, Emerson's "perpendicular granite walls stripped like athletes for exhibition." The two most famous of these are El Capitan and Half Dome. El Capitan is perhaps the largest block of granite in the world. It rises more than 3,500 feet straight up from the valley. Half Dome (which was never a whole dome) is even taller. Its pinnacle is 4,748 feet above the valley floor—nearly a mile. Four Empire State Buildings stacked atop one another would not reach the summit. There are many others—Cathedral Rocks, Sentinel Rock, Sentinel Dome, North Dome, the Three Brothers—towering above the valley. The perpendicular granite walls are so tall that the rim and the floor of the valley have different climates. At the rim, the temperature is lower; different plants and animals thrive. The walls even create different climates on the valley floor itself. The north is the sunny side of the valley. Except at the height of summer, the base of the cliffs on the south side of the valley is always in shade. In the spring, wildflowers bloom on the north side of the valley. Less than a mile across the valley floor, deep drifts of snow remain.

The cliffs of Yosemite do not stand in silence, at least not in the spring and early summer. During those seasons, the granite walls are decorated with the sights and sounds of waterfalls, some of the highest and most beautiful in the world. The waterfall nearest the west end of the valley is Bridalveil, which drops 620 feet. The prevailing winds that blow the water from the falls across the face of the cliff give it the appearance of a veil and inspired its name. Across the valley is Ribbon Fall, which plunges from El Capitan without interruption for 1,612 feet, a height ten times that of Niagara. The Merced River goes over two beautiful falls en route to the valley floor, first Nevada, a drop of 594 feet, and then Vernal, another 317 feet. There are others as well, but the most famous of all is Yosemite Falls, which first drops 1,430 feet from the rim and then, after a series of cascades, another 320 vertical feet. Its total height, 2,425 feet, makes it the second highest waterfall in the world, behind only Angel Falls of Venezuela.

In the spring and early summer, all of these falls, but especially Yosemite, are extraordinary sights. In describing the waterfalls of Yosemite, Freeman Tilden wrote that "they flow as streams as far as they can go, and end their careers by jumping." But the jump is not the end. The streams that jump merge in the valley with the Merced River. The Merced heads down the canyon to the west and ultimately flows into the Hetch-Hetchy aqueduct in the San Joaquin Valley, which serves as a source of water for San Francisco. The wild water that begins as snow on the peaks of the Sierras ultimately arrives, tame as a housecat, in a bathtub on Mission Street. And after the tub is drained, this same water may evaporate, travel back across the San Joaquin as a cloud, and fall as snow in the High Sierras, only to melt in the spring, flow down to the rim, and jump again.

The most astonishing beauty in the valley is the vertical: the sheer granite faces and the waterfalls that grace them. But the horizontal—the valley floor—is beautiful as well. The broad meadows of the valley teem with wildflowers; the forests are filled with sugar and ponderosa pine. The Merced, flanked by willow and cottonwood, meanders from the east end of the valley to the west. Wildlife is abundant: mule deer, coyotes, and thousands of songbirds.

The rhapsodies about Yosemite all fall short of the mark. Pictures come closer. Millions of Americans have seen Yosemite through the photographs of Ansel Adams, who said that he knew his destiny when he first experienced Yosemite. Adams' devotion to Yosemite was such that a mountain in the park was named for him. Many have also seen Yosemite in the paintings of Albert Bierstadt. But no painting and no photograph can fully capture the beauty of Yosemite, its scale, its grandeur. For that, you must go there, as Bobby and I did.

* * *

While reading about Yosemite, I thought what it must have been like to be the first to see it, the first to come into the valley and view El Capitan, Half Dome, and Yosemite Falls. I imagined walking into Yosemite Valley with no forewarning, having never read a word or seen a picture, having no idea what lay ahead.

American Indians have known of Yosemite Valley for at least 5,000 years, but most historians agree that no white man saw the valley until 1833 or entered it until 1851. In the fall of 1833, Tennessean Joseph Reddeford Walker led a band of about fifty men into the Sierras from the east. The men were fur trappers in search of beaver. Winter came early that year. By late October, the snow was already deep at high elevations. Game was scarce; the men stayed alive only by eating the meat of the horses that died along the way. Their situation desperate, they followed a stream to the south in the hope that it would lead them out of the mountains. But the party was disappointed; they found no escape route. Instead, to borrow Tilden's words, the stream flowed as far as it could go and ended its career by jumping. Zenas Leonard, Walker's clerk and chronicler, wrote of waterfalls that "precipitate themselves from one lofty precipice to another, until they are exhausted in rain below. Some of these precipices appear to us to be more than a mile high."

Walker looked down through his spyglass and saw the far different climate on the valley floor below. The meadows were deep in golden grass, the oaks red and yellow. Through the center flowed the Merced, the river of mercy. Walker knew the valley offered salvation: fish and game for the men and grass for the horses. He studied the vertical walls with his spyglass, searching for a passage to the valley floor. Seeing none, he sent out scouts. They too failed, finding it "utterly impossible for a man to descend, to say nothing of horses."

The party continued west through the mountains, supplementing their diet of horse meat with acorns, which may have saved their lives. As they came through the mountains, Walker and his men made another discovery—trees described by Zenas Leonard as "of the red-wood species, incredibly large—some of which would measure from 16 to 18 fathom round the trunk." These could only have been giant sequoias.

The men then crossed another stream and followed it south to its junction with the Merced, west of the valley. Had they turned upstream, it would have been a simple matter to follow the river into the valley. The Walker expedition instead turned downstream in search of lowland rivers and beaver. Two dozen horses had died, and the entire group had nearly perished. Despite it all, Leonard wrote that "every man expressed himself fully compensated" because of the "natural curiosities" they had seen.

Walker's decision to turn downstream instead of up postponed the full exploration of the valley by nearly two decades. When the first white men walked up the Merced into the valley in 1851, they were in search of Indians, not beaver. James Savage had come overland to California in 1846 and served under John C. Freemont. Savage then made a career as a thief, leading a large gang that specialized in stealing horses and cattle in the San Joaquin Valley. Gold was discovered in the foothills of the Sierras in 1848, leading to the California gold rush of 1849. To aid in his search for gold, Savage recruited Indians. He secured the necessary business and social alliances by marrying five different squaws from five different tribes. Savage gave the Indians beads and cloth for the gold they found. His take was often $20,000 a day.

By the spring of 1849, Savage had put up a store to supply the prospectors streaming into the area. The store was built at what later became known as Big Oak Flat, about thirty miles west of Yosemite Valley. To avoid conflicts between miners and the Indians under his control, Savage then moved farther east into the mountains, but the Indians who lived upriver considered him a trespasser and attempted a raid. Further encroachments led to more attacks by the mountain tribes. In December of 1850, Savage discovered that Indians had plundered two of his posts, killing three of his clerks and stealing his horses and cattle. Savage wanted to retaliate immediately. A consummate entrepreneur, he also saw an opportunity for personal gain. He called on the governor and convinced him to create the Mariposa Battalion. The 180 men who volunteered provided their own horses and firearms. The state paid for their food and other provisions, all purchased from Savage himself, the only supplier in the area.

In March of 1851, Savage and the battalion pushed east into the Sierras. They planned to find the mountain tribes and offer them a choice—peace, land, and food if they agreed to move to a reservation on the plain, war if they refused. Savage sent an envoy to Chief Tenaya of the Ahwahneechees, who came into Savage's camp alone. Savage warned that the entire tribe would be destroyed if they did not agree to his terms. Tenaya capitulated and left the camp to retrieve the tribe's members. The next day, he returned and reported that they would come but the deep snow would slow their journey.

After several days had passed and no Indians had arrived, Savage and a group went in search of them. Before long, they came upon a band of about seventy Ahwahneechees, mostly women and children. Tenaya explained that this was all who were willing to go to the plains. Savage and his men pressed on in an effort to find the rest of the Indians. The trail they were on led to what was later named Old Inspiration Point. Here the majestic valley came into view, and the men beheld what lay before them. Then they continued on to the valley floor and camped near the base of what is now Bridalveil Falls. Across the river and meadow to the north was the giant granite cliff that would soon become known to the world as El Capitan.

The valley was not yet called Yosemite Valley, but it did not go unnamed for long. That night, around the campfire, a young physician named Lawrence Bunnell suggested that they call the valley Yosemite, the name of one of the bands of the Ahwahneechee tribe. Some in the group objected to an Indian name and proposed Paradise Valley as an alternative.

One of the doctor's friends spoke in favor of the name Yosemite, and a vote was taken. Yosemite prevailed, and Yosemite it remains.

Many in the Mariposa Battalion were unmoved by the magnificence of the valley. Savage in particular had no poetry in his soul; he was interested only in tracking Indians. But the beauty was not lost on young Bunnell, who later wrote: "The grandeur of the scene was but softened by the haze that hung over the valley—light as gossamer—and by the cloud which partially dimmed the higher cliffs and mountains. This obscurity of vision but increased the awe with which I beheld it, and as I looked, a peculiar exalted sensation seemed to fill my whole being, and I found my eyes in tears with emotion." Bunnell and other members of the battalion named many of the features of the valley: Half Dome, Royal Arches, Clouds Rest, Vernal Falls, Nevada Falls, and El Capitan.

After the discovery of the valley in 1851, word spread. In 1855, J. M. Hutchings, a San Franciscan who was preparing to launch a new monthly periodical, led the first group of tourists to Yosemite. The trip was hard, but once in the valley the group spent "five glorious days in luxurious scenic banqueting." Photographers—Carleton Watkins and Charles Weed—and landscape artists—Albert Bierstadt and others—soon came to the valley. Through their artistry, the valley's beauty became known throughout the world. In 1864, just 13 years after the Mariposa Battalion first walked into the valley, Abraham Lincoln signed into law a bill entrusting Yosemite Valley to the State of California for public use, resort and recreation, to be inalienable for all time.

* * *

John Muir was born in Scotland in 1838 and came to America with his family when he was eleven. As a young man, Muir left the Midwest and set out on a lifetime of exploration. Yosemite, however, was not part of his plan. Muir started his journey after the Civil War, walking from Indiana to Florida. He intended to sail for South America to explore the Amazon. Unable to find a ship, he decided to go to California instead. He booked passage to Panama, walked across the isthmus, then caught a steamer up the coast to San Francisco. Muir disliked cities and crowds, so the day after landing he asked a stranger how to get out of town. The stranger asked where he wanted to go, and Muir responded: "To any place that is wild." The stranger pointed east. According to Michael Cohen, Muir then "followed his wild body into the wilderness." He caught the ferry to Oakland and set out on foot across the San Joaquin Valley. He arrived in Yosemite in 1868, four years after Lincoln signed the Yosemite Grant.

When Muir first walked into the valley, he reacted as Dr. Bunnell had nearly two decades earlier. Muir described himself as "bewitched, enchanted" and spent his first eight days exploring the wonders of the valley. Out of food and money, he then hiked back down the Merced, where he found a variety of jobs in order to support his simple needs so he could spend time in the valley and the mountains around it.

Through the decades that followed, Muir became Yosemite's leading advocate. According to Freeman Tilden, Muir was preeminent among the "large-souled men and women who from the very first days devoted themselves to the preservation of the integrity of Yosemite." Tilden called Muir the Western Thoreau. But unlike the reclusive Thoreau, "Muir was expansive—couldn't wait to tell the world about it."

Muir devoted much of his life to exploring the Sierras, hiking thirty miles a day and making numerous first ascents of the region's peaks. His friend John Burroughs observed that Muir's "communion with the mountains has stamped and molded his spirit; you can see the effects in his face and in the wistful, far-away look in his eyes; he hears their call incessantly." Muir headed to the high country for weeks at a time, returning when it suited his fancy. He pitied those who were bound by "clocks, almanacs, orders, duties." He studied the physical features of the valley and the high country and originated the theory that the valley was formed by glaciers. His view was dismissed by contemporaries with more formal training but is now accepted universally. In her history of Yosemite, Margaret Sanborn wrote of Muir: "No one has made a more extensive, prolonged, and reverent study of Yosemite Valley and the high country than John Muir. No one understood it better. Nothing was too insignificant for notation; the lisp of a snowflake alighting; fern fronds uncoiling; the distant calls of Canada geese winging high above the valley on winter nights; the silence following each big storm; the lunar bows in Yosemite Falls at full moon; the night shadows of trees and rocks cast by Venus' light."

In 1871, Ralph Waldo Emerson and a group of companions from New England traveled west to Yosemite. Muir was thirty-three, half Emerson's age, but the two became friends. Muir had read Emerson's poems and essays and wanted desperately for him to write about Yosemite. Muir felt that Emerson was the one man who could "interpret the sayings of these noble mountains and trees." After the two had spent days together in the valley, Muir issued a formal written invitation for Emerson to go on an extended camping trip to the high country: "I invite you to join me in a month's workshop with Nature in the high temples of the great Sierra Crown beyond our holy Yosemite. It will cost you nothing save the time and very little of that, for you will be mostly in eternity." Emerson was tempted; he was captivated by the younger man's passion. But he was in his late sixties, his health was frail, and his companions intervened. There would be no trip to the high country with Muir.

More than three decades later, Muir would have better luck when Teddy Roosevelt came to the valley in 1903. The roles were now reversed; Muir was in his mid-sixties and Roosevelt, our youngest president, was forty-four. The first night of Roosevelt's visit, a grand banquet was planned. Chefs had traveled from San Francisco for an event with all the pomp and circumstance befitting such an occasion. During the course of the evening, however, members of the presidential entourage noticed that Roosevelt had taken his leave. That night, by prior arrangement, he and Muir camped beneath the giant sequoias. Roosevelt later wrote that this was "like lying in a great solemn cathedral, far vaster and more beautiful than any built by the hand of man." The next morning, Muir and Roosevelt headed for the high country above the valley. They camped that night near the south rim. Roosevelt was thrilled when he woke in the morning and his blankets were covered with snow. He later declared that his escape with Muir and the long evening the two spent beside their campfire in the high country were the high points of his trip to the West.

Bobby and I often sit in silence by the campfire, hypnotized by the sight and sound of the flames. There was probably little silence around that campfire a century ago. John Burroughs, a friend of both of these great men, testified to their capacity for conversation. Of Muir, he said: "You must not be in a hurry, or have any pressing duty, when you start his stream of talk." But the President could hold his own. Again according to Burroughs, "Roosevelt talks his way through other people's talk like a snowplow going through a snowbank." But whatever the two men talked about, the break from presidential duties was just what Roosevelt needed. When they returned to the valley the next day, a reporter noticed a change in the President. Roosevelt had seemed tired and worried upon his arrival, but now he was bright and alert, the Roosevelt of old.

Muir wrote eloquently of the beauty of Yosemite and fought vigilantly to preserve that beauty for future generations. He was instrumental in the effort to make Yosemite America's second national park in 1890 after Yellowstone had become the first in 1872. In 1892, Muir became a founder of the Sierra Club and was unanimously elected to serve as its president, a role in which his efforts to protect the park continued. Even after Yosemite became a national park, the valley itself still belonged to the State of California as a result of the 1864 Yosemite Grant. Muir lobbied Roosevelt, and in 1906 the valley was receded to the national government and became part of Yosemite National Park. From his early years working as a shepherd in the park, Muir also knew the damage caused by permitting livestock in Yosemite. He fought against the use of park lands for grazing, describing sheep as "hooved locusts." Muir's last battle was to preserve the Hetch-Hetchy Valley, a slightly less spectacular version of Yosemite Valley twenty miles to the north. California Congressmen had proposed damming the Tuolumne River at the foot of the valley to provide water for the city of San Francisco. Muir headed the opposition, but the forces of commerce prevailed. In 1913, Congress passed the Raker Act authorizing the damming of the pristine Sierra valley. A year later, Muir died at the age of 76.

* * *

Bobby and I planned to return to the valley later in the day, so we didn't linger long before heading on our way. Our next stop was Glacier Point, which overlooks the valley from the south rim. To get there, we drove south on Wawona Road and then turned east, winding our way up into the high country. Along the way, we came to a car pulled over on the side of the road. The driver had gotten out and was peering into the woods. We stopped and looked out the window to see what he saw. Clinging to the side of a tree was a black bear cub. It was shy and adorable, a far cry from the vicious grizzlies of my dream. My bear dream, like most of my dreams, defied reality. No grizzlies live in Yosemite, the last one having been killed in 1895. Ironically, the name Yosemite is derived from the Miwok Indian word for grizzly bear. The cub on the tree posed briefly for pictures, then backed down and scampered into the woods.

On our first five trips to the West, Bobby and I saw a grand total of two bears—the cub in Yosemite and another black bear in the Tetons. We hiked nearly 200 miles, but we saw both bears while sitting in rental cars. On our sixth trip, our second to Glacier National Park, we saw bears for the first time without a vehicle to protect us.

Glacier Point provides the easiest access to the rim overlooking the Yosemite Valley. A short walk from the parking lot leads to a precipice that looks down on the valley floor 3,250 feet below. This walk, I submit, is too easy. To see a place this magnificent should require effort. Otherwise the experience is diminished. Here the magnificence is out of all proportion to the effort. The view from the rim is extraordinary. Cars moving along the road in the valley look like toys. The Merced River appears to be a tiny rivulet. Across the valley are Yosemite Falls, Indian Canyon, and North Dome. To the east is the profile of Half Dome, along with Clouds Rest, Starr King, and the taller peaks along the park's eastern border. To the west, to the left, is the brow of El Capitan. The panorama is so amazing it seems artificial, the product of special effects rather than the forces of nature.

Easy access to a spectacular spot in a popular national park spells trouble because it spells crowds. Bobby and I arrived in late morning, and Glacier Point was packed with the type of tourists that never stray far from their cars. Like John Muir, Bobby and I don't like crowds. Thoreau felt the same way. He wrote that he "would rather sit on a pumpkin and have it all to myself, than be crowded on a velvet cushion." Bobby and I stayed less than an hour at Glacier Point and then headed south for our next stop, the Mariposa Grove of Big Trees.

* * *

Mariposa Grove in the southern tip of the park is the largest grove of giant sequoias in Yosemite, with 500 mature trees ranging over elevations from 5,500 to 7,000 feet. I insisted on taking Bobby there because of my experience hiking through the grove in 1989. On that day, I had arrived at the south gate of Yosemite in early afternoon. It had been raining as I headed up into the Sierras, but by the time I reached the gate the rain was mixed with snow. As I gained still more elevation driving up to the grove, the mixture gave way to a beautiful snowfall, huge soft flakes floating down. The fresh snow was already several inches deep by the time I parked and began my hike. I was alone with the trees, trees that are some of the oldest and largest that have ever lived on the face of the earth. That was my first time to see the giant sequoias. The silence as I gazed up in wonder was absolute.

For those who have not seen them, it's hard to believe the big trees are real. In fact, the first reports of giant sequoias were not believed. The explorers who provided details concerning the height and girth of the big trees were written off as hucksters and charlatans. Even proof positive was rejected. A twenty-foot cross-section of a sequoia trunk was shipped east in 1875 for the Centennial celebration the following year. It was disparaged as a California hoax.

A giant sequoia is, by volume, the largest organism that has ever lived on Earth. It begins as a seed that weighs $1/91,000^{th}$ of a pound and, after many centuries, becomes a mature tree of two million pounds. The largest sequoias exceed thirty feet in diameter, a hundred feet in circumference, and three hundred feet in height. A single sequoia could yield as much lumber as an acre of virgin forest filled with more ordinary trees. The cinnamon-colored bark of a mature sequoia is two feet thick and virtually impervious to fire. Sequoias need fire, which clears out undergrowth and assists in seed germination.

Muir described the sequoia as "nature's forest masterpiece—the noblest of the noble race." He once spent a day with a pocket lens atop a large sequoia stump and counted more than 4,000 rings. Sequoia stumps are good for more than ring-counting. One was used as a ballroom floor; it accommodated 48 dancers.

The most famous of the sequoias in Mariposa Grove is the Grizzly Giant. It is more than a hundred feet in circumference but stands a mere two hundred feet tall, its top having been flattened through the centuries. The lowest and largest of the Grizzly Giant's limbs is more than seven feet in diameter, broader than the trunk of any tree in the forest other than a sequoia. The exact age of the Giant is unknown. Some experts have expressed the view that it took root more than 3,000 years ago. If so, it was a sapling when David penned the Psalms, an adolescent when Zacchaeus climbed the sycamore, and a massive giant when Charlemagne conquered the Saxons. Whatever its age, the Grizzly Giant is living and growing still. Muir said he never knew a sequoia to die of old age.

Even when they die, sequoias still remain. Along the road near the entrance to Mariposa Grove lies the massive Fallen Monarch. When I first saw this long-dead tree stretching hundreds of feet along the road, I wondered when it had fallen. I then came to a plaque near the base of the tree showing a photograph of a battalion of cavalry mounted on horseback in formation on the fallen trunk. The picture was taken in 1899. For the giant sequoia, the procession from dust to dust is a long one indeed.

During Emerson's visit to Yosemite in 1871, Muir made a last attempt to camp with him in Mariposa Grove. After Muir's invitation for an extended trip into the high country was rejected, he secured a promise from Emerson to camp together beneath the big trees. When the party arrived at the grove, however, Emerson's New England friends again intervened, citing fears that the frail poet would become sick if he slept outdoors. Muir responded that there was "not a single cough or sneeze in all the Sierra," but Emerson's companions stood firm. The outing was cancelled. Muir still had the joy of hiking among the big trees with Emerson, however, and during their walk Muir told him: "You are yourself a sequoia. Stop and get acquainted with your big brethren."

As part of an effort to draw tourists to the grove, two brothers—the Scribners—were hired to cut a tunnel in a sequoia in 1881. The tunnel was eight feet wide, nine feet high, and twenty-six feet long (the diameter of the tree). The brothers were paid seventy-five dollars. For decades, tourists enjoyed being photographed in their cars in what became known as the Wawona Tunnel Tree. Despite the tunnel, the tree remained healthy. Tilden was pleased to report in 1951 that it was still standing seventy years after the Scribners had cut their tunnel. In the heavy snows in the winter of 1968-69, however, the tree fell, though the tunnel may not have been the cause. Because cars had gotten bigger but the tunnel had not, the road had been rerouted around the base of the tree. The traffic had likely damaged its shallow roots.

Soon after the Wawona Tunnel Tree fell, David Brower founded Friends of the Earth. Brower sent to each of the charter members a seed from the fallen tree with this message: "One day, about two-and-a-half millenniums ago, when things were just right for it, a small seed began the process of putting together the exact amounts of air, water, soil, and solar energy to form what would be the Wawona Tree. Most of the seed was a wing, to carry it far in the wind. Within the seed itself was a wealth of vital, unique, secret information, packed with great efficiency in a very little space. It would inform the tree and all its parts, specifying . . . a long list of things a tree ought to know, each essential, none superfluous." The trees that grow from the precious few sequoia seeds that are successful know the things a tree ought to know for a long, long time.

For Bobby and me, our visit to Mariposa Grove was much less satisfying than my memorable hike through the snow seven years earlier. The trees were still the same—still unbelievable—but on this day the grove was hot, dusty, and crowded. The horde of tourists in the grove included many in Bermuda shorts and black socks, chattering like jays, cameras bouncing on their bellies. To me, this bordered on sacrilege. But then again, other than the socks, there was little to distinguish them from us. We hiked through the grove for an hour or two and then drove back to the valley.

* * *

We entered the valley on the road along the south side, towering cliffs to our right. We pulled into one of the parking lots and walked to the base of Yosemite Falls. In April seven years earlier, the valley floor was covered with snow when I walked to the falls, and they were as powerful as they were beautiful. An enormous wall of water crashed to the valley after dropping nearly half a mile from the rim above. The noise was deafening. The spray made a frontal approach impossible. In September, however, it was different. The winter's snow had melted long ago, and Yosemite Falls was reduced to a trickle. We were like Horace Greeley, who declared he had been swindled when he came to the valley in autumn and the waterfalls were dry.

Bobby and I next went to the Ahwahnee, the grand old hotel on the north side—the sunny side—of the valley. The Ahwahnee is a magnificent structure, born out of Park Service embarrassment following a visit by Lady Astor, who refused to spend the night in the valley because she found the hotels too primitive. The Ahwahnee was built of native stone and timber, granite and lodgepole pine. It was completed in 1927 and has served as the prize spot for guests to the valley since then, with a three-year hiatus during World War II when it served as a Navy hospital.

As part of the celebration of Troop 12's 500th campout in 1993, Daddy's former Scouts contributed money for a special gift. One of the organizers suggested a bronze bust of Daddy to be placed outside the troop's headquarters. I objected, pointing out that Daddy was not a bust kind of guy. He would be embarrassed. I proposed instead a raft trip on the Middle Fork of the Salmon River in Idaho, knowing I would get to go, albeit on my own nickel. A large group of former Scouts and their children, nearly forty in all, ultimately went on the Middle Fork with Daddy. I took Ann Lowrey, who was ten at the time and the one and only girl on the trip. But sending Daddy to the Middle Fork didn't cost nearly as much as his former Scouts had contributed, so my parents were given a second trip, a ten-day tour of California on which they spent two days in Yosemite and a night at the Ahwahnee. It was their only time to see the valley.

After walking through the hotel, Bobby and I went to the meadow outside, where a wedding was beginning. It was late in the afternoon on a magnificent fall day. The temperature had dropped into the sixties. The setting was more beautiful than any church. More than a century ago, Muir came to the same conclusion, writing that "no temple made with hands can compare with Yosemite." But Bobby and I didn't look like we belonged in any temple. In stark contrast to the wedding guests in their finery, we were dirty and unshaven, wearing shorts and boots. We skulked along the fringes, hiding in the shadows.

The afternoon was growing late, and we still had to climb the trail back to May Lake. There was time for one final stop in the valley. We walked out to the meadow just south of El Capitan and stared up at the massive granite face. When John Burroughs visited Yosemite, he described this scene: "El

Capitan stands there showing its simple sweeping lines as you approach, like one of the veritable pillars of the firmament. It is so colossal that it seems near when it is yet far off." Bobby and I spotted tiny specks of bright color on the face of the cliff. With our binoculars, we were able to identify the specks: rock climbers. Climbers from all over the world come here to take on what many consider the holy grail of their sport, ascending routes with colorful names: the Nose, Realm of the Flying Monkeys, Lurking Fear, Squeeze Play, Pacemaker, New Jersey Turnpike. The minuscule size of the dots of color emphasized the colossal size of the wall. Most climbers take several days to make the ascent, sleeping at night from hammocks hanging from the sheer wall. From our view in the meadow, reaching the top seemed like a superhuman accomplishment, but a paraplegic has done it, as has a nine-year-old.

Before leaving, Bobby and I wanted to take photographs of El Capitan aglow in the late-afternoon sun. Neither of us is a photographer, which is a shame because of the countless magnificent photos we could have taken on our trips. For this trip, we had bought wide-angle, panoramic disposable cameras, but they were of little use here. We had not taken into account that Yosemite is as much vertical as it is horizontal.

We returned to the car and left the valley, retracing our route to the May Lake trailhead. We stopped along the way at a store to fill up our water bottles. The store was closed, but there was a faucet in back. Seeing the wedding guests at the Ahwahnee had reminded us of our growing grubbiness, so after topping off our water bottles, we washed our hair under the ice-cold water. Semi-clean and refreshed, we continued up Tioga Road, climbing again into the High Sierras, more than twice as high as the valley floor.

Most visitors to Yosemite never get beyond the valley. But the valley is only eight square miles and accounts for less than one percent of the park's twelve hundred. Beyond the valley, in the high country of the Sierras, wonders abound. Muir described it well: The park outside the valley includes "the headwaters of the Tuolumne and Merced Rivers, two of the most songful streams in the world; innumerable lakes and waterfalls, and smooth silky lawns; the noblest forests, the loftiest granite domes, the deepest ice-sculptured canyons, the brightest crystalline pavements, and snowy mountains soaring into the sky twelve and thirteen thousand feet, arrayed in open ranks and spiry pinnacled groups partially separated by tremendous canyons and amphitheaters; gardens on their sunny brows, avalanches thundering down their long white slopes, cataracts roaring gray and foaming in the crooked rugged gorges, and glaciers in their shadowy recesses, working in silence, slowly completing their sculptures; new-born lakes at their feet, blue and green, free or encumbered with drifting icebergs like miniature Arctic Oceans, shining, sparkling, calm as stars." You could spend a lifetime exploring the vast backcountry of Yosemite, hiking its trails, fishing its waters, and climbing its peaks. Yosemite Valley is one of the most beautiful places on Earth, but it is also loved too much by too many. In the backcountry, there is solitude as well as beauty.

We parked at the May Lake trailhead and hustled up the trail to make it back to camp before dark. With no packs, it was a piece of cake. We made it just at sunset. Trout were rising in the lake, dappling its surface. We fired up our stove to cook dinner: freeze-dried, spicy Santa Fe chicken. This wasn't exactly the "luxurious scenic banqueting" enjoyed by Hutchings and his tourists a century and a half earlier. To the contrary, the Santa Fe chicken was barely edible. We choked it down and settled in for another night by the campfire. The temperature had dropped into the forties. We huddled close to the flames for warmth.

CHAPTER
4

On the Virtues of the Campfire

I love campfires. To me, an evening spent around a good campfire is one of the greatest joys in life. It is time to be treasured. I love sitting beside a fire in the woods or the mountains, or even in our backyard, where we have a fire ring on our patio. The campfires Bobby and I shared in Yosemite were our first, but there have been many more since then. The times the two of us have spent beside campfires have been some of our very best times.

* * *

More than a half century ago, the Mississippi legislature engaged in a great debate regarding the sale of liquor by the drink. A young lawmaker named Soggy Sweat was called upon to share his wisdom on the subject. He responded with what came to be known as the Whiskey Speech. I repeat the Whiskey Speech here in full, in part because it bears on the subject at hand, but mostly because it's both amusing and wise. Here it is:

My Friends:

I had not intended to discuss this controversial subject at this particular time. However, I want you to know that I do not shun controversy. On the contrary, I will take a stand on any issue at any time, regardless of how fraught with controversy it might be. You have asked me how I feel about whiskey. All right, here is how I feel about whiskey.

If when you say whiskey you mean the Devil's brew, the poison scourge, the bloody monster that defiles innocence, dethrones reason, destroys the home, creates misery and poverty, yea, literally takes the bread from the mouths of little children; if you mean the evil drink that topples the Christian man and woman from the pinnacle of righteous, gracious living into the bottomless pit of degradation, and despair, and shame, and helplessness, and hopelessness, then certainly I am against it.

But,

If when you say whiskey you mean the oil of conversation, the philosophic wine, the ale that is consumed when good fellows get together, that puts a song in their hearts and laughter on their lips, and the warm glow of contentment in their eyes; if you mean Christmas cheer; if you mean the stimulating drink that puts the spring into the old gentleman's step on a frosty, crispy morning; if you mean the drink that enables a man to magnify his joy, and his happiness, and to forget, if only for a little while, life's great tragedies, and heartaches, and sorrows; if you mean that drink the sale of which pours into our treasuries untold millions of dollars, which are used to provide tender care for our little crippled children, our blind, our deaf, our dumb, our pitiful aged and infirm; to build highways and hospitals and schools, then certainly I am for it.

This is my stand. I will not retreat from it. I will not compromise.

* * *

So what does Soggy Sweat's speech have to do with campfires? Maybe it's a stretch—I do like the speech—but I submit that campfires are like whiskey. Used excessively or carelessly, campfires cause destruction and misery. They destroy property and ruin lives. But a modest campfire, tended responsibly, is a wonderful thing. It too serves as "the oil of conversation." When good fellows get together, it too brings "the warm glow of contentment in their eyes." I count among my fondest memories times spent around campfires with good fellows after a day of hiking or canoeing.

Some of my memories are of glorious times of great humor, the conversation lubricated into the wee hours by good drink and a good fire, laughing until the tears rolled down. Stories are best told around a fire. Jokes are funnier. The fire brings out the best in our deliveries. Emerson wrote that part of success is "to laugh often and much." I have been a great success by campfires.

But I have also had memorable times of seriousness beside campfires. Escaping from the working world to the wilderness, even for only a few days, inevitably causes Bobby and me to think about deeper issues than we usually have time to consider back home. In the wilderness, to quote Enos Mills, the John Muir of Rocky Mountain National Park, "there is room—glorious room—room in which to find ourselves, in which to think and hope, to dream and plan, to rest and resolve." Bobby and I do all of this on our travels. Around our campfires, we talk about the usual: work, politics, and stories from our pasts, of Lucky Dog and the like. I learned most of what I have written so far about Bobby while sitting by campfires. But he and I also talk about more serious things—our beliefs, our regrets, our dreams. The campfire acts as a sort of truth serum, and barriers come tumbling down. We reveal more of ourselves than we are accustomed to revealing at home in the "real world."

Sometimes we talk of religion. It was William Thomas Cummings who wrote that there are no atheists in foxholes. I suspect that there are few atheists in Yosemite. I am hardly a devout person and not much for organized religion. I cannot pretend to know things that, to me at least, are unknowable. I am skeptical of those who claim to have all the answers. Yet it is hard not to see the hand of a divine creator in Yosemite. A minister friend of mine told me this is called natural revelation, the precept that Yosemite and places like it prove that God exists. I know that forces of nature caused the uplift of the Sierras and carved Yosemite Valley, and I know that the process occurred over many millions of years. But it is difficult to believe that this process was entirely unplanned, that there was no divine guidance, that the grandeur we see today is the product of pure, dumb luck. The masterpiece is simply too magnificent. In *Of Men and Mountains*, William O. Douglas wrote that "when man ventures into the wilderness, climbs the ridges, and sleeps in the forest, he comes in close communion with his Creator." In the splendor of the mountains, in a place like Yosemite, it is hard to believe that there is no creator.

Bobby and I talk of many things around our fires, but we always return to one common refrain—our mutual desire to change our lives so that we can spend more time in the wilderness, more time around campfires. We know, as E. R. Jackman has written, that "life in a city, or even a town, isn't too good for us. A jangling phone, a blasting horn, the blasphemy of a jukebox, the hundred interruptions of daily business life—these things do not build character or provide peace of mind." Bobby and I regret the undeniable truth that we are bound by "clocks, almanacs, orders, duties" and thus are among those Muir pitied. We live in a society in which much is artificial and even more is superficial. We want to make the world of campfires our real world.

As we ponder our predicament—the recognition that our time in the mountains is the exception to the rule of our lives—we often fall silent. Rick Bass has written of the same emotion we feel: "Several of us—the older ones, I notice—study the fire for a while. We've been in towns; up here is where we want to be. Circulating among strangers and spending time with concrete under our feet when there are perhaps only a few years left does not sound very attractive to us." On every trip, Bobby and I wonder how to change things. Like Thoreau, we want "to live deep and suck out all the marrow of life." But then we fly home to our world of deadlines and commitments, and the years roll by. I would love to be able to escape from practicing law, from selling my time by the tenth of an hour. I often enjoy the challenge of my work, and I have it far better than most. I must acknowledge that. But all the same, I would far rather sit beside a campfire in Yosemite than at my desk in Jackson. Even at its best, practicing law is extremely stressful. Not so in the mountains, where, as Muir observed, "cares drop off like autumn leaves."

Around campfires is not the only place where Bobby and I dream our dream of a future with unlimited time in the wilderness. Back home, our thoughts often return to the mountains, to the desire to change our lives so we can spend more time in places like Yosemite. We yearn for what these places do for us, how they focus us on what is real, how they make us feel alive, how they give us peace. But spending more time in the wilderness isn't easy. There is always some responsibility tugging at us, some reason not to go. Bobby's thoughts on the matter resulted in a pearl of wisdom that is sad but true. He wrote that "the only difference between a rut and a grave is the depth."

A good fire is about the only thing I know of that appeals to all five senses. I can sit for hours staring at a good campfire, studying the colors and watching the flames. I love to listen to a campfire crackle and pop and hiss. A campfire has a special smell; it reminds me of my childhood, of Daddy, of his coming home from campouts when I was still too young to go. Perhaps above all, a campfire feels good. On a cold night in the mountains, a campfire is a necessity. Otherwise the only choice is to crawl into your sleeping bag right after dark. And a campfire lets you cook things that taste good. Meals in the outdoors taste better than they do anywhere else.

The natural progression of a campfire seems to match the conversation of those around it. As the fire is built and grows, the talk grows with it. When the flames are at their peak, the jokes and stories come rapid fire. The laughter is at its loudest. Then, as the hour grows late and the fire dies down, voices become quieter, silence lingers. Finally, as the last embers fade away, there is nothing but silence. One by one, the campers by the fire break away from the circle and wander to their tents. Sometimes one person remains, a solitary figure huddled close to what remains of the coals, savoring the night and the quiet and the stars.

Rick Bass has written that he "loves the way campfires break up—the slow release of that bond, the flames becoming coals, becoming almost nothing, relinquishing us back to the night." When I'm with good friends, I never want the campfire to break up. I am always the last to leave. Sometimes one of my friends lasts as long as I do, but sometimes I remain by the fire alone. When that happens, I huddle by the coals, wanting the night to last. Aldo Leopold wrote of this special time, sitting alone beside a dying campfire: "On a still night, when the campfire is low and the Pleiades have climbed over rimrocks, sit quietly and listen . . . and think hard of everything you have seen and tried to understand. Then you may hear it—a vast pulsing harmony—its score inscribed on a thousand hills, its notes the lives and deaths of plants and animals, its rhythms spanning the seconds and the centuries." I love the last minutes by the fire, looking up at the stars and down at the coals, until the cold finally drives me to my tent.

In recent years, campfires have become a subject of controversy. As use of the wilderness has increased, the need to protect the wilderness has increased as well. There are times when campfires are unwise and places where they should be prohibited altogether, particularly at high elevation. But I reject the view of those who oppose campfires under all circumstances. The author of a trail guide I read recently took an unqualified position against campfires; he even argued that burning dead wood gathered from the forest floor somehow detracts from the wilderness experience of those who come after, I guess because they see less dead wood. This strikes me as much too radical. To my mind, the enormous joy of good company around a good campfire far outweighs any infinitesimal harm to the environment a carefully tended fire may cause. Without a campfire, backpackers miss one of the best things about camping, perhaps the very best. I am a firm believer in leave-no-trace camping, but a few campfire rings in the vast wilderness leave much less trace than the trails crisscrossing that same wilderness. With very rare exceptions, those who choose to go into the wilderness treat it with respect and reverence, build modest campfires, and tend them with care. And the forest replenishes the supply of dead wood on the ground at a much faster pace than legions of backpackers can burn it.

* * *

On this night by the fire in Yosemite, Bobby and I reviewed the day's events. We agreed that we had driven too much, walked too little, and spent too much time with too many people. But we had also seen some of the most beautiful places on Earth. We had seen Yosemite Valley from the top and bottom on a cloudless day, and we had hiked among the massive sequoias of Mariposa Grove, trees that were enormous long before America became America.

Before turning in, we walked down to the meadow below our campsite for an unobstructed view of the sky. If you have not been in the west on a dry, clear, moonless night, far from city lights, you have never really seen the stars. The sky is filled with them. There seems to be more white than black. The Milky Way paints a bright swath across the heavens. This was just such a night. Astronomers have concluded that there are billions upon billions of stars in the universe, more than one for every person who has ever lived on Earth since the dawn of time. Of this total, only a comparative few are visible on even the clearest of nights. From our vantage point south of May Lake, however, it was as if we could see them all.

On our raft trip through the Grand Canyon, Daddy and I slept under the stars, never putting up a tent. Every night, before we dropped off to sleep, we lay in our sleeping bags and counted the shooting stars. It was like that again this night in Yosemite. We stared up at the sky, picked out constellations, and spotted a meteor tracing across the sky. I reminded Bobby that the light we were seeing from distant stars left there thousands of years ago. Since then, it has been hurtling in all directions at 186,000 miles a second, nearly six trillion miles a year. Just as the light we were seeing was generated thousands of years ago, the light these same stars were generating this night, many trillions of miles away, will not be seen on Earth until thousands of years from now. And if one of them happens to explode, as stars sometimes do, the explosion will remain unseen and unknown on Earth for those same thousands of years. Contemplating the wonder of it all made me feel small and insignificant, but I didn't mind.

Bobby and I walked back up to camp, made sure the fire was out, and crawled into the tent. On this night, for the first night of our trip, there would be no noise outside the tent at three in the morning. I slept until Bobby's alarm watch sounded just before dawn.

CHAPTER 5

Campfires Without Borders

In 2003, the year after the last of the trips described in this book, Bobby took an extended, involuntary camping trip without me. His destination was Camp Sather, a military expedition base adjacent to the Baghdad International Airport. Long after returning from his deployment to Iraq, Bobby wrote the following about his experiences there.

* * *

When I flew to Baghdad, I took only a few personal items with me from home. The one thing I took that proved most valuable and most enjoyable was something intangible: the experience gained from our hiking trips about the virtues of the campfire. In Baghdad, I learned about another virtue: the wonderful effect a campfire can have on strangers thrown together in a strange land in a time of war.

My first couple of months in Iraq consisted of working what seemed around the clock performing our mission and taking steps to protect the base. You talk to people only briefly under such circumstances and exchange the basics, learning where they're from and what they do back home but little else.

With Thanksgiving approaching, the days grew short. A blackout was imposed at night because of the random rocket attacks on the base. The only opportunities to relax were in the loud Morale, Welfare, and Recreation tent, where you could play cards, listen to music, or watch a movie, or in the quiet tent called Rosie's Café, where you could read a book until your eyes got heavy.

With December came a new commander and a new agenda. The nightly blackout was lifted because our lights could not be seen from where the rocket attacks were launched. A squadron was assigned to renovate a shattered building next to the runway to replace the mobile command shelter and provide a conference room for briefings and meetings. Next to the building was a pit that looked like maybe flowers had been grown in it during more peaceful times. When I saw the flower pit, I knew right away what to do with it.

Over the course of the next few days, I was able to get my hands on a small, dull chainsaw and gather enough wood for a debut campfire on a cold December night. Although others viewed my project with skepticism and even some criticism, all of that ended when the fire was lit and its mysterious magic took hold. Soldiers and airmen drawn to the flames would first sit on the ledge around the pit and stare at the glow. As they warmed up, so did the conversation. There wasn't any alcohol to oil it, but none seemed to be needed.

As word of our campfires spread, the number of visitors grew. Everybody would come to bathe in the glow of the fire and escape to a different world, talking freely, laughing, and building intimate friendships. It was like we were sharing a secret. People began treating each other differently, and better. When walking through the camp during the day, I would often be asked, "Hey, Major, is there going to be a campfire tonight?"

As time went on, the fire pit became the camp's social meeting hub. We would cook on the cedar coals, drink alcohol-free beer, and smoke cigars. Our Baghdad campfires, and all the stories I heard and told beside them, could fill another book. Around one of our fires, we conceived and designed, and then later built, a Tiki Bar atop the remodeled building.

When our deployment ended, and we were set to leave and our replacements were set to arrive, we burned all the wood that was left and swept the fire pit clean. It was as if the campfires had become part of us, and it was time for them to pack up and go home too. I don't know what it was like for our replacements. It sure wasn't the same. We heard later that the new commander ordered the Tiki Bar to be torn down.

CHAPTER
6

The Rest of Yosemite

Bobby and I have learned much over the course of our trips to the West. We have learned to minimize time in the car and maximize time on the trail. We have learned to avoid crowds. We have also learned that it makes no sense to fly across the country and stay only a few days. But Yosemite was our first trip, and we hadn't learned any of those things yet. The previous night, as we sat by the fire, we realized we should have given ourselves more time. Our third day in Yosemite was to be our last, at least on this trip. We had to make the most of it, follow Thoreau's advice, and suck out all the marrow.

We started our day by waking early to see the sunrise. When Bobby's alarm went off, we pulled on all our warm clothes and walked the short distance to the ridge southeast of the lake, where we sat, shivering, as the dawn broke. The huge brow of Clouds Rest gradually came into focus. The sun topped the crest. The birds in the trees around us came to life, singing their greetings to the day. We sat in silence, watching, listening. The line distinguishing sunlight from shadow gradually moved down the slope of Mt. Hoffman to our west. The sunrise show over, we retreated to our campsite and stoked the fire to warm ourselves.

The night before, we had decided to spend the morning climbing Mt. Hoffman, its peak 1,500 feet above the lake. We were very near the center of the park. The trail guide promised that the summit rising above May

Lake would give us dramatic views of the Sierras in all four directions. Before we started our climb, however, I had another move to make.

* * *

Let me now pause to discuss a delicate subject and the source of my principal discomfort on our trips. Here's the problem: Away from home, especially at high altitude, my gastrointestinal system shuts down. Food goes in at the top, but nothing comes out at the bottom. Traveling always seems to have this effect on my digestion system, and I wonder: How does it know? How does my alimentary canal know I'm not in Jackson? This condition never afflicts Bobby. Every morning, like clockwork, he strolls out of camp, a grin on his face and a trowel and roll of toilet paper in his hand. He returns shortly and questions me with mock concern about my condition. But this morning, for the first time on our trip, I made the morning trip as well. The Santa Fe chicken, which had tasted so bad the night before, had at least served some purpose. I walked out of camp with trowel and paper and returned shortly with a new bounce in my step.

* * *

When I returned, I discovered that I didn't have my sunglasses. Reviewing events from the day before, I realized I had left them in the car. In most circumstances, I would have made do without them. But Mt. Hoffman is almost entirely treeless, and I knew I would be miserable with no shades. While Bobby cleaned up after breakfast, I hustled to retrieve them. I jogged down the trail and hiked back up as fast as I could, making the round trip in less than an hour, faster than our one-way climb thirty-six hours earlier. We had not started the day's hike, and I was already tired.

Before we began our climb, Bobby and I decided to hike around the lake. We walked under the hemlocks on the eastern side and then made our way along the north shore to the base of the mountain. We scrambled along the western shore, hopping from boulder to boulder. This was the deep end of the lake, the steep mountain slope continuing below the water's edge. The water was perfectly clear down to the rock bottom in the depths below. We counted the trout suspended below the surface. We wished for a fly rod or spinning rod but had neither.

On our first four trips, Bobby and I twice camped beside trout-filled lakes and watched the trout dapple the surface, rising to feed. It happened here in Yosemite, and it happened again in the Tetons. We also took fishing tackle with us on two of the four trips, but they were the wrong two. We hiked with our fishing gear at Glacier and in the Cascades but did not catch a single fish on either trip. Finally, on our fifth trip, to the Wind River Range in Wyoming, we had both fish and rods to catch them.

We walked back along the south shore to camp and prepared for our hike up Mt. Hoffman. As we packed our lunch, a strong wind began to blow. We looked up at the mountain and saw dust blowing across its face. Neither of us was keen on the idea of being exposed on a steep slope in high wind, and we knew little about the trail to the summit. We chickened out, again blaming our lugless boots. We decided to break camp, head down to the car, and take a different hike. I hesitated to give up on Mt. Hoffman, not because I was braver than Bobby, but because changing our plans meant that my early morning trip down to the car for my sunglasses had been unnecessary. But at least my needless act was a small one. At least I didn't volunteer for the Navy to avoid the draft just before the draft was cancelled.

On the way down the trail, I had a thought. When I die, why should my family spend thousands on a fancy casket just to bury it in the ground? Wouldn't it be better, I asked Bobby, to spend the casket money on plane tickets so my family could hike up this trail and scatter my ashes in May Lake? They could remember me by a beautiful place, a place where I had camped, and not waste money on an undertaker. Bobby generally agreed, but he did me one better. He suggested cutting the crematorium out of the deal as well. His plan was for my family to pitch my carcass into a dumpster and get some ashes out of the fireplace. My loved ones could pretend the ashes were me when they scattered them in May Lake. With or without Bobby's modification, I think it's a good idea. But I now have other potential sites for the ceremony: Elizabeth and Cosley Lakes in Glacier, Phelps Lake in the Tetons, Blue Lake in the Cascades, and Island Lake in the Wind River Range.

I also came across another idea for disposing of my corpse when my time comes. Accomplishing it would cost more than abandoning my remains in a garbage bin, but it would put them to better use. And like scattering my ashes in an alpine lake, it would require neither a shovel nor a chainsaw. The idea comes from writer/conservationist/Vietnam warrior/erstwhile eco-terrorist/ bear lover Doug Peacock, about whom Rick Bass wrote in *The Lost Grizzlies*. According to Bass, Peacock carried a card in his wallet, a sort of organ donor card with a twist. The card provided instructions to whoever happened to come across Peacock's body after he got through using it. The card states:

FEED THE BEARS

I _____, being of sound mind but dead body, do hereby bequeath my mortal remains to feed the Grizzly Bears of North America. Respect my body. Do not embalm! (A little mustard would be appreciated.) My family and friends have been instructed in how to deal with my corpse. They may be reached at phone _____; address _____.

Please put me in a deep freezer if I must be held for a few days. Should my family refuse to claim me, or should I be indigent at the time of my demise, please explain to the County that I can be mailed to a wilderness (as evidenced by the presence of grizzlies and/or wolves) for a lot cheaper than I can be buried in a pauper's grave.

Please remove my eyes, kidneys and heart for use by the living, but retain my liver because I think Grizz would like that the most. I love you all. See you in the spring!

Perhaps Peacock was not committed to this plan of action because he evidently had not yet filled in the blanks when Bass wrote *The Lost Grizzlies*, but I think it's a great idea. Better to feed the bears than the undertakers. Better to be part of a grizzly's food chain than buried six feet under, at least if the grizzly doesn't start eating you before you're dead.

* * *

We walked the mile and a quarter down to the trailhead, my third time to hike the trail this morning and sixth altogether. We got in the car, returned to Tioga Road, and drove a few miles west to Porcupine Flat. It is so named because of the prickly mammals that frequent the area, but we didn't see one. We then set off on foot, our destination the summit of North Dome on Yosemite Valley's north rim.

The first part of the hike was down a grade through a thick forest of pine and red fir. Less than a mile from the trailhead, we crossed Porcupine Creek. In early summer, the creek can be high; a log crossing is required. By this time of year, however, it was almost dry. We were able to hop across the tiny stream, which was no more than four feet wide. Before we continued on our way, we spotted several tiny trout, their size proportional to that of the stream. We wondered how they got here, where they were going, what their future held. With winter approaching, their prospects looked bleak. Surely what little was left of the creek would freeze solid.

Just before the two-mile mark, the trail started to climb. We wound our way up, at times through forest, at times over open rock fields. We reached the top of Indian Ridge right at noon and detoured up the slope to an unusual rock arch, the only one of its kind in the park, where we stopped for lunch. It was another perfect day, temperature in the high sixties and not a cloud in the sky. There were no crowds here. We had not yet seen a person on the trail.

Crowds and traffic are enormous problems in the national parks, especially at the height of summer. But surveys show that most park visitors—perhaps eighty percent—never get more than a quarter of a mile from a paved road. Our experience proves the point. Once on the trail, Bobby and I leave the crowds behind. We see other hikers occasionally, but never many. Even here in Yosemite, one of America's most popular parks, we found this to be true.

The trail dropped sharply from Indian Ridge to its destination. In several spots, the path was steep and the footing tricky. Bobby and I agreed that this was not a trail for the careless. We continued to descend, and North Dome and the valley came into view. As we got closer, we saw movement on the top of North Dome—more hikers. When we reached the top of the dome, our sense of accomplishment was shattered. The group of hikers consisted of a couple and three young children, none over eight years old, all barefooted or wearing sandals. The kids had hiked the same trail we had. "Little bastards," Bobby muttered under his breath.

North Dome gave us our third view of the valley, this one from the north rim. We had seen it from the south rim and the valley floor the previous day, but this view was more rewarding for two reasons—it wasn't crowded, and it took effort to get here. The valley floor stretched out to the west. We could see smoke from the fires of the campers more than 3,000 feet below. To our left, the massive face of Half Dome, almost directly across the valley, seemed close enough to touch. From left to right, east to west, were Tenaya Canyon, Merced Canyon and Illilouette Gorge. We had bird's-eye views of them all. We asked one of the parents of the three kids to take our picture. Then they headed back up the trail, leaving us to enjoy the sights alone. The view from here was no more spectacular than the view from Glacier Point, but having it to ourselves, after hiking nearly five miles to get here, made it far more satisfying. We explored the surface of the dome, took some more pictures, then began the long walk back.

On most day hikes in the mountains, the trailhead is the low point. You start in a valley, climb into the mountains, and then return. You hike up in the morning and down in the afternoon, doing the hard work first. This trail, however, was just the opposite. North Dome was the low point of the hike, and the return was uphill nearly all the way. Instead of retracing our steps, we decided to take a longer route back. Just north of North Dome, we turned west on the North Rim trail, heading for Lehamite Creek. This part of the walk was downhill, which we knew would only increase the climb ahead of us. Along the way, a massive fir had fallen across our path. A trail-wide slice had been sawed out to clear the way. Someone had counted more than 450 rings in the tree's cross-section, marking them by the hundred. This was just an infant compared to the sequoias; it sprouted about the time Magellan sailed around the world.

We came upon Lehamite Creek in a beautiful, tree-shaded canyon. The only sounds were the trickling of the stream and the wind in the trees. We then turned back northeast for the return to the trailhead. We now moved steadily uphill, hiking through meadows and forests in the late-afternoon light. As the day grew short, we began spotting mule deer in the woods on either side of the trail. A mile and a half from the car, we rejoined the path that led to the trailhead. After another half hour, we again reached

Porcupine Creek. As we approached, I spotted a mule deer doe with her head down, drinking from the creek. Bobby and I were hiking in our accustomed position, with me in the lead. I motioned for him to be quiet and catch up. We edged forward together to see how close we could get. The doe detected movement and looked up. We froze. The doe stared at us; we remained motionless. She decided all was well and resumed drinking. We crept forward again. The process repeated itself twice more. Finally, when we had closed to within fifteen feet, she twitched her ears and sauntered away into the woods. We watched in silence until she disappeared among the trees. When she was gone, Bobby and I looked at each other and smiled. In *My First Summer in the Sierra*, Muir wrote that "wherever we go in the mountains, or indeed in any of God's wild fields, we find more than we seek." The doe at Porcupine Creek was late-afternoon lagniappe.

We trudged up the last half mile of the trail, reaching the car at dusk, and plopped down in the car seats, exhausted. It had been a great hike on a great day. We headed east on Tioga Road and stopped at the Tuolumne Meadows Ranger Station for souvenir tee shirts for our families. This stop became an obligatory part of our trips, a small price for leaving our families behind when we go on our travels. We continued east, passed through the gate at Tioga Pass, then stopped to eat at a place called Parker's. Our meal of mulligan stew and apple pie was our best of the trip. After dinner, we wound down out of the Sierras and turned back north, retracing our route toward Reno. The mountains lay to our west; the plains stretched away to the east. It was another cloudless, starlit night. As has happened on all of our trips, we fell into a silent melancholy, sad that our time in the wilderness was coming to an end. Bobby is more affected by this condition than I am. He gets more excited before our trips, or at least seems to, and so has farther to fall.

John Prine is one of my favorite songwriters, his "Souvenirs" one of my favorite songs. When Prine was first performing live, he thought he was supposed to have a new song every week. He wrote "Souvenirs" in his '65 Malibu on the way to do a show. It starts with these words: "All the snow has turned to water; Christmas Day has come and gone. Broken toys and faded colors are all that's left to linger on." When our trips come to an end, Bobby is still like a child on Christmas. Only now it's Christmas night, and the colors are faded.

Our flight home was not until noon the next day, so we could have camped again at Washoe Lake. But we didn't want to risk another attack in the night, and we were overdue for hygiene. We got a motel room in Minden, Nevada, and flipped a coin to see who would take the first shower. Returning to civilization at the end of a great camping trip is always sad, but it is not without rewards. The first hot shower is chief among them. Also on the list are the first cold beer, the first good meal cooked by someone else, and the first night in a warm bed. Simple pleasures we take for granted take on added meaning after days without them.

We had time the next morning before our flight for a side trip to Lake Tahoe, with water as clear as that in May Lake. We drove along the eastern shore of the lake, stopped for a big breakfast, and then headed for the airport in Reno. Our gas gauge was on empty. Bobby, the worrier, wanted to stop and buy three dollars of gas just to make sure. I, the tightwad, wanted to coast in on nothing but fumes. We compromised and put in a dollar and a half.

On the long flight home, first to Salt Lake and then to New Orleans, Bobby and I reviewed the trip. We agreed that it was great but that it could have been much better. At a bar in the Salt Lake airport, I proposed two toasts—one to Bobby for having the idea and the other to Herb Kelleher for the cheap plane tickets. At some point on the trip home—I don't remember exactly when—the two of us made a pact. We would make this an annual event. No matter what, we would go on a camping trip every year.

After making this vow, we talked of future trips. Our next destination remained undecided, but several things were clear. On our next trip, we would spend more time on the trail. We would find out where the crowds go and go elsewhere. Like Muir a century and a half earlier, we would aim for "any place that is wild." And we would stay longer. We would give ourselves more time to strip away the layers of civilization that shroud our souls, more time to shed what Rick Bass calls the "work-caused spirit-funk." Our trip to Yosemite had been too short, but at least we had shed some of it. And now there would be more trips.

Our flight didn't land in New Orleans until nine o'clock. Even at that hour, it was ninety degrees, with humidity to match. The weather reminded us that our time in the mountains was at an end, that we were back in our real world.

CHAPTER
7

Glacier National Park
– September 1997

Bobby and I spent less than an hour deliberating before picking Yosemite in 1996. The end of the Southwest anniversary special demanded that we act with dispatch. In 1997, however, we had all the time we needed to choose a destination. Over a period of months, Bobby and I scoured maps and magazines and talked to friends. Ultimately we picked Glacier National Park, based on a recommendation from a very close friend.

In the late 1980s, our family got to know Jerry and Kathy Drake of Jackson and their four children, Ruthie, Brian, Jonny, and Chad. Ruthie, the oldest, became our babysitter of choice when she was in high school. After Ruthie graduated, we turned to Brian. Then came Jonny. In the fall of 1993, during his junior year in high school, Jonny became our regular babysitter. Our children, who were nine, six, and three, loved him. The following spring, Jonny told us his parents had decided to move to Columbia Falls, Montana. Jerry is a petroleum geologist, and the oil and gas business in Mississippi was virtually dead. He had decided to start a new career in Montana, where Kathy's brother lived. As for Jonny, he was not thrilled with the idea of leaving Mississippi and his girlfriend right before his senior year of high school. Not only was he a star on the soccer team, but he was also trying to get an appointment to one of the military academies. Service academy appointments require not only exemplary qualifications but also support from a Congressman. Jonny was a shoo-in for an appointment from Mississippi. As a new resident of Montana, however, he would go to the bottom of the list. We talked it over and decided to ask the Drakes if Jonny could spend his senior year with us. They agreed, and we had a great year with Jonny, who was far more mature and considerate than most high school seniors. Friends told us we were generous for welcoming Jonny into our home, but we got far more from the arrangement than we gave. We had the company of a delightful young man, role model for our children, and built-in babysitter, and the only cost was an increase in our grocery bill to satisfy Jonny's enormous appetite. When Jonny graduated in May of 1995, our family and his crying girlfriend put him on a train bound for Montana. He spent a month there with his parents before reporting for duty at West Point.

During his year with us, our whole family became very close to Jonny. Over the next four years, he split his holidays between Montana and Mississippi, often bringing friends from West Point to stay with us. In May of 1999, all five of us traveled to West Point for Jonny's graduation. He was then assigned to a base in Germany, where he commanded a field artillery unit. He later served tours in Afghanistan and Iraq.

Jonny shares my love for the outdoors. During the time he spent in Montana with his parents, he got to camp and hike in Glacier. When Jonny came to Mississippi in May of 1997, he told me about the trails he'd hiked and showed me the pictures he'd taken. Until then, Bobby and I were still mulling several alternatives, but after I talked to Jonny and saw his pictures, I decided on Glacier. Bobby, as I noted earlier, lets me decide.

* * *

The process that formed the mountains in what is now Glacier National Park began sixty million years ago, when a slab half a mile thick slid from west to east across the top of a softer layer of rock. The length of the slab's journey was thirty-seven miles. This phenomenon, called the Lewis Overthrust, formed a range of mountains running from north to south. Many of the mountains have a conical shape and resemble Mayan temples. The overthrust exposed sedimentary rock that was formed in the bed of an ancient sea. Some of the rock is more than a billion years old, among the oldest on Earth. After the mountains were formed, ice, wind, and water began carving them. In the last Great Ice Age, the region was filled with massive glaciers formed by the compression of heavy snows over many years. Gravity pulled the glaciers downhill, shaving off chunks of mountains, deepening gorges, and polishing hard rock to a sheen. The larger glaciers formed U-shaped valleys, leaving natural amphitheaters called cirques in their wakes. When the glaciers retreated, they left mounds of debris at their feet called terminal moraines. The mounds created alongside the glaciers are lateral moraines. The terminal moraines often acted as dams, creating many of the lakes in the park. After the Great Ice Age, smaller glaciers created hanging valleys and waterfalls.

Within the park, there are two different continental divides. Precipitation falling on the west side drains to the Pacific. The snow that feeds the streams in the southeast corner of the park makes one of the longest journeys on the continent. These streams flow into the Missouri River, which converges with the Mississippi above St. Louis, which then empties into the Gulf of Mexico below New Orleans. The snow that falls in the southeast corner of Glacier two thousand miles from Jackson ultimately turns to muddy water and passes by the city of Vicksburg fifty miles west of Jackson. This accounts for all but the northeast corner of the park. Precipitation falling in this region heads north and east to the Hudson Bay and the Arctic Ocean. A single mountain in the center of the park called Triple Divide Peak sends water coursing in all three directions. It is a ritual for climbers who reach the top of the mountain to unzip their pants, pirouette while relieving themselves, and feed three different oceans.

The climates and appearances of the land in the three watersheds are distinct. Far more precipitation falls on the western slopes. The lower elevations on the west side of the park are akin to a Pacific rain forest, with huge trees growing in close formation, lush vegetation, moss, and ferns. The southeast is windswept, arid, and barren. The northeast is a cross between the two.

A New Yorker named George Bird Grinnell is recognized as the father of Glacier National Park. Grinnell, the editor of *Forest and Stream* magazine, later to become *Field and Stream*, first went to Montana in 1885 to evaluate the plight of the Blackfeet Indians. Grinnell was captivated by the beauty of the mountains and glacial landforms and declared the region the Crown of the Continent. When Grinnell returned to the East, he enlisted friends and colleagues in an effort to set aside the region as a national park. Grinnell's efforts succeeded in 1910 when President Taft signed the bill creating Glacier National Park. The new park, which now comprises more than a million acres, was the sixth of America's national parks.

The region of mountains and lakes formed by the Lewis Overthrust is bisected by the 49th parallel, which in 1818 became the border between the United States and Canada. The Canadians saw the wisdom of preserving the land as a national park before we did. Waterton Lakes National Park was established on the north side of the border in 1895. In 1932, the United States and Canadian governments voted to give the two parks one name: Waterton-Glacier International Peace Park.

Early visitors to Glacier traveled by horseback because there were no roads into the backcountry. In 1932, the park became accessible to cars for the first time. That year, after more than a decade of work, the Going to the Sun Road, a scenic drive that may well be the most spectacular in the world, was completed. The road, the high point of which is the Continental Divide at Logan Pass, crosses the park from east to west just as Tioga Road crosses Yosemite.

A number of glaciers in the high country can still be seen today, but they are not what give the park either its beauty or its name. Many of the park's grandest features are the result of glaciers, but the glaciers that created them melted long ago. Their lasting contributions include the glacial cirques, alpine lakes, and waterfalls that fill the park. Added to this backdrop are the living things—towering trees, gorgeous wildflowers, and abundant wildlife. There are no giant sequoias here, but the larches, hemlocks, firs, and cedars are beautiful if not gargantuan. During the short summer, the meadows are filled with flowers of every color, more than a thousand species in all. Among them are bear grass, Indian paintbrush, calypso orchids, shooting stars, and Lewis's monkey flowers, all with blooms showier than their names. Glacier is also the home of an incredible array of large mammals—bighorn sheep, mountain goats, mule deer, white-tailed deer, elk, and moose. Packs of wolves make their home here, having migrated south from Canada. Black bears are plentiful. Finally, and most famous of all, is *ursus arctos horribilis*, the grizzly bear. Glacier is the home of the largest concentration of grizzly bears in the lower 48 states. In a recent study, rangers confirmed that more than four hundred grizzlies live in Glacier. But surely there are more; surely some grizzlies keep their lives in this wilderness hidden from man. Smaller animals abound in the park as well: beaver, marmot, otter, and pika. The lakes are filled with trout and the skies with birds, including bald and golden eagles.

Because of its incomparable beauty and more than seven hundred miles of trails, Glacier is a paradise for hikers. In the fall of 2000, *Backpacker* magazine published the results of a poll of its readers about their favorite national parks. Nineteen parks were rated in four categories—scenery, wildlife, solitude, and trail quality. Glacier was the landslide winner, finishing first for scenery and trail quality, third for wildlife, and eighth for solitude. The magazine described Glacier with the following accolades: "Scenery that'll suck the breath out of your lungs. Quiet so intense you'll wonder if your ears still work. Enough wildlife to make a zookeeper drool with envy. Exactly what you'd expect from . . . a place so close to heaven."

Friends of mine who know of my trips with Bobby have asked me to compare the places we've been, to rank them like *Backpacker* did. To me, this is like drinking a fine Cabernet one year, another fine Cabernet a year later, and then being asked to declare which is better. I find it almost impossible to choose. *Backpacker* magazine, in contrast, had no trouble at all. Of the nineteen parks the magazine ranked, Yosemite finished a distant eleventh, its overall ranking hurt most by finishing next to last for solitude. It suffers from being located in America's most populous state. Glacier is far less accessible.

Here's how I size up the two parks based on my limited experience. Yosemite Valley is the most spectacular place I've ever been. In terms of breathtaking magnificence, sheer jaw-dropping beauty, no single spot in Glacier, or anyplace else that I've seen, quite equals the valley. But Yosemite Valley is nearly always crowded, and beyond the valley I give the edge to Glacier. Of the places Bobby and I have gone on our trips, Glacier is the only one to which we've returned.

In the article announcing the results of the *Backpacker* poll, David Peterson answered the question: Why Glacier?

> The scenery, of course. Often you hear a place effusively proclaimed "the most beautiful spot on Earth!" confirming only that beauty is relative. Here it is absolute, and a key contributor to Glacier's wild magic. But there's more. There's the delicious clean air and turquoise water and scarcity of backcountry traffic. There's the maniacal night-music of wolves and loons and, most profoundly, the palpable presence of grizz.

Ah, the grizzly, that most feared of carnivores, that bear of my dreams. The palpable presence of grizz sharpens the senses; it makes the wilderness wild. As John Murray has written, "Those who have packed far up into grizzly country know that the presence of even one grizzly on the land elevates the mountains, deepens the canyons, chills the winds, brightens the stars, darkens the forest, and quickens the pulse of all who enter it."

For the first half century of the park's existence, no grizzly bear killed a person within its borders. There were occasional maulings, some resulting in serious injuries, and from time to time a hiker disappeared without a trace. But until the summer of 1967, there had never been a confirmed human death caused by a grizzly bear. Then, in the most extraordinary of coincidences, two different grizzlies killed two different nineteen-year-old girls in two different locations on a single August night. The girls were both working in the park that summer. One was killed on an overnight camping trip near Trout Lake in the western lowlands of the park. The other was killed by another bear several miles to the northeast in the high country near Granite Park Chalet on the Highline Trail. Both tragedies were attributed to sloppy practices of the Park Service. In one case, rangers had been slow to react to a rogue bear that had become increasingly aggressive toward people. In the other, the bear had been drawn to the area by the custom of letting grizzlies, for the amusement of visitors, feed on the garbage and leftover food from the chalet. This practice, which was seen in hindsight as extremely dangerous, was permitted before that August night because of the more than five decades without a single confirmed fatality.

I know all of this because, a month before our trip to Glacier, Jonny Drake sent me an excellent book called *Night of the Grizzlies* by Jack Olsen. Olsen's book explores in great detail the events of that night in August 1967 and the cause of the two fatal attacks. Foolishly, just before our trip to Glacier, I read it. Jonny had sent me the book from West Point, where he was beginning his third year. As our trip took shape, he and I tried to figure out a way for him to go to Glacier with us. But in September of his junior year, Jonny couldn't go home to go camping.

We did manage to include one Drake on our trip to Glacier. Brian, who is two years older than Jonny, had moved west with his parents in 1994, transferring from Mississippi College to the University of Montana in Missoula. In order to join us, he drove up from Missoula and skipped two days of classes. We also included a fourth hiker on our trip, David Sawyer, an emergency room doctor from the Mississippi coast and a close friend of Bobby. To a casual observer, David would appear to be the calmest and most sensible of our Glacier foursome. Several years earlier, however, David had done something that seems utterly senseless to me. Though he was already a successful physician, David decided to go to law school. He commuted to New Orleans and got his law degree from Tulane even though he had no intention of ever practicing law. I would not have gone to law school just for fun.

* * *

On September 17, 1997, Bobby, David, and I met at Bobby's house for the drive to New Orleans. This time, nobody was in the hospital; our trip was safe. We again flew to Salt Lake City, but this year our second leg took us north to Kalispell instead of west to Reno. Bobby claims he remembers seeing the northern lights on our flight to Montana. I don't remember seeing a thing. Brian and his dad, Jerry, came to the airport to meet us. We picked up our rental car, a Lincoln Town Car Bobby had reserved, and headed to the Drakes' house. It was nearly midnight when we got there.

We awoke the next morning to a steady rain. The sky was solid gray with no relief in sight. To save time, we had assigned Brian the task of buying food before our arrival. Brian has a prodigious appetite. During Jonny's year with us, when I teased him about how much he ate, he claimed that he was anorexic compared to Brian. Bobby, David, and I surveyed our provisions covering the floor and counter of the Drakes' kitchen in Montana. The supply of food was enormous. Brian had bought enough for four Brians. Also among the provisions was a blue can of GAZ for Bobby's stove. Bobby had mailed it to Montana because pressurized fuel cannot be taken on commercial flights and he was afraid he wouldn't be able to find the right kind in Glacier.

By the time we got to Montana, we also had a highlighted, dog-eared trail guide written by Erik Molvar entitled *Hiking Glacier and Waterton Lakes National Parks*. Later, in order to write about our trip, I pulled out the trail guide to help me recall the details of the trails we hiked. I found a bee smashed flat and stuck to the picture on page 120 of the book. The bee must have lost its life when I closed the book after stopping to check our bearings on the trail to Ptarmigan Tunnel on our second day in Glacier. The book's description of this trail starts on page 121. The flattened bee remains in the book as a souvenir.

Like our Yosemite backcountry permit, Molvar's guide contained advice about bear encounters. This advice appeared under a heading in all caps entitled "A FEW WORDS OF CAUTION" at the front of the book. Having just read *Night of the Grizzlies*, I studied Molvar's words of caution with special interest. He advised that "in areas of dense brush along trails, it may be necessary to announce your presence to bears. Bear bells may be worn for this purpose; clapping and shouting at appropriate times works just as well." This brought to mind the joke about distinguishing black bear scat from grizzly scat. Black bear scat is usually filled with berries; it may also contain fur and bones from the small rodents on which black bears occasionally feed. The scat of a grizzly may contain berries and fur and bones as well. In those respects, it's hard to tell the two apart. But grizzly scat is easily distinguished by one unique feature: It contains small bells. Molvar's guide contained not only words of caution, but also a message of reassurance: "Remember that a bear will try to avoid contact with humans, so if you meet a bear along the trail, the odds are good that he will turn and flee." When I read this on the flight to Montana, I was not so reassured. I wondered to myself: What exactly did he mean when he said the odds are "good"? The bear will flee 99 times out of a hundred? Or two times out of three?

We had not planned to backpack in Glacier. Instead, we intended to stay in campgrounds and take long day hikes. The decision about whether to backpack or car camp involves unavoidable trade-offs. The fundamental benefit of car camping is the ability to take everything you want without having to carry anything on your back. You can take a cooler filled with beer. You can plan a menu without regard to weight or the need for refrigeration. You can eat steaks and burgers rather than freeze-dried Santa Fe chicken. You can have pancakes and bacon for breakfast instead of instant oatmeal. You can also throw in lounge chairs to make time around the campfire more comfortable. Even a table. But all of this convenience comes at a price. Roadside campgrounds in national parks are never empty, and there is much to be said for having solitude at day's end and a campsite all to yourself. And the most magnificent camping spots are also denied to the car camper. Camping alone beside a high alpine lake is far preferable to sharing a roadside campground with a horde of strangers. Backpacking also gives you much greater freedom. You can take longer hikes deeper into the wilderness, see country that can't be reached on a day hike. But then again, there is much to be said for hiking with no pack on your back.

On our early trips to the West, we did a fair amount of both types of camping but gravitated to backpacking. Yosemite was a mix of backpacking and car camping, mostly the latter, as was our trip to the Tetons. Our first trip to Glacier was all car camping. Our trip to the Cascades in 2000 was entirely backpacking, as was our trip to the Wind River Range and our second trip to Glacier in the years that followed. On balance, I come down in favor of backpacking. Only by backpacking is it possible to camp alone in breathtaking scenery. To me, the benefits are worth the cost of foregone creature comforts and having to carry everything you need on your back. If you can't bring yourself to make this compromise, there are alternatives. You can use pack animals—horses, mules, or llamas—to lighten the load. Or you can take to the water and go canoeing. In a canoe, you can escape from roads and crowds and also take most anything you want.

* * *

We had big plans for our first day in Glacier, but the weather was spoiling them. The downpour was steady. We entered the park at West Glacier and climbed the Going to the Sun Road past Lake McDonald. At ten miles long and nearly five hundred feet deep, Lake McDonald is one of the largest in the region. It was carved by a huge glacier that filled the entire valley in the last Ice Age. We were traveling in two vehicles. Brian and I were in the Drakes' old Toyota pickup truck, which used to be mine. I sold it to them before they moved to Montana. Bobby and David followed in the Town Car. We planned to leave one vehicle at the Loop, a hairpin turn on the road several miles west of the Continental Divide. The four of us would then head up to Logan Pass at the Divide in the other vehicle. From there we planned to hike the Garden Wall, perhaps the best known trail in the park.

The Garden Wall, a magnificent geologic feature formed by the Lewis Overthrust, forms the Continental Divide. The trail follows the west face of the wall and provides magnificent views as well as frequent sightings of the area's wildlife. Marmots and pikas are common, as are mountain goats and bighorn sheep. Grizzlies are often seen. George Ostrom, who hiked many thousands of miles in Glacier over more than sixty years, once coaxed his wife into joining him to hike the Garden Wall by promising her there would be no grizzlies. They saw eight, more than one a mile, on the trail to Granite Park Chalet. Most of the grizzlies were a safe distance away, but one stood astride the trail. Ostrom and his wife avoided the trail bear by cutting across a switchback.

The section of the trail to the chalet is much more level than most mountain trails. Along the way are views across the valley of Mounts Clements, Cannon, and Oberlin, as well as Birdwoman Falls. The trail circles to the east of Haystack Butte and passes a spur trail to Grinnell Glacier, which was discovered by and named for George Bird Grinnell. At the chalet, near the site of one of the grizzly attacks in 1967, there are views of Heavens Peak across the valley and the Livingston Range to the north. After passing the chalet, we planned to turn west and drop steeply down to the Loop, ending nearly twelve miles from where we began.

But alas, we saw none of this. As we gained elevation driving east toward the Divide, the rain turned to snow. Soon we were in a blizzard. Then we came to barricades that blocked any further ascent up Going to the Sun Road. We spoke to a ranger, who told us the road would be closed at least for the rest of the day. After that, he said, who knows? This was a major setback. Not only were our plans for the day ruined, but we had picked hikes on the east side of the park for the next two days. We retreated west, dropped below snow line, and stopped to reassess. We decided to take a shorter, low-elevation hike to Avalanche Lake and then drive around Glacier rather than through it to get to the east side. We would take Highway 2, which tracks the southern boundary of the park and crosses the Divide at Marias Pass, the lowest route over the Rockies between Canada and Mexico.

The trail to Avalanche Lake is an easy hike to a spectacular destination. Thus the trail is usually crowded, but the weather on this day kept most hikers at bay. We put on our rain gear, walked through cottonwoods and cedars, and crossed Avalanche Creek, the beautiful stream fed by the lake. The trail continued up a gorge filled with moss and western hemlocks. On the creek bank, we saw water ouzels, John Muir's favorite bird, and watched as they dove fearlessly into the rapids. Along the way, Brian and I discussed the relative merits of Montana and Mississippi. Mississippi has no mountains, much less mountains like these. We agreed that Montana is far more beautiful. With respect to women, however, Brian insisted that it was just the opposite. To start with, there were far fewer women in Montana. As of 2000, Mississippi had 2,766,500 residents in its 46,914 square miles, just over sixty people per square mile. Montana had 882,000 residents spread over 145,556 square miles, just over six per square mile. Not only were women far scarcer in Montana, but Brian was certain that, at least on average, they were much less attractive, or at least didn't try as hard. Brian, who was 22 and single, was clearly frustrated about his prospects. He missed Southern girls. But his frustrations were temporary. Shortly after our trip, he met Jennifer Miller from Kalispell. By the time of Jonny's graduation from West Point in May of 1999, Brian and Jen were engaged. They married that summer and now have four children.

After a walk of nearly three miles, we reached Avalanche Lake. By then, the rain had stopped. A pair of men were fishing in the shallow end of the lake and had caught a handful of cutthroat trout. We had brought our fishing gear to Glacier, but because of the rain we had not bothered to bring it on the hike. We followed the trail along the south shore to the head of the lake. Towering cliffs surrounded us on three sides. Bearhat Mountain rose to the east and Mount Brown to the west. Between the two a steep cliff rose to the hanging cirque to the south formed by Sperry Glacier, which is not visible from the lake. The melt from the glacier creates the many waterfalls that cascade down the face of the cliff. The steep face is the site of the avalanches that give the lake its name.

After reaching the end of the trail, we retraced our steps to the vehicles. We shed our rain gear, returned to the park entrance, and turned south on Highway 2 for the drive around the park. We drove to the southern tip of Glacier, where the highway and park boundary turn to the northeast. After we crossed the Continental Divide at mile-high Marias Pass, the look of the land changed dramatically. To our north in the park was the Two Medicine area, which the Blackfeet regarded as the backbone of the world. This corner of the park lies in a rain shadow. Most precipitation falls west of the Divide, emptying the clouds before they get here. Vegetation here is sparse. The mountains are rocky and barren. Eighty-mile-an-hour winds roar through the mountain passes at high elevations. In contrast to the many shades of green on the western slopes, the dominant color here is brown.

* * *

At the southeast corner of the park, we passed into the Blackfeet Indian Reservation. Bobby and David were leading in the Town Car; Brian and I trailed in my old pickup. We passed a sign warning to be on the lookout for free-range cattle. Free-range chicken I'd heard of, but not free-range cattle. Around the next curve, we saw brake lights ahead. Bobby had come to a halt in the Town Car. We stopped behind him. I couldn't see what the problem was and lowered my window. Bobby laid on his horn. Then the Town Car slowly pulled into the left lane to ease around an obstacle in the right lane. There she was, the free range cow of which we had just been warned. Her business end was aimed toward us; she was nonchalantly relieving herself. This struck me as perhaps the ultimate expression of freedom for a free-range cow. Bobby told me later that he pulled to within inches of the cow's hindquarters before honking. The cow, focused on the task at hand, didn't even flinch. But when she had finished, she took her revenge. As Bobby slowly drove past, the cow aimed an agile side kick at the passenger door. With my window down, I heard bovine hoof strike Lincoln sheet metal. We saw Bobby flinch and David slide away from the attacker. Brian and I were smiling spectators for the whole event. We waited for the belligerent free-range cow to get off the road and continued on our way.

* * *

We headed north on Highway 89 to Babb, then turned west into the park. Our destination was the campground at Many Glacier, the terminal point on this road. Along the way, we passed Lake Sherburne. Brian said he had seen grizzlies on the beach north of the lake the last time he was here. We then passed Many Glacier Hotel, which the Great Northern Railway built in 1914 as a destination resort. It sits among jagged peaks on the shore of Swiftcurrent Lake in a spot that looks like a postcard from the Alps. We reached the campground right at dark. After we stopped, we inspected the Town Car for hoof damage. There was none, but the trip was still young. It had started raining again, and a dense fog filled the valley. We studied the sky and unanimously voted to rent a tiny cabin rather than put up tents. Then we went to the Swiftcurrent Motor Lodge for beer and pizza. After dinner, we returned to our cabin, climbed into our sleeping bags, and listened to the rain on the roof. All we could do was wish for better weather in the morning.

I woke before sunrise and lay there, listening. Nothing. The rain had stopped. Leaving the other three asleep, I went out for a short walk in the valley. Our wish had been granted. The bad weather had moved off to the east. The sky was clear, the fog gone. Mountains that were concealed the previous evening towered above. A full moon hung over the massive face of Grinnell Point to the south. In the cold of the not quite dawn, I heard a bull elk bugle. Things were looking up.

I returned to the cabin, where the others were starting to stir. Our menu called for bacon and pancakes. Bobby wanted to use his stove to justify shipping the GAZ to Montana. As the self-appointed cook, however, I chose to use mine, the simpler but heavier propane stove I hauled up to May Lake in Yosemite. When it was time to flip the first batch of pancakes, I realized we were in trouble. I thought I had packed everything, but we had no spatula. Bobby came to the rescue. On our first four trips, for no apparent reason, Bobby took a huge Bowie knife, as big as a machete. We had absolutely no use for it on three of our trips, but this morning we used it to flip pancakes.

When I sent a draft of this chapter to Bobby to review, he took umbrage at the suggestion that taking his Bowie knife on our trips was foolish and explained why he was attached to it:

> Listen, you can make fun of me for bringing my Bowie knife, but we have used it more than those frickin fishing poles. The knife was given to me when I was about six years old by my dad. Remember, this was the Davy Crockett era, and I was a big Davy Crockett fan. Wore the coonskin cap, had the musket, and would take off for the day with a packed lunch into the woods across Bayou St. John, where we lived in New Orleans. Sure couldn't do that now. Besides, kids are more interested in play stations and computers. Anyway, I saw the knife in Toy Center, and it was about $25 back then. A lot of money, so I never expected to get it. Well, I got it for my birthday and was sure surprised. When my dad was taking it out of the scabbard, he dropped it and cut his leg. He did grind the blade down before he let me have it. I later wondered why he gave me such a dangerous implement. Funny, but he had purchased a $10,000 whole life insurance policy on me several months before. Maybe he figured that $25 had the possibility of yielding great returns should I sever an artery while across the levee in the woods and bleed to death before somebody found me. The knife went everywhere. When we moved to Mississippi, it went on all the outings and camping trips on the river. I even took it with me when I went to Vietnam. So there. That's a run down on the pancake flipper.

After cleaning the breakfast dishes, we packed a lunch and headed up the trail. Our destination was Ptarmigan Tunnel, five miles to the northwest.

The hike would require a climb of nearly 2,500 feet. The trail rose steeply at first and then swung to the west on the south face of Allyn Peak. Across the valley to the south were Swiftcurrent Valley and the towering face of Mount Wilbur. Streams fed by the rain and snow that had fallen the previous day crossed the trail at frequent intervals. As we swung around the face of Allyn Peak and turned north, Brian and I spotted a golden eagle riding a thermal above us. We heard a wolf howl in the distance.

The trail at this point was surrounded by thick underbrush. David was wearing bear bells, but he was hiking with Bobby some forty yards behind Brian and me. Molvar's trail guide warned that we were in the midst of prime grizzly habitat. I also recalled his advice that "in areas of dense brush along trails, it may be necessary to announce your presence to bears." To announce our presence, I decided to sing.

I first sang Merle Haggard's "Big City" about wanting to be turned loose and set free somewhere in the middle of Montana. If only for a few days, that's just what had happened to us. Then I chose James Taylor's "Sweet Baby James" and sang about sitting by the fire as the moon rises, thinking about women and glasses of beer. When I sang "as if maybe someone could hear," I wondered if any bears could hear. My third choice was John Prine's song about his ancestral home, Paradise, Kentucky, where the coal company tortured the timber and stripped all the land. I closed my performance with Steve Earle's "Ft. Worth Blues," his ode to Townes Van Zandt. I sang about all the places in the song, including up beyond the Great Divide, where the sky is wide, the clouds are few, and a man can see his way clear to the light. The Big Sky of Montana above us was wide, and there were no clouds at all. The views were magnificent, the air pure. Even the acoustics were good. We walked through a stand of spruces. They looked and smelled like Christmas trees. If bears were near us, my singing scared them away.

Near the halfway point, we stopped at the bridge over Ptarmigan Falls, a beautiful series of rapids on Ptarmigan Creek coming down from the canyon to the north. Here the trail split. One branch headed to the west to Iceberg Lake in a glacial cirque surrounded by 3,000-foot cliffs. We took the other branch, following Ptarmigan Creek upstream to the north. For the next mile and a half, the trail climbed moderately. On the slopes to our west, we spotted a small herd of bighorn sheep. We watched them awhile, hoping for some head-butting, but they declined to entertain us. It was nearly noon when we reached the lake that feeds the creek. Ptarmigan Lake is in a barren cirque at the foot of Ptarmigan Wall. We stared up at the wall above it. We could barely see the tunnel at the top of a series of switchbacks climbing up the steep grade. The first half of the climb was over open rocks. Above that, the mountain was white from the snowfall the previous day. We headed up the switchbacks, stopping often to rest and enjoy the views behind us to the south. We passed from the rocks to the snow and finally arrived at the tunnel, breathing hard.

The tunnel was blasted through Ptarmigan Wall in 1931 to provide access to the Belly River country to the north. The south end of the tunnel offers spectacular views of Mount Wilbur. We paused here and then headed north through the tunnel. On the other side, we found an entirely different world. The south face was warm and sunny. Even at the tunnel's entrance, the snow was no more than a few inches deep. But on the north side, we entered a winter wonderland. Even at mid-day, the face of the mountain above us blocked the sun. A cold wind blew. The snow was deep. The views to the north, toward Canada, were spectacular. Elizabeth Lake lay in the valley half a mile below us. The summits of Natoas Peak and Mount Merritt loomed high above it.

We descended on the trail north of the tunnel, winding along the west face of the ridgeline east of the valley. We decided to walk far enough to get out of the shadow of the mountain and descend far enough to get out of the snow. Then we would stop for lunch.

Building a trail here was no small task. The path swinging around to the northeast from the mouth of the tunnel is a comfortably wide rock ledge built into the sheer face of the mountain. The builders even added a low rock wall on the downhill side of the trail. As we descended, we discovered we were not the first to walk the trail since yesterday's blizzard. We were not even the first to enjoy the view. In a protected spot, where the wind could not disturb it, was the clear imprint of a wolf's paw. The wolf had been facing west, toward the valley and the mountains beyond. This was the direction from which we had heard a wolf howl as we climbed up the trail.

We dropped below the snow line into the sunshine and stopped for lunch. A golden mantle squirrel appeared, looking for handouts. The view here was wondrous. The turquoise waters of Elizabeth Lake were now directly below us. Tucked into a valley to the southwest was Helen Lake. The Belly River connected the two, carrying water bound for Hudson Bay. Mount Merritt rose between the lakes, its peak towering more than 5,000 feet above them. Dotting the mountain's eastern face were several glaciers, most prominently Old Sun Glacier. The colors were glorious, with sharp contrasts going up the slope from green forest to brown mountain to white snow, with the blues of the lake and sky at the bottom and top. This was scenery, to quote *Backpacker*, "that'll suck the breath out of your lungs." George Ostrom, who tricked his wife into hiking the Garden Wall with a no-grizzly promise, and who hiked thousands of miles in Glacier after coming here with his parents in 1936, described this as the single most awesome scene in the park. I stood next to Bobby, who was soaking in the scene. "Unfrickinbelievable," he said.

* * *

I know how inadequate my words are to describe this place, or the other places Bobby and I have been. I have quoted the words of others, better words than my own, but they are still just words. Descriptions and statistics—the height of a mountain, the color of the sky, all the purple prose that can be penned, all the pretty words that can be strung together—are not the same as being there. They are not even close.

On the cover of the paperback edition of *A Walk in the Woods* by Bill Bryson, a review of the book declares that "the best way of escaping into nature is to read a book like *A Walk in the Woods*." Perhaps the reviewer, a writer for the New York Times, intended his comment as irony. The best way of escaping into nature, as all who've done it know, is to *escape into nature*. Reading any book, even the best of books, is a poor substitute. Americans read too little, but they escape into nature even less.

Looking back on that September day in Montana, I wonder how many Americans have been to this special place, how many people have seen what we saw. Not many, to be sure. And so, let me preach a bit. If your health permits, there is no good reason, absolutely none, for not coming here, for not seeing this. A hiking vacation is about as cheap as they come. Even with equipment, which can be reused time after time, a trip like this costs only a fraction of the price of going to Disney World. And it is far from impossible to reach this glorious place. When I climbed the trail to Ptarmigan Tunnel, I was a middle-aged man in middle-aged shape. The hike was just hard enough to make me feel I earned the view. And the earning is part of the pleasure. As Aldo Leopold observed in *A Sand County Almanac*, "things worked for have a higher value than things assured." So come here. Hike up Ptarmigan Wall. Stand where we stood and see what we saw. Don't just read about it. Do it.

When I have been to a magnificent place like this, it is my nature to want to share the experience, to tell my friends, to urge others to go. Perhaps this instinct is unwise. When he wrote *A Sand County Almanac* more than a half century ago, Leopold adopted a tone of pessimism, writing that "all conservation of wildness is self-defeating, for to cherish we must see and fondle, and when enough have seen and fondled, there is no wilderness left to cherish." I take a more optimistic view and cite Glacier as proof. Glacier is a popular national park. It is visited annually by thousands. Hundreds of miles of trails have been carved into its backcountry. Yet the wildest of America's wildlife—the timber wolf and grizzly bear—live here and thrive. They are proof that Glacier, for all the fondling, is still wilderness. They stand as testimony that man can cherish without destroying.

* * *

We left this spot reluctantly, trudging back up the trail toward the icy north face of Ptarmigan Wall and the mouth of the tunnel. We then descended the switchbacks on the talus slope to Ptarmigan Lake. Just below the lake, we discovered that a visitor had been on the trail since we passed here this morning. Something big and strong with sharp claws had been digging on the edge of the trail. A few strands of silver-tipped hair were hanging from a shrub beside the fresh diggings. I resumed my singing as we continued down the trail.

We had given some thought to making a side trip to Iceberg Lake on our hike down from the tunnel. When we got to the trail junction, however, the four of us agreed we had neither the time nor the energy. At Ptarmigan Creek, we stopped, pulled off our boots, and soaked our feet in the icy water. I couldn't bear to leave my feet in the water for more than a few seconds at a time, but the sensation was still sublime.

We reached the trailhead at four o'clock, loaded up, and headed east. Having two vehicles gave us the capacity to hike from point to point without returning to the same trailhead. We stopped at the Many Glacier Hotel and left the Town Car. Our plan for the next day was to hike a trail from Going to the Sun Road across Piegan Pass and down to the hotel. The four of us continued on in Brian's pickup truck. I volunteered to ride in the back. The temperature was dropping, so I bundled up. We drove east to Babb, turned south on Highway 89, and then turned west at Saint Mary on Going to the Sun Road. Along the way, we stopped to buy beer and firewood to ensure a sufficient supply of both for the next two nights. We pulled into Rising Sun campground just before dark, picked a spot, and put up our tents. We grilled chicken for dinner and settled in around the campfire.

I don't recall anything much from the talk around the fire that night, which I regret, for I'm sure things were said that would be worth recounting. But I didn't take notes, physical or mental, because the notion of writing about my travels with Bobby hadn't yet occurred to me. I doubt we discussed anything of seriousness. From my experience, there is an inverse relationship between the number of people around a campfire and the likelihood of a serious conversation. I do remember one slightly serious note—Brian's talking about wanting to find a woman to marry. Spewing a string of profanities, Bobby forbade him from considering it. Bobby, however, had one piece of good news to report. He had left a couple of minor emergencies at work, and his boss had insisted he bring a cell phone with him on our trip. Bobby had even been directed to take the phone on our hikes into the mountains, as if there would be a cell tower on top of Ptarmigan Wall. But even here at Rising Sun, close to civilization, Bobby remained incommunicado. Bobby showed us his cell phone; on its face were the words "no service." He was pleased. No good could come from a phone call here.

The next morning, we woke early. For the second day in a row, I cooked a big breakfast. Again, I used my stove. Bobby's was ready, just in case, but I didn't need it. I made bacon, eggs, instant oatmeal, and wheat toast. Bobby and David, both of whom are health nuts, turned up their noses at my eggs. Because it was a special occasion, we convinced Bobby to eat one. David refused even to taste them. I had three. That left eight for Brian; he ate them all.

After cleanup, we put all of our gear into our two tents and zipped them shut. Everything would be there all day with no one to watch over it, easy to steal if someone wanted to. But thieves rarely go camping. With the exception of a three-dollar water container someone inexplicably snatched from a hiding place in the Cascades on our trip in 2000, Bobby and I have never been victims.

We again loaded into my former pickup and headed west on Going to the Sun Road. To our south was Saint Mary Lake, with the oddly named Almost a Dog Mountain towering above its shoreline. I guess Lucky Dog was almost a dog when Bobby got through with her. Wild Goose Island lay in the middle of the lake. Just beyond the western shore, we stopped at Siyeh Bend and got out to begin our hike. Our walk today would take us up to Piegan Pass, 1,500 feet above the trailhead. On the north side of the pass, we would descend nearly 2,500 feet, hiking along the east side of the Garden Wall and passing alpine lakes. With a side trip to Grinnell Lake, we would cover nearly fourteen miles before reaching our destination at Many Glacier Hotel. Maybe not a full day for John Muir, but a full day for middle-aged flatlanders with office jobs. We hoped the Town Car would be where we left it. I double-checked to make sure I had the keys in my day pack.

It was another magnificent day, not a cloud in the sky, the temperature close to fifty. We were hiking in shorts with fleece pullovers. We had left our rain gear behind. Each of us, however, had one item we had not taken on the trail to Ptarmigan Tunnel the previous day—a fishing rod. Near the end of our hike, we planned to reel in brook trout from Lake Josephine and Swiftcurrent Lake. Brian had bought us an assortment of lures and flies; we were ready. I have already written of the futility of our fishing efforts, but we had high hopes at the beginning of the day.

We began our walk beside beautiful Siyeh Creek and then climbed through a forest of towering firs and spruces. For the first mile of the trail, we headed southwest, climbing through the trees. Then we turned due north toward Piegan Pass. The dense woods gave way to open meadows. To our east were the crests of Going to the Sun Mountain and Matahpi Peak. To the west was Piegan Mountain, a glacier of same name clinging to its eastern slope. Straight ahead to the north were Mount Siyeh and Cracker Peak. We were on the lookout for bears and other large mammals, but they were in hiding. We settled for birds and squirrels.

After walking nearly three miles, we came to a trail junction. The right fork led to Siyeh Pass at nearly 8,000 feet. We took the left fork, crossed a small creek, and wound along the open slope of Cataract Mountain, with magnificent views to the south. We could see Siyeh Bend, where we had started, and the slopes of Heavy Runner Mountain across Going to the Sun Road.

As we hiked along this slope up to the pass, we climbed into the snow, just as we had on the steep grade up to Ptarmigan Tunnel the day before. But on the sunny south face of Cataract Mountain, like the south face of Ptarmigan Wall, most of the snow had melted. Even when we reached the pass, the snow was no more than a few inches deep.

At the pass, we climbed on top of some snow-free rocks to eat lunch. The ambience was grand. Piegan Pass is a barren col separating the Saint Mary drainage from that of the alpine lakes in the Many Glacier region. We could see for many miles to both north and south. The trail guide told us to be on the lookout for mountain goats capering on the surrounding slopes. The views were spectacular, but we spotted no movement. No goats were capering.

After finishing our ham sandwiches and apples, we started down the slope. Like yesterday, the snow on the north slope below the pass remained deep. Because of the steepness of the grade, the trail followed a series of switchbacks. The heavy snow could have made the switchbacks difficult to follow, but fortunately someone had gone before us. A set of prints in the deep snow led the way down the trail. We followed them along the first of the switchbacks. Not long after we started, however, the prints left the trail. Disregarding the switchbacks and severe slope, the tracks headed straight down the mountain. We looked down at the precipice, wondered how the hiker did it, and continued crisscrossing, moving slowly to keep from losing the path. As the trail dropped in elevation and we descended toward the snow line, we left the deep drifts behind. When we next crossed the tracks of the hiker who had gone before us, the snow was only a few inches deep. Now we knew how the hiker had managed to head straight down the mountain. In the deep snow higher on the slope, we had assumed the tracks were made by boots. But now we saw that the tracks were not made by boots, or by shoes of any kind. David, our expert on animal tracks, studied the prints. After a minute's inspection, he declared that we were following a grizzly. Just how close we were, David couldn't say, but the tracks sure looked fresh to me. We peered ahead, searching the landscape, but saw nothing. As we continued our descent, I resumed my singing.

The trail below the pass was magnificent. The Garden Wall, dividing the continent, towered above us to the west, crowned by Bishop's Cap. Looking north down the valley, we could see Mount Gould and the southern slopes of Mount Grinnell. We walked through open parklands, with waterfalls to our west and streams crossing the trail. The summit of Allen Mountain soared above us to the northeast. A small pond, turquoise with glacial silt, lay tucked against the Garden Wall. A hawk soared in the blue sky overhead. From time to time, I would stop and slowly pirouette a full 360 degrees, soaking in the views in all directions, trying to burn them into my memory.

Surveying the scene, Brian declared with conviction, "This is the *shit*." A strange way to express it, perhaps, but we all understood. Brian's shorthand summed up what we were all feeling: This was what we came for. This was what made the effort worthwhile. How fortunate we were to be in this place, on this day, with these friends. Bobby smiled at Brian, nodded, and offered his agreement. "This *is* the shit."

We soon came to Morning Eagle Falls, a magnificent cascade on Cataract Creek, which runs down to the lakes in the valley. We had seen no sign of the bear since leaving the snow field just below the pass. But along this creek, we found, to quote David Peterson, "the palpable presence of grizz." We frequently had to step over berry-filled bear scat in the middle of the trail. As the four of us stood looking at one of the large piles, I thought of what Brian and Bobby had said. I altered the emphasis and shifted from figurative to literal. "Actually, *this* is the shit," I said.

Suddenly Bobby had a moment of great revelation. He realized that something he had regarded as a truism wasn't true at all. He announced this epiphany to the rest of us: "Well, I'll be damned, it isn't true after all. I always just assumed it did."

I took the bait: "What's it? Did what?"

Bobby explained: "A wild bear. Shit in the woods. And it doesn't. It shits in the middle of the frickin trail." Bobby smiled down at the bear shit with pride.

Brian stirred the pile with a stick. I suggested we check the scat's temperature to see how fresh it was, to find out if we were in imminent danger. It seemed like a good idea, but nobody else volunteered, and I sure wasn't going to do it. The four of us looked at each other and stuck our hands deeper into our pockets. We continued down the trail, not knowing whether we were following a family of bears or a single, prolifically shitting bear, and not knowing how far ahead of us the bear(s) were.

A number of factors increase the risk of a grizzly attack. A mother with cubs is most dangerous. Adolescent bears are a greater risk than adults. A bear protecting a fresh kill is likely to be aggressive. Coming too close to an unsuspecting bear greatly increases the risk as well. This often happens where thick underbrush blocks the bear's vision and something drowns out the noise of approaching hikers. And that's exactly where we found ourselves. The underbrush on both sides of the trail was thick, and the rapids on Cataract Creek, freshened from the snow and rain, were louder than David's bells and my singing.

We walked along the trail beside the creek. My senses were razor sharp. I strained to hear even the slightest telltale noise. My peripheral vision seemed to expand. Every slight movement I detected on either side of the trail brought me to an immediate halt. I strained to analyze every sound I heard, or thought I heard. More than once I mistook a four-ounce bird for a four-hundred-pound bear. Then something came to another of my senses. As I rounded a curve in the trail by the creek, I smelled something awful. It was a putrid smell, the way my dog smells when she's found a dead animal in the woods and rolled in the remains. I came to a stop. I sniffed. I looked. I listened.

Grizzlies are magnificent creatures, but they are not picky eaters. They like their meat fresh, but they will eat it rotten. As a result, they stink. Hikers who have survived grizzly attacks often recall the overwhelming funk that filled the air as they were being mauled. They remember the horrific breath of the beast that was gnawing on them. But the smell could not be as bad as the sound. Edward Abbey wrote that "in all of nature, there is no sound more pleasing than that of a hungry animal at its feed. Unless you are the food."

When Brian caught up with me on the trail, he stopped. Sniffing the air, he grimaced and confirmed what I was thinking: "Grizzly bear." Strangely, I was not the least bit frightened. Instead, I adopted a Calvinist, Presbyterian view and chose to believe that my fate was predestined. If the bear was going to eat me, there was nothing I could do about it and thus no point in worrying. But there was no bear attack, and we never knew whether the smell was from a grizzly, a grizzly's prey, or an animal that just happened to die close to the trail. Making as much noise as possible, we continued on our way. When we took our next break, I read aloud Molvar's comments about this section of the trail: "Grizzly bears abound in the low-elevation meadows; care must be taken not to disturb these majestic creatures." Bobby noted the strange choice of words. "Disturb *them*? I ain't disturbing nothing."

Reaching the valley floor, we passed Feather Plume Falls. The trail split, and we took the west fork to Grinnell Lake. The waters of the lake are a milky green as the result of glacial silt. On the south end of the lake is Grinnell Falls, fed by the melt from Grinnell Glacier on the slope above. We rested briefly on the shore. The views, as they had been all day, were splendid. We continued down the trail nearly a mile to the southeast corner of Lake Josephine. Across the clear water were the towering profile of Mount Gould and the glaciers on its face. We walked out onto a gravel bar along the eastern shore. After hauling our fishing rods all day, we finally put them to use. But they were of no use. Just as no wildlife had been capering, no fish were biting. While we fished, we took off our boots and soaked our tired feet in the clear, cold water. After nearly an hour of unsuccessful casting, we gave up and trudged on toward Many Glacier Hotel. We wound around tiny Stump Lake, then walked along the eastern shore of Swiftcurrent Lake. The trail, which was often boggy and wet, passed through a dense fir forest. At times, there were gaps in the trees, offering views of the lake and the eastern slope of Grinnell Point. We fished briefly in Swiftcurrent Lake, but again we had no luck.

Shortly before five o'clock, we trudged up the last hill to the parking lot. The Town Car was still there. I plopped down in the driver's seat, exhausted. But it was a good tired, a physical tired. It was far better than the mental exhaustion at the end of a long day at work, what Rick Bass describes as "the other kind of tired. Tired of the big city, the long hours, the coffee machine fill-ups, the pressure, the office, the end-of-day fatigue, the computer terminal, the telephones, the traffic," the tired that leaves you "listless, like a dog that has been kept in a kennel too long." The tired we were feeling now—the physical, wilderness kind—was the opposite of the mental, city kind. We were exhausted but exhilarated. It had been a magnificent day. The weather had been perfect and the scenery spectacular. We had seen no grizzlies, but their presence, to quote John Murray, had "elevated the mountains, deepened the canyons," and most assuredly had quickened our pulses.

We had seen very little wildlife, but we soon had a surprise on that score as well. As we headed east in the car toward the park entrance, we spotted a gangly, adolescent bull moose munching on plants in a creek near the road. We pulled over and got out to watch him. After a few minutes, he tired of watching us watch him and loped away into the trees.

We retraced the route we had driven the previous day, out to Babb, south on Highway 89, and back into the park to Rising Sun. We decided to recover the pickup that evening rather than leave it overnight even though we would pass by the trailhead the next morning on our drive across the park. We weren't worried that someone would try to steal the eleven-year-old Toyota, but we didn't think we could get all four of us and all of our gear into the Town Car. Brian and I dropped Bobby and David at the campground and continued west to the trailhead to get the truck. We took a couple of well-earned beers apiece for the forty-minute round trip.

While Brian and I were gone, Bobby and David were supposed to build a fire and start preparing dinner. When we got back, however, we found that Bobby had spent the time drinking. And he was drinking hundred-proof bourbon instead of six-percent beer. The whiskey had given Bobby renewed energy and loosened his tongue. He served as the principal entertainment for the night.

Bobby and I have very different attitudes about food. I relish a good meal. I like salt, butter, chocolate, and red meat. Bobby eats only to survive. He is more concerned with fat grams than flavor. I range from ten to twenty-five pounds overweight. Bobby looks like a refugee. I wear pants that are thirty-six inches in the waist with a thirty-inch inseam. Bobby is just the opposite. His pants are thirty inches in the waist, and he needs a thirty-six-inch inseam for his stork-like legs. And Bobby has no ass at all. He says he has a dog ass—just a back with a hole in it.

Our different attitudes about food have sometimes resulted in disagreement about the menus for our trips. On all of our trips, Bobby has threatened to feed us with MREs procured from the Air Force base on the coast. He has spoken of the convenience and nutrition of these Meals Ready to Eat, but he never mentions flavor. Before the trip to Glacier, Bobby again began pushing MREs. Via email, I asked my other connection to the military, Jonny Drake, for his opinion. Jonny wrote back: "Let me put it this way. The brass calls them Meals Ready to Eat. Enlisted men call them Meals Rejected by Ethiopians."

Based on Jonny's advice, I banned MREs from our official menu, but Bobby brought a couple anyway. After our fine last dinner of Caesar salad, grilled rib eyes, and creamed corn, Brian complained that he was still hungry. Bobby took a sip of bourbon and smiled. This was the chance he'd been waiting for. Acting for all the world like a drunken used car salesman, Bobby pulled out an MRE, held it up for Brian to see, and began extolling its virtues. Bobby focused first on efficiency, pointing out that an entire meal, with enough food to feed a hungry GI, was included in this single package. Then he spoke of nutrition, claiming the government's premier dietitians had combined various ingredients to ensure a balanced meal meeting a fighting soldier's every need. I observed the scene in amazement. Bobby was never this eloquent, or this passionate, in the cases the two of us had tried together. Having set the stage, Bobby then pried open the lid. Brian looked on in anticipation, licking his lips. He was young, naive, and hungry, and he didn't know Bobby. He had bought the whole shtick. David shied away, but I had to sneak a peek. It was like driving past a car wreck. You know you shouldn't look, that you'll regret it, but you look anyway. What I saw looked disgusting; the main dish was miniature wienies in a mauve-colored sauce. Only Bobby and Brian ate them. When they finished, I insisted they carry the empty container far away from our campsite. The smell reminded me of what we thought was a grizzly on the trail by Cataract Creek.

There always seems to be more drinking on the last night of a trip. It's part of sucking out the marrow before returning to the real world. This night was no exception. Brian and I focused on our cooler full of beer. He vowed to stay up until it was empty. But the effect of the beer on us paled in comparison to the effect of the bourbon on Bobby. He was far ahead of us, and there was no catching up. Bobby is amusing even when he's sober. On this night, our last night in Glacier, Bobby was in top form. As for David, he was ready to serve as camp doctor in case one of us stumbled into a tree or as designated driver in case the tree injury was too severe for him to treat.

We had a grand time around the campfire that night. We recounted our hike, reanalyzed the bear shit, and laughed over old stories. The high point of the evening was a joke Bobby told about a blind lumber inspector with no arms. Under normal circumstances, this is a three-minute joke, tops. But Bobby's presentation was significantly prolonged by the whiskey. He took fifteen minutes, embellishing the story, adding details and digressions. Brian and I were a receptive audience, our appreciation aided by the empty beer cans piling up beside the cooler. By the time Bobby got to the punch line—"a shithouse door on a tuna boat," maybe you've heard it—I was laughing so hard I was crying. Brian fell off the cooler. The bemused Dr. Sawyer studied the three of us. He seemed less entertained by Bobby's joke than by its effect on Brian and me.

At about 10:30, David called it quits and headed to his tent, shaking his head at the three drunks. Bobby soon stumbled after him. As I watched Bobby weave his way to the tent door, I was reminded that the shortest distance between two points is a straight line. Bobby took the long way. Brian and I were having too much fun and didn't want to turn in. I guess we got a little loud, because a few minutes later a woman in a nearby tent called out, in a thick German accent, "Be quiet. I am trying to sleep." She sounded like Marlene Dietrich "vanting to be alone." Brian gave up on his quest to finish all the beer, and we retired to my tent.

The next morning, three of us awoke with heavy heads. Bobby was suffering the most, as he should have been. We had brought food to cook for breakfast but decided on this last morning to eat in the restaurant on the road into the campground. It would take less energy, and there would be no clean-up. It was just a short walk to the restaurant, but Bobby and I didn't even have the energy for that. Bobby crawled into the driver's seat of the Town Car; I walked around to the other side.

I had parked the previous evening with the passenger side only a foot or so from a large boulder. Bobby cranked the engine, hit the gas, turned the wheel sharply to the right, and hit the boulder. There was a crunching sound, rock on metal. Bobby got a sick look on his face, that telltale "I'm a dumbass" look. But Bobby flirted with personal responsibility only briefly. Human nature took over. In a matter of seconds he transitioned from guilt to anger to blame. By the time he turned and faced me, *I* was the dumbass. "Why didn't you tell me there was a rock beside the car?"

I wasn't buying it, not for a second: "Cause I didn't know you were blind."

After Bobby and I realized we weren't going to agree on whose fault it was that the dumbass hit the boulder, we got out of the Town Car to check for damage. He wasn't as lucky as he had been after his confrontation with the free-range cow. This time, there was a dent and scrape on the right rear door. Bobby rubbed his temples. At breakfast, he hardly said a word, either because he'd just hit a rock, because he was mad at me because he'd just hit a rock, because he had a vicious hangover, or because our trip was ending. He was a shell of the man who had entertained us by the fire the night before.

Even today, Bobby insists it was my fault, that I should have known he didn't know the rock was there, that I should have known he was going to jerk the wheel to the right and hit it. He points out that he could have known about the rock only if he had parked the car the night before or if he had walked around the car before getting into the driver's seat. I think what really irritated him was my attitude. I would have been more sympathetic if he hadn't tried to blame me.

In addition to my attitude and his hangover, Bobby was irritated because the Town Car should have been rented to me, not him. I don't remember this, but he says I made the reservation but he put the car on his credit card while David and I collected our gear at baggage claim. He also wants you, the reader, to know that I didn't offer to help cover the repair costs. Well, I want you to know that he never asked.

Bobby says the rock incident cured him of any guilt for abandoning me during the sprinkler attack at Washoe Lake. I'm willing to say the two incidents make us even, but in the ledger of life he obviously feels I still owe him. Just recently, he threatened to slip an Ambien into my nightcap on a rainy night, remove the rain fly, and see how long it would take me to wake up.

After our store-bought breakfast in Glacier, we returned to our campsite, took down our tents, and loaded the car and truck. Not wanting to listen to Bobby bitch about the boulder, I rode in the truck with Brian. We headed west on Going to the Sun Road, crossing the park on the route we had tried to use the day we got here. It was another beautiful day, our third in a row. We again passed Saint Mary Lake, but this time we continued west past Siyeh Bend. We climbed up toward Logan Pass, Piegan and Pollock Mountains to our right, Heavy Runner and Reynolds Mountains to our left. The scenery was spectacular. We scanned the mountains looking for wildlife, but there was still no capering.

We stopped at Logan Pass to walk along the west side of the Garden Wall, the trail we had planned to hike our first day. The alpine tundra at the pass is a favorite spot for wildlife to congregate. Mountain goats are common. Oblivious to cars and people, they loll about in the sun like dogs. But there were no goats on this day. It was as if they had heard we were coming and disappeared. We walked north on the trail, Going to the Sun Road far below us to our left. But we didn't go far. The trail was crowded, and we were listless. Three-fourths of us were hung over. We returned to the vehicles and descended west from the pass.

Driving down from Logan Pass, Brian and I discussed his time as a football player. Brian was a star linebacker in high school and played as a freshman at Mississippi College, but he gave it up when he transferred to the University of Montana. I asked if he missed it. Brian said he missed his teammates. Anything else? I asked. The hitting, Brian confessed. He missed hitting people. He described the satisfaction of a perfect tackle, standing over a dazed ballcarrier. I guess it's the way I feel after a good cross-examination. I suppose we're still cavemen at heart.

The views of the western slopes as we descended toward the Loop were amazing. We passed by Mount Oberlin on our west with Logan Creek between the road and the mountain. The face of Haystack Butte loomed to our right, framed against the bright blue sky. We passed the Loop, the rapids of McDonald Creek below us. Shortly after reaching the eastern shore of Lake McDonald, we stopped for another short hike. We were starting to show signs of life. We walked across Going to the Sun Road and headed for Fish Lake, two and a half miles away. From the name, we figured we would surely catch fish there. The hike was through a thick forest of cedar, hemlock, larch, white pine, and Douglas fir. The trees were beautiful, but the views were limited. The lake itself was a disappointment.

Reeds and trees crowded the shoreline, making casting nearly impossible. We caught no fish in Fish Lake. In our weakened state, we surrendered quickly and headed back to the car.

It was now time for lunch. We drove a few miles back up Going to the Sun Road to a spot on McDonald Creek. We walked along the creek bank below a series of rapids to a pair of large flat rocks that were a perfect spot for a picnic. After eating, we stretched out for a siesta. I lay there watching the creek, listening to the music of the rapids. The water glistened in the sunshine. In Norman Maclean's masterpiece *A River Runs Through It*, he wrote: "The river ahead came out into the sunny world like a chatterbox, doing its best to be friendly. It bowed to one shore and then to the other so nothing would feel neglected." Frank Smythe's words are also fitting: "All streams are talkative, and a hill stream is the greatest chatterer of all. It is never boring, yet always soothing . . . . Do not think as you lie beside it, but let it think for you." I should have taken this advice. As I lay beside McDonald Creek, I was thinking our trip was too short. End-of-trip funk was creeping in. I wasn't ready to go home.

Finally, reluctantly, we rose from the rocks. We strolled along the creek bank before returning to the vehicles to head for the airport. When we made the obligatory tee shirt stop at West Glacier, I noticed that Bobby was putting a package in the mail. I asked him what he was doing, what he had bought, and why he was mailing it instead of taking it with him. He mumbled something under his breath; he obviously didn't want me to know. This made me even more curious, so I grabbed the package to see for myself. It was the blue can of GAZ, still sealed, still unused. Bobby had mailed it to Montana and was now mailing it back to Mississippi. This was more proof that he was the dumbass.

After Bobby paid the postage, the four of us left the park for the last time. We headed for the airport and turned in the damaged Town Car. Bobby, David, and I bade farewell to Brian. The three of us were headed back to work, back to our real worlds. He was headed back to school.

I had wondered before our trip if Brian might be reluctant to skip school to go with us, joining three middle-aged men on a camping trip. At the beginning of the trip, the four of us hardly qualified as close friends. I had just met David and hadn't seen Brian in years. We were twice Brian's age, and he had never met Bobby or David. By the end of our time in

Glacier, however, all was changed. We had adventured well, and we were good friends. And I was convinced that Brian had just as much fun as we did. His little brother Jonny later confirmed this. He told me Brian said he had more fun with us than he ever had on a camping trip.

Our flight home didn't land in New Orleans until midnight, but it was still hot and humid, just like the year before. Bobby, David, and I drove east to Bobby's house, arriving at two a.m. I had planned to spend the night there, then head to Jackson in the morning. When we got to Bobby's, however, I was still wide awake. I decided to keep going and turned north toward home.

Seeing white-tailed deer along roads in Mississippi is common, but this night was exceptional. In my drive up from the coast in the predawn hours, I counted more than thirty deer. I saw bucks alone and groups of does with their fawns. A few miles south of Jackson, I spotted a flock of wild turkeys in a meadow beside the highway.

This was more wildlife than we had seen in four days in the park billed by *Backpacker* as brimming with "enough wildlife to make a zookeeper drool with envy." But no matter. Though the wildlife was scarce, I had no complaints. Kenneth Brower, son of the first executive director of the Sierra Club, wrote that "the best times of my life have been in wild places." Our trip to Glacier had been one of the best times of my life.

CHAPTER
8

Grand Teton National Park - September 1998

A year after our trip to Glacier, we returned to the West, this time to the Tetons in northwest Wyoming. The Tetons, perhaps the most spectacular mountains in the lower forty-eight states, were given their name by a French Canadian fur trapper in the early 1800s. Tetons is French for breasts or, if you prefer a more literal translation, tits.

Little is known about the details of the naming of the Tetons. The identity of the fur trapper is unknown. Where and when he took the notion to name these mountains for a woman's breasts remain mysteries. My guess is that it happened around a campfire, the conversation lubricated with liquor. Whiskey and a long period of abstinence likely combined to enhance the lonely trapper's imagination. But this is only speculation, as is the tale that follows. Join me on this foray into fiction.

* * *

The setting is a broad, sweeping valley located between two mountain ranges running from north to south. The range to the east is modest in height and appearance. To the west, however, the towering mountains rise abruptly from the valley floor. These are, it has been said, mountains without foothills. The valley has not yet been given a name, at least not by the white men who have only recently seen it for the first time. It will later come to be known as Jackson Hole.

To make the scene more real, I have decided that you and I should be first-hand observers. And so that our presence will remain undetected, we are wearing disguises. Our costumes are quite convincing. We are tiny in size, we have feathers, and we can fly. We are posing as a pair of sage grouse. We will have a bird's-eye view.

It is late in the afternoon on a beautiful, crisp fall day. We are moving south along the valley floor, stopping occasionally, pretending to feed on seeds. This pretense is part of our cover. To our right, to the west, winds a beautiful river flowing parallel to the mountains. It will come to be known as the Snake. The sun has already dropped behind the towering summits that rise above the river into the sky.

As we move south, a strange noise comes to our ears. Our pace slows; we proceed carefully, fluttering from sagebrush to sagebrush. The sound is that of grown men. They are singing, and singing badly. As the wind shifts and begins blowing from the south, the tune is carried our way. A chorus of off-key voices reaches our ears. We hear the words: Frere Jacques, Frere Jacques, Dormez-vous? Dormez-vous? The scene is touching, even poignant.

There are four men altogether. They are huddled close to a campfire to ward off the late-afternoon chill in the shade of the great mountains. We slip behind the nearest sagebrush just as the last chorus of their wretched singing dies away. We are able to recognize the four men by their garb and their accents. These are French Canadian fur trappers, lured here by the bountiful beaver along the Snake and the creeks that feed it. They have had much luck. A tall stack of pelts lies nearby. From the fire comes the delicious aroma of grilling meat. We peek around the sagebrush to get a closer look. An elk hindquarter is sizzling over the fire on a makeshift spit. We are both hungry. After all, we only pretended to eat the seeds. There are live elk in the vicinity as well. The rut has begun, and we frequently hear the mating calls of bull elk, the bugle that is unique in all of nature. These elk are part of the massive herd whose descendants still winter in Jackson Hole.

You and I lean in, listening to the campfire conversation. Though they were singing in their native tongue, the French trappers are now, for our benefit, speaking almost entirely in English. From their conversation, we soon learn their names: Jacques, Francois, Baptiste, and Pierre. They are passing around a jug; all save Pierre are partaking. With both liquor and a campfire, there is ample oil for conversation. The campfire talk of men has changed little through the ages. We know it's just a matter of time before the talk of these men will turn to women, and soon enough it does.

Baptiste speaks first, fondly describing a winter spent with the Mandan Indians in Dakota Territory. The Mandans were a friendly, hospitable lot. The braves of the tribe were the most gracious of hosts. They believed they could gain knowledge and wisdom from their white visitors by permitting the Frenchmen to sleep with the tribe's squaws. Motivated purely by self-interest, the trappers encouraged this pagan belief. Reminiscing about how they outsmarted the braves, Jacques observes, "They were right, you know; we *were* the wise ones." Baptiste and Francois nod in agreement, laughing. Baptiste recounts an evening spent with a young raven-haired squaw whose hospitality was particularly vigorous. He recalls with pride that he shared his wisdom with her repeatedly. He looks over his shoulder and stares longingly toward the east, toward Dakota, a wistful smile on his lips. Francois responds with a similar tale, claiming even greater prowess. He brags that his partner's cries of ecstasy confused the Mandans in the adjacent hut, who mistook them for the war whoops of an attacking tribe. The others are skeptical, but they let it go. Now it is Jacques' turn. He has no choice but to call his colleagues and raise them, so he launches into a real stem-winder. He tells of a long night spent with a pair of beautiful Mandan maidens. To lend credence to his story, he provides the most intimate details. When the dawn broke, according to Jacques, both lovely maidens were satiated with knowledge. As he finishes his tale, you and I turn and wink our tiny birds' eyes at each other, silently sharing the recognition that these men, like men through the ages, are lying. I cover my beak with a wing to stifle a laugh.

In every group, there seems to be a naysayer, a self-appointed pessimist. Having him along is both good and bad. He adds a necessary dose of realism, but he's just no fun. In this group, the naysayer is Pierre. As the other three gleefully exaggerate their exploits with the young Mandan squaws, Pierre sits glumly, staring at the campfire. When at last he speaks, it is to point out, as he so often does, that the glass is half empty. He first reminds his trapping partners that warm hospitality was not the only gift they received from the Mandans. The lusty Mandan squaws also presented them with four raging cases of syphilis. A few years earlier, Pierre reminds them, the members of Lewis and Clark's Corps of Discovery had wintered with the Mandans and received the same hospitality and the same affliction. Pierre would be the one, you and I think to ourselves, to add an unpleasant non-fiction fact to this story. Pierre also points out that it has been six long months since they headed west from Dakota Territory. For half a year, one hundred and eighty lonely nights, they have not laid an eye, much less anything else, on any woman. The memories of the Mandan women are growing faint with time. Only the syphilitic symptoms remain. You and I scowl bird scowls at Pierre. Every party has a pooper, we think to ourselves.

The four now sit in silence, Pierre having spoiled their festive mood. Six months is a long time to go without female companionship, especially for a Frenchman. Women—actually the lack of women—have come to occupy the trappers' thoughts in every waking hour, not to mention the hours while they sleep. These are virile young men and full of life, and life should include the company and comfort of beautiful women. The six long months of abstinence have taken a heavy toll.

At last, Baptiste looks up to the heavens. He spots a billowing cloud, slightly pink in the twilight sky. One side of it is rounded, with a wisp of vapor protruding from the center of the semicircle. Pointing to the cloud, he speaks to the others: "The cloud—it looks like a teton, no?" Francois looks up and mutters his assent: "Aye, an enormous, pink teton." Jacques nods in agreement. But Pierre, he has no imagination: "It is but a cloud. It looks the way clouds look." You and I squint up at the cloud. We twist our heads from side to side, trying to see what the Frenchmen see. We are inclined to agree with Pierre, but why must he spoil their fun?

Not to be outdone by Baptiste's cloud, Jacques looks around for a discovery he can claim as his own. A smile brightens his face as he points to an anthill not far from our perch. Its red color is highlighted by the glow from the sunset. Jacques stares at the anthill with a combination of lust and nostalgia. The color is the thing. He announces his finding with a flourish. "Mandan teton, eh?"

Baptiste regrets that the thunder from his cloud has been stolen, but he has to agree. "Aye," he says, recalling an especially buxom Indian maiden. To Baptiste, the glass is half full. He has forgotten that the maiden had the face of a bison. Francois agrees as well. He stares at the anthill, his mind racing back to the memorable winter in Dakota, to all the young maidens who willingly accepted his knowledge. Maybe they weren't the loveliest, but their attitudes were keen. When Francois, still in a trance, looks away at the horizon to the south, he makes his own discovery—two heaping mounds of buffalo dung in the foreground. The mounds are conical; their shape is lovely, pert even. They sit side by side on the valley floor, perfectly symmetrical, separated by no more than an inch. Francois is delighted. Baptiste and Jacques have spotted single tetons, but he is the first to claim a double. Pointing to the mounds of dung with pride, Francois proclaims in a voice so loud it spooks a mule deer bedded down a hundred yards away: "Deux tetons." He doesn't have to tell the others that tetons are supposed to come in pairs. "Et décolletage," he continues, French for cleavage.

The three others stare at the two mounds. Though they are more than a little jealous of Francois for this discovery, Baptiste and Jacques are honest men, and the resemblance of the dung heaps to a woman's breasts is uncanny. They nod and agree: "Deux tetons," they repeat in unison. Pierre stares at his three companions, wondering if they have gone mad. From behind the sagebrush, you and I wonder the same thing. The three madmen stare at the two exquisite mounds of buffalo dung, reminiscing silently about better times. They are lost in thought, their minds in a long-ago time, a faraway place. The jug makes another revolution. All draw deeply, all but Pierre, who views the jug's contents as the cause of the insanity surrounding him.

Baptiste and Jacques know that Francois's discovery will be hard to top, but Baptiste has the advantage. The four men sit in a circle around the fire. Baptiste faces due west, toward the majestic mountains. He stares up at the peaks, backlit by the setting sun. He studies their magnificent shapes, pointing erect toward the sky. Suddenly it comes to him. These mountains are not a cloud made of vapor. They will not be dispersed by the wind. These granite slopes are not a mere anthill or mounds of buffalo dung. They will not be washed away by the next rain. Nor do their tops rest a mere six inches above the valley floor. Au contraire. These mountains, to borrow words from a great song written nearly two centuries later, have points all their own sitting way up high, way up firm and high. And there are not just two of them. Suddenly Baptiste leaps to his feet; he points at the three towering mountains dominating the center of the range. He cries out, at the top of his lungs: "Les Troix Tetons." Francois and Jacques, who are facing north and south respectively, turn their gaze to the jagged peaks. They both smile. These are tetons alright; huge, immutable tetons. Tetons of the firmament. Francois's buffalo dung is forgotten.

Pierre remains seated, facing east. We stare at him, awaiting his next move. Though the others pay him no mind, to us he has become the central character in the unfolding drama. He pokes the fire with a stick, refusing to become an accomplice to the absurd spectacle. Without turning to look, he asks in a patronizing tone: "Troix tetons?" Always the first to find fault, Pierre reminds the others that tetons are like martinis—one is not enough, he says, a clear reference to the cloud and anthill that started this silly contest, but three are too many. Six months earlier, when Mandan pairs were plentiful, his three compadres might have agreed. But it has been a long, lonely six months. As far as Baptiste, Jacques, and Francois are concerned, the more tetons, the merrier. They continue to gaze up at the mountains. Several minutes pass in silence. Finally, Pierre can contain his disgust no longer. He rises to his feet, turns around, and looks to the west. In a voice that will brook no disagreement, he proclaims that these are mountains: big, cold, hard, gray, rock mountains. They aren't tetons, they don't look like tetons, and they most assuredly wouldn't feel like tetons. His voice dripping with sarcasm, he invites the others to climb to the top and find out for themselves.

To the other three, who have now been staring longingly to the west for more than ten minutes, this borders on heresy. They have been listening to Pierre's bellyaching for the same six long months they have been without women. His surliness has been the poorest of substitutes. This is the last straw. He will burst their bubbles no more. Cursing and spitting, they drive him from the camp. He saddles his horse, glad to be taking his leave from this asylum on the range. He gallops away toward the east, leaving the Tetons and the madmen behind. He will never be seen again.

The three like-minded Frenchmen then settle back in beside the campfire. The tension has eased; Pierre's departure was overdue. We agree, though Pierre was the only sane one in the bunch. The three no longer sit in a circle around the campfire. Instead, they line up on the east side of the fire, all staring up at the beautiful, womanly curves of the mountains Baptiste has just named. Day slowly turns to night. The mountains are dark for a time, but then a new light appears from behind the men, from the east. It is the rising moon. The mountains shine again. As they stare up at the summits, Jacques experiences an epiphany of sorts. He points up toward the tallest of the peaks, beautiful in the moon glow. He clears his throat to get the others' attention, and then he speaks. This, he says, is a magnificent mountain, the crest more than 7,000 feet above where they now sit. Based on his experience as a mountain man, he estimates its peak is 13,770 feet above the level of the great seas. You and I, who know the facts, marvel at his accuracy. A mountain of such splendor, Jacques submits, deserves a name of its own. A beatific smile spreads across his face. With only the faint glow of the firelight, it would be easy to overlook the fact that he is missing half his teeth. To Jacques, however, his mouth is half full. He climbs to his feet, his eyes never leaving the summit. He spreads his arms, still gazing up to the west. Baptiste and Francois turn and look up at him expectantly. As if knowing that his words will live forever, Jacques lets the moment build. At last he speaks, and speaks solemnly. He utters but three words: "Le Grand Teton." The others smile and nod. The name is perfect. This magnificent mountain, this pillar of the firmament, is now the Grand Teton. And so it will be, forevermore.

The story now at an end, the mountains named, you and I take our leave from the contented Frenchmen and fly west toward the old mountains with their new name. We never make it to the base of the slopes, choosing instead to roost in a willow on the east bank of the Snake River, just downstream from a murmuring rapid. Tomorrow morning, we will remove our costumes and return to our homes. We will resume our normal roles, mine as a lawyer and writer of non-fiction and yours as a reader and whatever else you are or hope to be.

* * *

Before beginning the story of our trip to the Tetons, however, let me mention that these are not the only mountains to be named for a woman's breasts. In the San Juans in southwest Colorado, a beautiful cone-shaped mountain with a short protruding pinnacle atop its summit has been named Nipple Peak. In his treasure of a book *The Lost Grizzlies*, Rick Bass wrote that this mountain "is so aptly named that it causes a stirring in the heart and the groin, the size of it so immense and the shape of it so perfect." Imagine: aroused by a rock. Such, I submit, is the power of woman. But enough of this digression.

Nearly ten million years ago, in what is now northwest Wyoming, the earth cracked along a forty-mile-long fault running from north to south. The rocks on both sides of this crack began to shift, one side rising, the other falling. The side that rose became the Tetons. The side that dropped became the broad valley east of the Tetons, later to be named Jackson Hole. Even now, the Tetons continue to rise and Jackson Hole continues to fall, though the movement is imperceptible. The Tetons are growing a foot every three or four hundred years. Jackson Hole is dropping slightly faster than that.

Like the mountains of Yosemite and Glacier, the Tetons are heavily glaciated. The cause of glaciers is simple—more snow falls than melts. Over time, the snow compresses into ice. During the periodic Ice Ages after the Tetons were formed, massive glaciers formed in the mountains. The most extensive glaciation occurred during the most recent Ice Age, known as the Pinedale Period. The glaciers that formed in the high country during this period slid down the major canyons. The glaciated canyons include those bearing the names Cascade, Garnet, Avalanche, and Death. The glaciers deepened the gorges as they went, scoured the rock walls, and permanently altered the landscape in their wakes. Writing of glaciers, John Muir observed that "nature chose for a tool not the earthquake or lightning to rend and split asunder, not the stormy torrent or eroding rain, but the tender snow-flowers noiselessly falling through unnumbered centuries . . . . Laboring harmoniously in united strength they sculptured, fashioned, modeled all the range, and developed its predestined beauty."

When they reached the foot of the mountains on the eastern slopes of the Tetons, the massive glaciers formed extensive moraines. These moraines in turn created the string of lakes that line the base of the eastern slopes. On a calm day, the mirror image of the wondrous jagged mountains towering above the lakes can be seen as reflections on the surface. A viewer standing on the eastern shores of these lakes gets a double dose of the horns and peaks and knife-edged ridges as well as the flower-filled canyons that run between them.

Many mountains in the lower forty-eight states, including more than a hundred in Colorado alone, are taller than any of the Tetons, but none of them is more spectacular. The reason is the Tetons' suddenness. The gradual increase in elevation seen in other ranges—the preamble to the highest slopes—is missing here. As if without warning, the Tetons rise straight up from the floor of Jackson Hole, offering one of the most spectacular sights in America. This sight has led to rhapsodies that rival those offered to Yosemite. The view of the Tetons from Jackson Hole led surveyor Dr. Ferdinand Hayden to christen them the "summit of the world." In 1883, President Chester Arthur visited the Tetons and Jackson Hole on a fishing trip. A member of his entourage wrote of their first view of the valley and mountains: "There burst upon our view a scene as grand and majestic as we had ever witnessed. Below us, covered with grasses and flowers, was a lovely valley. Along the whole westerly edge of this valley . . . towered the magnificent Teton Mountains, their snowy summits piercing the air."

The views of the Tetons are magnificent from both the east and west, but the view from the east, from Jackson Hole, is both more famous and more spectacular. That is because it is on this side of the range that the earth cracked. As a result, the mountains slope away more gently to the west. Jackson Hole is about 6,500 feet above sea level. As Jacques correctly surmised, the Grand Teton rises more than 7,000 feet from the valley floor. He also pegged the height of its summit precisely—13,770 feet above sea level.

As mountains age, their peaks become rounded, their knife-like edges smooth. Among the mountains of the world, the Tetons are quite young, in fact the youngest in the Rocky Mountain chain. Hundreds of millions of years from now, their appearance will be far different from what we see today. Someday, they will even have the smooth, rounded appearance of the Appalachians, the oldest of America's mountains and some of the oldest on Earth. When that day comes, the Tetons really will look like tetons.

During the vast eons before the Tetons began to rise, this entire region was repeatedly covered with shallow seas. The seas left behind a thick, flat layer of sedimentary rock atop the granite basement rock. When the mountains heaved upward, they pushed the layers of sediment upward with them. Ancient layers of sedimentary rock that were left behind by the seas—dolomite, shale, sandstone and limestone—can still be seen on the tops of the peaks on the west side of the range and its north and south ends. On the east side, however, these sedimentary layers have been stripped away by wind, water, and, most profoundly, the scouring action of glaciers. The stripping exposed the more resistant and much older granite that forms the Grand Teton and the surrounding peaks in the center of the range. Though these mountains are the youngest in all of America, the rock that forms them is nearly as old as Earth itself.

Native Americans first ventured into Jackson Hole and the Tetons some 12,000 years ago. Because of the severity of the winters in the unprotected valley, the visits were limited to late spring, summer, and fall. The appearance of the valley and mountains to these first visitors was much the same as we see it today. The U-shaped canyons formed by the Pinedale glaciers bisect the mountains from east to west. The canyons are filled with mountain streams fed by snow melt and the few remaining glaciers clinging to existence in the shade at high elevations. In the valleys and canyons are magnificent rock gardens. Waterfalls cascade over the polished granite sides of the canyons, dropping hundreds of feet. Beginning in June, the valley floors are abloom with wildflowers. The profusion of color progresses from one species to the next, then moves up into the canyons as the summer wears on. Sagebrush buttercups are followed by yellow bells, steershead, and spring beauties. Others include larkspur, wild buckwheat, lupine, and scarlet gilia. Nature creates a kaleidoscope of all the colors of the rainbow and all the shades in between. In the higher elevations can be found the alpine forget-me-not, the official flower of Grand Teton National Park.

The Snake River snakes its way through the valley from north to south, coming down from its headwaters in Yellowstone. Beaver and river otter inhabit the Snake and its tributaries. The river is also home to herons, white pelicans, trumpeter swans, Canada geese, mallards, and cinnamon teal. The waters teem with trout, which lure fly fishermen as well as ospreys and bald eagles. The river's banks are lined with willow, cottonwood, spruce, and aspen, providing shelter for birds of many species and food and construction materials for the industrious beaver. The ponds they build create habitat for waterfowl and gathering places for hundreds of other species that make the valley their home.

Abundant wildlife thrives away from the river and ponds as well. Mule deer are common. Moose are frequently seen near canyon streams and in the valley lowlands. Though bears are less prevalent here than in Glacier, black bears are common. Grizzlies are rare but not unheard of. Among all the inhabitants of the mountains, the Tetons are best known for their elk. Nearly 3,000 of them, the largest herd in the world, spend their summers in the mountains and then descend to Jackson Hole when winter approaches. Smaller mammals also inhabit the mountains. Pikas live in the rock gardens. Fat marmots sun themselves before taking to their dens for winter. Chipmunks, red squirrels, and two species of ground squirrels are common, as are snowshoe hares. The park is home to muskrats, porcupines, martens, and weasels. Antelope, bison, and coyotes live in the valley.

In Glacier, the trees are much larger and denser on the western slopes, and the eastern side of the park is dry and barren in comparison. Here in the Tetons, it's just the opposite. The western slopes are drier, the trees smaller and scarcer. In the low elevations on the eastern slopes are dense evergreen forests. Lodgepole pines are the most prevalent, but Douglas firs are common as well. On the higher slopes, these trees give way to beautiful subalpine fir and Engelmann spruce and then to white bark pine. Just before tree line is a layer of krummholtz, the name given to stunted specimens that barely cling to life at the highest elevations at which trees can survive.

* * *

John Muir observed that nothing in nature is wasted; to the contrary, all of the natural world is "eternally flowing from use to use." And so it has been for Jackson Hole and the Tetons. In recent centuries, Americans have come here for countless reasons, some honorable and some not. In roughly chronological order, those who have spent time in Jackson Hole and the Tetons include American Indians, fur trappers, outlaws, homesteaders and cattlemen, hunters and fishermen, tourists and hikers.

Before the first white man discovered Jackson Hole and the Tetons, Indians were frequent visitors. The tribes who came here included the Utes, Nez Perce, Gros Ventre, Crow, Blackfeet, and Shoshoni. During the short summers, the Indians hunted the abundant wildlife in the valley and mountains and fished in the Snake. Because of the brutal winters, the Indians did not remain year round. The valley offers little shelter from the storms that sweep down from Canada. Heavy snowfalls and temperatures that dip far below zero are common. The mountains, where the climate is even more severe, often lie buried under more than ten feet of snow. At the highest elevations, to borrow John Murray's description of Colorado's mountains, there are but two seasons—winter and the Fourth of July. When fall came, the Indians thus sought shelter in valleys that offered better protection. In later years, one of the tribes chose to winter here not out of choice but to survive. Some tribes had begun trading with the white man for rifles. The Shoshoni, with no comparable weapon, were helpless when attacked. They took refuge in the Tetons, living in caves and hidden valleys.

Just as they had come close to the mountains of Glacier, Lewis and Clark's Corps of Discovery narrowly missed the thermal wonders of Yellowstone and the Tetons. In their journey west, the Corps passed within 75 miles of Yellowstone and 125 miles of the magnificent range of mountains to its south. From a different direction, Lewis and Clark might have seen the Tetons even from this distance. Because they rise straight up from the plain, the Tetons were used as an important landmark for early western travelers. On a clear day, they were (and are) visible from as far away as 150 miles.

Though Lewis and Clark missed discovering Yellowstone and the Tetons, a member of their Corps became the first white man to explore the region. Lewis's reports to Jefferson led hundreds of other young men to head west in search of riches. He wrote that "the Missouri and all its branches from the Cheyenne upwards abound more in beaver and Common Otter, than any other streams on earth, particularly that proportion of them lying within the Rocky Mountains." This report was widely circulated and had the same effect as the discovery of gold at Sutter's Mill four decades later. Many heard the call, gave up their lives in the East, bought traps, guns, and ammunition, and headed up the Missouri.

John Colter was the member of the Corps of Discovery who discovered the Tetons. In 1806, three years after their journey began, Lewis and Clark and their men were paddling downstream on the Missouri on their return from the Pacific. They met two trappers who were headed west to the headwaters of the Missouri and needed a guide. Although the men of the Corps had spent the last three years away from civilization and their homes and families, Colter liked the West. He asked the leaders for permission to take his leave and head back upstream with the two trappers. Lewis and Clark agreed, Clark writing that they were "disposed to be of service to any of the party who had performed their duty as well as Colter had." They paid Colter for his work and outfitted him with traps, canoes, powder, and lead.

By the following spring, Colter had split from the two trappers and again began the long journey down the Missouri to St. Louis, this time alone in a canoe. He met a boat carrying a large party of trappers and hunters under the leadership of Manuel Lisa, a St. Louis merchant. Lisa told Colter he planned to set up trading posts among the Indian tribes of the region. Once again, Colter was asked to serve as guide and, once again, Colter chose to remain in the wilderness rather than return to civilization. He climbed aboard Lisa's boat, where he found among its occupants three fellow members of the Corps of Discovery.

Where the Bighorn and Yellowstone Rivers converge, fifty miles east of present-day Billings, Lisa's men established their first trading post, the first building erected by white men in what is now Montana. As the post was nearing completion, Lisa requested Colter to travel to the tribes of the region—the Cheyenne, the Shoshoni, and the Crow—to encourage them to bring their furs to the post to trade. Though winter was approaching, Colter agreed. In November of 1807, he set off by himself, heading into lands no white man had ever seen.

Colter started his journey by traveling west along the Yellowstone River. He then turned south and descended into the valley of the Bighorn River, which was reputed to be the home of both the Crows and the Shoshonis. Colter crossed into what is now Wyoming and then headed west, following the North Fork of the Shoshone River. After days of walking, he came upon a land of rumblings and underground explosions, with boiling springs that emitted sulfuric gases. Colter named the river the

Stinking Water because of the smell. The region was subsequently dubbed Colter's Hell. Later still, it became Yellowstone.

After making this discovery, Colter turned southwest, probably crossing the Continental Divide at Togwotee Pass. If this was the route he took, the pass would have provided him with the first sighting by a white man of the Tetons. Colter walked down into the valley, becoming the first white man to enter Jackson Hole. The Indian tribes had abandoned the region for the winter, and Colter crossed the empty valley on snowshoes. After fording the Snake River, he headed up into the Tetons toward a pass at their south end. From here Colter looked down into a valley in present-day Idaho. The valley was later named Pierre's Hole for Pierre Tivanitagon, an Iroquois trapper. Colter then turned north on an Indian trail along the west side of the Tetons, but he again found no Indians. The valley below him, like Jackson Hole, was too exposed to the blizzards and winter winds from the northwest. The Indians were elsewhere. Near Henry's Fork, a tributary of the Snake, Colter finally found a village of Shoshonis. He told them of the new trading post and offered gifts. He then climbed back into the Tetons, crossing from west to east and returning to Jackson Hole. Traveling in the most brutal months of the year, Colter followed a trail through the mountains to the largest of the lakes at the foot of the eastern slopes, which later became Jackson Lake. He hiked north into the heart of Yellowstone country, past what are now Yellowstone Lake and Mammoth Hot Springs. He then turned east, retracing his route downstream along the North Fork of the Shoshone, ultimately arriving back at the trading post in the spring of 1808. The reaction of those present at the post is unknown, but they must have been astonished. Colter had walked 500 miles in the dead of winter, all alone, and crossed the Tetons twice. He had been the first white man to see not only the Tetons but Jackson Hole, Pierre's Hole, the Bighorn Valley, the Absaroka Mountains, and the wonders of Yellowstone.

Later that year, Colter again defied death. In the fall of 1808, he and John Potts, another member of the Corps of Discovery, were trapping in the Three Forks country of western Montana. Early one morning, they were surrounded by a large band of Blackfeet, the most fearsome of the area's tribes. Colter saw they had no chance to escape and pulled his canoe ashore to surrender. Potts tried to get away but was immediately riddled with arrows. The Blackfeet dragged his body ashore and hacked it to pieces.

The Indians then decided to make a game of killing Colter. They stripped him naked, gave him a short head start, and let him run for his life. Colter headed across the six-mile plain toward the Jefferson River, which had been named for the president by Lewis three years earlier. The plain was covered with prickly pear. Colter's bare feet were bleeding, but he outpaced all but one of the Blackfeet. As his only close pursuer came within striking distance, Colter whirled, snatched the Blackfoot's spear, and killed him. He then jumped into the river and hid under a log. When the rest of the Indians reached the river, they discovered their dead comrade and scoured the river and both banks. But Colter's hiding place was secure; the Indians gave up and left. Colter then climbed to the bank, naked and shoeless, his feet filled with prickly pear spines. Despite it all, he walked the 200 miles to Manuel Lisa's trading post in only seven days.

As it turned out, single life in the wilderness suited Colter far better than life as a married man in the city. Not long after his escape from the Blackfeet, Colter returned to St. Louis, took a bride, and settled down. A few years later, this extraordinary man, who survived a winter alone in the Tetons as well as the Blackfeet's savage game, died of jaundice. He was only thirty-eight.

Bobby views the life of John Colter as a lesson, a parable for modern man. When he was in the mountains, Colter lived off his wits and his will. His feats were Herculean. He was, any impartial observer would have to agree, a badass. But when Colter returned to the city and took a wife, everything changed. He got soft; his spirit, the spirit of the mountains, was broken. He gave up, turned yellow, and died. To Bobby, the lesson is obvious. For Colter, life as a mountain man was liberating and healthy, life in the city suffocating and lethal.

In the years after Colter's discovery of the Tetons, legions of fur trappers flocked to the beaver-rich waters in the region. The most famous were Bill Sublette, Jim Bridger, Kit Carson, Jedediah Smith, David Jackson, and Joe Meek. A number of businesses and partnerships flourished. One of the most successful was Smith, Jackson & Sublette, which sounds more like a law firm than a trio of trappers. Men came to the West by the score, seeking beaver in every pond, river, and tributary. They roamed the uncharted territory, hunting buffalo, elk, antelope, deer, and bear. They made peace with the Indians who were willing and warred with those who were not.

Early trappers played a central role in the exploration and settlement of the Rocky Mountains and northwest. As mountain man George Ruxton put it in *Life in the Far West*, "these alone are the hearty pioneers who have paved the way for settlement of the western country." Writing a century later, Hiram Chittenden concurred: "*They* were the 'pathfinders' of the West, and not those later official explorers whom posterity so recognized. No feature of western geography was ever *discovered* by government explorers after 1840."

The early trappers named many of the features in the West, often for themselves and their comrades. Jackson Hole was named for David Jackson, one of the partners in the successful fur partnership. A "hole" was the name given by trappers to a high-altitude valley surrounded by mountains. Jackson reportedly spent the winter of 1829 on the shore of the largest of the lakes in the valley, which was also named for him. A bay on Jackson Lake was named for John Colter. Leigh Lake, which lies at the foot of the Tetons just south of Jackson Lake, was named for early homesteader Richard Leigh, known to one and all as Beaver Dick. Jenny Lake, just to its south, was named for his wife.

During the heyday of the fur trade, the trappers gathered each summer in Pierre's Hole on the west side of the Tetons to trade furs, drink whiskey, and swap stories. Wagon trains traveled from St. Louis to Pierre's Hole with supplies for the mountain men. Money was scarce, so beaver pelts served as legal tender. With demand in Europe high, a beaver pelt could be traded for six dollars in goods.

After the annual rendezvous, the trappers would again scatter to their favorite spots in search of beaver. Many of the trappers had Indian wives and wives in the East as well. As a rule, neither was aware of the other's existence. The trappers lived off the land. According to Ruxton, they ate everything from "buffalo down to rattler, including every quadruped that runs, fowl that flies, and every reptile that creeps."

Some of the trappers made big money during the peak of the fur trade, but by 1840, times were tough. Fashion had changed, prices for pelts had dropped, and beaver had become scarce. The annual rendezvous faded into oblivion, and only a stubborn few continued to ply their trade. The era of the mountain man was over. At least for a while, the Tetons became wilderness again.

The trappers' summer rendezvous was never held in Jackson Hole. Completely surrounded by mountains, it was too inaccessible. This inaccessibility, however, is what attracted the men who came here in the decades following the Civil War. Ranches had proliferated in the West by then. The crime of choice among the region's outlaws was stealing horses. It was hard to survive in this land without a horse, and stealing a man's horse was considered the same as killing him. Horse thieves were thus punished like murderers and summarily hanged or shot. But in this huge land, the risk of getting caught was slim. Jackson Hole became a favorite hideout for thieves. It was not only surrounded by mountains but, once within, contained innumerable hiding places. The thieves made use of Indian trails that cut through the mountains and made pursuit virtually impossible. One favorite became known as Horse Thief Pass.

The era of the horse thief was followed by the arrival of cattlemen. Beginning in the late 1800s, homesteaders moved into the valley. Barbed wire was strung. Settlers soon began serving as guides for wealthy hunters and fishermen. By 1890, Jackson Hole had sixty-four permanent residents. After the turn of the century, the first dude ranch was established.

The early visitors to the Tetons undoubtedly appreciated their beauty, but they gave no thought to any formal action to preserve the mountains or the valley at their feet. They were there to make a living, by trapping beaver, stealing horses, or herding cattle. But here as elsewhere, increasing efforts to tame the wilderness led to a contrary movement to keep it wild. The first step toward preservation occurred in 1897, when President Grover Cleveland established the Teton Forest Reserve. A decade later, Teton National Forest was created. Two decades after that, in 1929, conservationists achieved a partial victory when Congress passed the bill creating Grand Teton National Park. The park as originally constituted, however, included only the eastern slopes of the range and a narrow strip along their base that contained Leigh, Jenny, Bradley, Taggart, and Phelps Lakes. Virtually all of Jackson Hole lay outside the park.

Before the park was established, John D. Rockefeller, Jr. had begun buying up land in Jackson Hole to hold until it could be turned over to the government for inclusion in the park system. Many were opposed to expansion of the park, particularly cattlemen who were convinced that their grazing rights would be abolished. The controversy raged; Congressional approval for inclusion of the Rockefeller lands was withheld. For more than a decade, Rockefeller continued to hold and pay taxes on 30,000 acres of land in the valley. Finally, after Rockefeller grew impatient and threatened to sell, President Roosevelt issued an executive order on March 15, 1943, creating Jackson Hole National Monument. Many in Wyoming were outraged by Roosevelt's unilateral act. The executive order was regarded as a blatant violation of the state's rights. Acts of vandalism followed. Ranchers led cattle across the land in the newly created monument. The Jackson Lake Ranger Station was gutted. A bill abolishing the national monument passed both houses of Congress, but FDR refused to sign it.

Over the years that followed, however, feelings subsided. Many locals began to see the wisdom of adding Jackson Hole to the park. On September 15, 1950, President Truman signed a bill adding land in the National Monument to Grand Teton National Park, more than tripling its size. The park now encompasses 310,000 acres.

* * *

Nearly 50 years after Truman signed the bill, we chose Grand Teton National Park as the destination for our third trip to the West, which Bobby and I were now describing to our families as an annual event. Until right before our trip, it looked like we would have a complete reunion from Glacier. Bobby, David and I would fly to Salt Lake City, then on to Jackson Hole. Brian would again skip classes, this time driving south from Missoula to meet us. Shortly before the trip, however, Brian backed out. His course load was just too tough, he couldn't reschedule a test, and he was trying to save all his money for an engagement ring. When I told Bobby that Brian was bailing out on us because of school and a woman, Bobby's reaction was predictable. He cursed me, though I was just the messenger, then demanded Brian's phone number so he could curse him directly. I thought Brian's reasons were legitimate. My only complaint was that he took the coward's way out: He sent an email instead of calling.

When I began writing about this trip, I told Bobby I couldn't remember how we chose the Tetons. Bobby said that I had picked the destination based on what the Tetons were named for. I knew that wasn't true; I didn't yet know what they were named for when we decided to go there. To get to the truth, I turned to David. He remembered sitting next to two girls on the flight home from Glacier the year before. The girls were returning from a hiking trip to the Tetons. They said the Tetons were not only spectacular, but they had seen abundant wildlife on every day of their trip. After seeing precious few animals capering in Glacier, the Tetons sounded inviting.

* * *

More than a century ago, John Muir wrote that "thousands of tired, nerve-shaken, over-civilized people are beginning to find out that going to the mountains is going home." Bobby is hardly over-civilized, but as we planned our trip to the Tetons it became clear that he fit Muir's description in all other respects. The constant demands of work and family had worn him thin. He was tired and nerve-shaken. He needed to go to the mountains. This need came through not only when we talked, but also in what he wrote. We were considering using one of our days in Wyoming for a raft trip on the Snake. I was in charge of finding an outfitter. A few weeks before our departure, I sent Bobby an update by email, reporting that I had tried to call an outfitter but got no answer. In less than an hour, Bobby responded to my email with one of his own. Bobby's response was in the style William Faulkner, who worked at the post office in his hometown of Oxford, Mississippi, would have used if he had ever gone postal. This is what Bobby wrote:

> Probably didn't get an answer because they are out on the frickin river doing what they want for a living in their short life span rather than sitting in an office dying every day waiting for the phone to ring and it's just some asshole on the other end with some two-bit problem that you now have to get involved with and screw up the rest of your schedule only to have to stay late to do a dumbass report for corporate with others you don't want to be around day in and day out, which only puts you further behind doing the no-redeeming-social-value projects you do like a frickin hamster knowing that anybody without any interest can do the same thing until you either retire too old to enjoy life or die prematurely without ever living the life you

want if only for a few years cause you got this other frickin anchor around your neck that's called a family that drains you for what little life you have left and doesn't think of you as anything but a paycheck and bitches and moans whenever you spend less money on yourself during the entire year including such things as camping equipment than you do on those ungrateful bastards in one weekend for five days out of an entire year to do something you enjoy with people you enjoy being with for a frickin change knowing in the back of your mind that it doesn't have to be that way, that you will probably only get more regretful with age wondering why you just didn't tell everybody to buzz off and go take that job in the park and go hit the road and live a real life seeing what there is out there taking in what God has created before life passes us by and we wake up and just snap and just blow the shit out of everybody going down in that final blaze of glory with at least the satisfaction that you took a few of the bastards with you.

Well, I thought, it's time for us to go. To keep from going postal, Bobby needed this trip, and he needed it now. He needed to escape the cacophony of commerce; he needed to go home to the mountains. He needed to give his spirit a good cleansing, to walk in the woods, to laugh by a campfire. He needed to spend time in a place in the world little affected by man, little changed by so-called progress. He needed to savor cool nights, to breathe clean air. At the end of a long, hot summer working in Mississippi, Bobby needed to head north, climb into the mountains, and escape from the crowd. Increases in latitude, altitude, and solitude would improve his attitude. He needed to get away from the real world to a world that really is real.

Will Dilg once wrote: "I am weary of civilization's madness and I yearn for the harmonious gladness of the woods and of the streams. I am tired of the piles of your buildings and I ache from your iron streets. I feel jailed in your greatest cities and I long for the unharnessed freedom of the big outside." Bobby had this same weariness, this same longing, and so did I.

* * *

Finally, at last, the day arrived, and it arrived early for me. I rose at 3:30 a.m., which was 2:30 where we were headed. I drove three hours to New Orleans to meet Bobby and David and catch the early morning flight to Salt Lake City. I could have flown out of Jackson, but from New Orleans, the connections were better and the fares cheaper. We landed in Salt Lake at 10:00, caught our connection, and were on the ground in Wyoming by noon. The airport in Jackson Hole is the only one in America that's in a national park. Some consider this a convenience, others an abomination. We loaded our rental car, drove to Jenny Lake Campground, and picked out a site.

Taking into account the lessons learned on our earlier trips, we expanded the length of this one. We would be in the Tetons for six days. We had analyzed and reanalyzed the trail guide—the only one I know of that actually contains a drawing of bear shit—but our plans were not set in stone. We hoped to spend several days backpacking in the high country along the Teton Crest Trail, but the forecast was not encouraging. As it turned out, in comparison to our other trips, this one earned low marks for weather but high marks for wildlife. The girls who recommended we come here had been right.

When we arrived in Jackson Hole, the weather was partly cloudy, the temperature in the sixties. After we put up our tents, Bobby and David studied the bear precautions in the trail guide to ensure that our camp would not be marauded while we were gone. We then set out on our first hike, a flat trek around Jenny Lake. With one side trip, the length would be eight miles.

Jenny Lake is two and a half miles long and a mile and a half wide. The lake was created when an enormous glacier slid downhill from Cascade Canyon to the valley floor. Because the valley slopes gradually from east to west, the valley floor acted as a dam. The glacier did not move out into the valley when it reached the foot of the mountains, but instead spread to the north and south. When the glacier melted, it left the elongated lake that exists today.

We walked around the south shore of the lake, the Tetons towering directly ahead of us. We then turned north, walking in the shade of the spruces and firs along the lake's western shore. The trail is one of the easiest and most popular in the park and thus was crowded. At the center of the lake on the west side, we came to Cascade Creek, which courses down from a glaciated canyon. The creek is fed by Lake Solitude and several smaller ponds high in the mountains. We took a left and walked along the trail that follows the creek up into the canyon. Cascade Creek is a classic mountain stream, with quiet pools separating the rapids. Not far up the canyon is Hidden Falls, over which the creek leaps before finishing its journey to the lake. From our vantage point, I guessed that the falls were more than a hundred feet high. It was mid-afternoon by now, and the falls were in complete shade. Storm Point, which towered above the falls to the northwest, was still bathed in sunlight.

We crossed Cascade Creek on a footbridge below the falls and climbed the steep trail four hundred feet up to Inspiration Point, which provides exceptional views to the east. Jenny Lake lies in the foreground, the terminal moraines that created it obvious from this viewpoint. In the distance are the relatively modest slopes of the Gros Ventre Mountains. Between the lake and the Gros Ventres lies the broad expanse of Jackson Hole. To our southwest were the summits of Mount Owen and Teewinot Mountain, both of which rise to more than 12,000 feet. After resting while we enjoyed the view and took pictures, we headed back down the trail. When we got to the lake, we continued along the western shore, leaving the crowd behind. The trail along the lake's edge wound through a forest of Douglas and subalpine fir. Near the northern edge of the lake, two mule deer does stood beside the trail. Both allowed us to approach within ten feet. They calmly posed for photographs, showing no concern as we whispered and pointed and clicked. We were determined to outlast the two does, and they finally sauntered away into the woods.

Hunting, with the exception of a limited hunt to thin the enormous elk herd, is prohibited in Grand Teton National Park. In fact, with this one exception, hunting is banned in all the national parks. And, somehow, the animals know it. They have become accustomed to people and have lost their fear. In the national parks, animals are less timid and more approachable than they are elsewhere. Seeing wildlife up close is wonderful, but it seems unnatural, contrived. Wild animals should be wild.

Beyond the north end of the lake, we crossed the creek that connects String Lake and Jenny Lake. String Lake is a small pond lying between the two larger lakes named for Beaver Dick Leigh and his wife Jenny. Leigh

Lake is sixty feet higher than String Lake, which in turn is forty feet higher than Jenny Lake. The short creek that runs from String Lake to Jenny Lake is filled with rapids. In the late afternoon, we stood on the footbridge that crosses the creek and enjoyed the sights and sounds.

We turned back south and walked along the eastern shore of Jenny Lake. It was nearly 7:00; we had to hurry to make it to camp before dark. Along the way, we admired the view of the Tetons across the lake to the west. From the closer perspective on the other side of the lake, the summit of the Grand Teton had been hidden by Teewinot Mountain and Mount Owen in the foreground. On this side of the lake, however, the tallest of the Tetons came into view. Its snow-capped peak was magnificent, but it looked nothing like a teton. But then again, the Frenchmen who named the Tetons had been away from the comfort of the real thing for many months. We had been away from home less than twenty-four hours.

When we arrived back at the tents, a strong wind was blowing. A storm seemed imminent. We had not yet bought propane for my stove, so we piled into the rental car and headed into the town of Jackson for dinner. On the drive, both going and coming, we saw elk in the open fields beside the road. It was nearly 11:00 when we got back to camp. I crawled into my sleeping bag and fell asleep immediately after my twenty-hour day.

The next morning, I woke at 6:15. The sun was not yet up when I stuck my head out of the tent. I pulled on my boots and some warm clothes and walked to the entrance of the campground, where I heard a bull elk bugle in the distance to the south. I cupped my ear; he bugled again. It was just like day two at Glacier: déjà vu all over again. The sun then topped the Gros Ventres to the east, illuminating the face of the Grand Teton and the lesser slopes surrounding it. The snow on the slopes glittered in the morning sun.

On my walk back to the tent, I stopped in the bathroom on the south end of the campground. When I came out, five mule deer were staring at me. As I turned to walk toward our tents, they walked slowly ahead of me, as if they had been waiting for someone to herd them. When I stopped at the tents, the deer continued, disappearing into the trees.

I fired up the stove with the propane we had bought in town the night before, fixed a cup of coffee, and watched ground squirrels play. By now, Bobby was up. As we sat quietly, six more mule deer—two groups of three—came through our campsite and walked right past us. A coyote howled in the distance.

Not a bad start—the bugle of a bull elk, the howl of a coyote, eleven mule deer, and sunrise on the Grand Teton. Soon David emerged from the tent, rubbing his eyes. I told him he should have set his alarm.

Our plans for the day depended on the weather. After breakfast, we walked to the ranger station to get an update. The ranger had discouraging news—the forecast was for snow above 8,000 feet. We were reluctant to backpack in the high country in the snow and decided to spend another night at Jenny Lake and take a day hike up Paintbrush Canyon. Our destination would be Holly Lake, 6.2 miles away. We would climb to 9,400 feet, a gain of some 2,700 feet, and then return. We might be hiking above the snow line, but we wouldn't be camping there.

We drove several miles north to the Leigh Lake trailhead, parked our car, and hiked nearly a mile along the eastern shore of String Lake. We crossed the bridge just below the south end of Leigh Lake and began climbing into the hills. The trail swung to the northwest, giving us excellent views of L-shaped Leigh Lake and the island near its north shore. Climbing through these hills, we saw another doe and two nearly grown fawns. In a tree beside the trail, we spotted a grouse. A real grouse.

As the route became steeper, we passed a woman of about fifty coming down the trail. I studied her backpack and commented on her heavy load. She said I should have seen it seven days ago. I asked where she had been, and she described a route all over the high country of the Tetons. I felt like a wimp.

Popcorn snow—a cross between snow and hail—began to fall. Lucky for us, the popcorn kernels were no bigger than pebbles. Shortly after the snow began, we came upon two hikers leaning against rocks and looking down the hill. A bull moose and cow were about fifteen yards below the trail. The cow was eating, the bull resting. Like the mule deer in the campground, the moose were not the least bit bothered by our presence. They behaved like compliant props in the grand national park show. I could picture them ambling to the park gate at dusk, punching their time cards, and shedding their costumes. They would then meet the other "animals" for a beer and tell stories about the tourists they had fooled.

This was the first time I had been this close to a moose. The bull moose was enormous. Moose are far and away the largest members of the deer family. A mature white-tailed buck may weigh 250 pounds, a large bull elk 800 pounds. A full-grown bull moose stands seven and a half feet at the shoulder and weighs as much as 1,800 pounds. But for all their size, moose are not majestic. We studied them for a time and decided they looked like a cross between a camel and a horse, with faces only a mother moose could love.

From this point, we moved steadily uphill. The snow continued to fall. Distance in the mountains is deceiving. We paused to talk to a couple from Michigan coming down the trail; they estimated it was a mile from where we were to Holly Lake. Fifteen minutes later and a half mile closer to the lake, we passed two men on the trail and asked them the same question. They said we had two miles to go.

Not long after passing these hikers, we came to a beautiful rock garden on the north side of the trail. We heard squeaking noises coming from the rocks and stopped to investigate. The source of the noise was pikas, dozens of them. Many had grass and leaves and wildflower stems in their mouths. The snow had spurred them to action; they were getting ready. A single pika stores as much as a cubic yard of food to make it through the long, cold winter.

* * *

Overlooking proper equipment can have serious consequences. Sometimes the consequences are foreseeable, sometimes not. We had not brought gloves on our hike up Paintbrush Canyon. The foreseeable consequence of the oversight was cold hands. The unforeseeable consequence was a head injury.

After we topped 9,000 feet and began the final approach to the lake, the snow began falling harder. The temperature was in the thirties. I was hiking in the lead, then David, then Bobby. As I rounded a curve, I heard a sound behind me, the sound of boots slipping on the trail, struggling to gain purchase. Then a thud; the boots had failed. Bobby had slipped on the wet trail and landed face down. With no gloves, he was hiking with his hands in his pockets. When he slipped, he couldn't get them out in time to catch himself. By the time we turned around, Bobby was pulling himself up to his hands and knees. David and I were just starting to laugh when Bobby looked up. We caught ourselves. The look on Bobby's face was the same as when he had crashed the Lincoln into the boulder in Glacier. But there was one difference; this time, there was blood. A steady stream was running down Bobby's Roman nose, dripping off the end. Bobby tilted his head forward to keep the flow from running into his mouth. The blood kept me from being a smartass and telling Bobby he was a dumbass.

David, our camp doctor, went to Bobby's aid. David had a bandana and used it to wipe away the blood and examine the wound. Bobby had a nasty gash over his left eyebrow. While David was tending to Bobby, I found a rock imbedded in the middle of the trail with a sharp edge above ground level. On the edge was a single drop of fresh blood. I looked back at the victim, from whom the blood still flowed.

David had medical supplies back in camp, but he had brought none in his day pack. The bandana was now soaked with Bobby's blood. No solution was apparent, but then we were rescued. A man came walking up the trail through the snow, like a St. Bernard bearing brandy. He immediately produced an ancient first aid kit. He said he had been hiking with it for twenty years, toting it all over the mountains of the West, never once opening it. He was pleased that it would finally be put to use. David put sterile pads on the wound, wrapped Bobby's head in decades-old gauze, and slapped on adhesive tape to keep the gauze in place. Bobby looked like the guy playing the fife in the painting of the Revolutionary War fife and drum corps. The bleeding had stopped, and Bobby was now more embarrassed than hurt. We offered to turn around, but he refused. The three of us pressed on to the lake, our hands no longer in our pockets.

We soon arrived at Holly Lake, a beautiful glacial tarn with Mount Woodring rising above it. The trail continues from here to Paintbrush Divide and Lake Solitude and then turns south, becoming the Teton Crest Trail. The lake, however, was our turnaround point. We stopped briefly for lunch, but it was too cold and wet to stay long. We turned back and headed down in the spitting snowfall.

Loop trails are far preferable to returning the way you came. There is no backtracking, and you don't walk the same route twice. All the same, the views coming down a trail are different from those going up. We doubled our pace going downhill. We saw no more wildlife but enjoyed the views down the canyon and across Jackson Hole. To the south were Rock of Ages, the Jaw, Mount St. John, and Rockchuck Peak. We crossed and recrossed the creek that comes down the canyon to the head of Leigh Lake. Because of the time we had wasted dealing with Bobby's bleeding head, we kept a steady pace, not stopping to rest until we got back to the bridge over the creek that connects String and Leigh Lakes. The three of us then hustled back to the car and returned to camp.

As soon as we got to the campground, our attention returned to Bobby's injury. David peeled off the adhesive tape, unwound the gauze from Bobby's head, and inspected the wound. Stitches were needed, David pronounced. He told Bobby there were two options. We could drive back into town and try to find a hospital or clinic or, if Bobby was game, David could field dress the wound right here. David had taken an inventory of his medical supplies. There was good news; he had a suture kit. But there was bad news as well: no anesthetic. Bobby and I reacted differently to this revelation. Bobby groaned; I grinned. Realizing the enormous potential for entertainment value, I encouraged Bobby to let David sew him up. "Be a man," I goaded him. "It will make for a great story." I was already looking forward to telling it. Bobby pointed out that it was not my head, but the shaming worked. Bobby decided to man up.

* * *

The senior partner of the fur trapping partnership of Smith, Sublette and Jackson was famous mountain man Jedediah Smith. Like John Colter, Smith was a nineteenth-century badass. Like Bobby, Smith suffered a head wound that was stitched up in the wild, though his injury was more severe than Bobby's. On his way to the Rockies, Smith and his men surprised a grizzly bear in a river bottom. The bear turned on Smith before the men could raise their rifles. According to a report of the attack, the grizzly took Smith's head "in his capacious mouth close to his left eye on the one side and close to his right ear on the other and laid the skull bare to near the crown of his head." One of Smith's ears was torn from his head. The bear was shot and killed and Smith's life was saved, but his wounds were grievous. But Smith was no quitter. He enlisted one of his men to sew

. back together, and the skin that had been peeled from his skull was . attached. That still left the missing ear. The amateur doctor insisted that nothing could be done, but Smith wanted two ears. He asked the seamster to do the best he could, and the ear was reattached. Reports indicate it healed nicely, though there are no before and after pictures to prove it.

* * *

Had I known at the time of Smith's experience, I would have used it to persuade Bobby to let David sew up his head. I would have cited the courage of the mountain man and appealed to Bobby's aspiration to be a mountain man himself. Instead, Bobby got the encouragement he needed in another form. While I gathered firewood, he ransacked my pack, helping himself to the bottle of Dewar's I had brought from home. He took several big gulps, sat for a few minutes to let the Scotch take effect, then pronounced himself sufficiently anesthetized for the surgery to begin. Bobby probably had the advantage over Smith on this score. By all accounts, Smith was a mild man and a Christian, one of the few in the mountains. In all likelihood, he was far too honorable to steal his buddy's whiskey before the sewing on his head began.

I was right about the entertainment value of the campsite procedure. I give Bobby credit. He never screamed or cried. He asked for more Scotch just once. I looked on and provided commentary, wincing dramatically each time the needle went in. I counted the stitches as David tied them and frequently asked Bobby if it hurt. Bobby's responses went from profane to profaner. I asked David to predict the extent of the scarring. He studied Bobby from several angles and concluded that any change would be an improvement. Bobby's face as David ran the needle through his head reminded me of a woman's expression during childbirth. But David made quick work of it—quicker than birthing a baby—and Bobby was soon back on his feet. The head wound would not alter our trip, and the scar would give Bobby a memento.

After the sewing ended, we had an addition to our group: Mike Kitchen, who works at the shipyard with Bobby. Mike had come to Jackson Hole by himself to fish. The weather was ruining his fishing, so he decided to spend the next two nights and days with us. Bobby and I got a fire started while David and Mike went off in search of wine. I studied Bobby's stitches in the firelight, and we invented better stories to explain his injury. I proposed one involving extraordinary heroism, with Bobby saving us from fearsome grizzlies at incredible personal risk. Anything, I said, was better than admitting he fell in the middle of the trail and hit his head on a rock. David and Mike returned with two bottles of Merlot, the rain held off, and we stayed by the fire until late in the night. From time to time, I would aim the flashlight at Bobby's forehead, shake my head, and predict hideous scarring. Bobby responded with an anatomically impossible suggestion.

Rain came during the night. The morning dawned with a solid gray curtain stretching across the sky. Just before sun up, a large animal walked through the camp and nearly knocked Mike's tent down. It was probably another mule deer, but there were elk nearby as well. We walked to the ranger station and got another gloomy forecast. None of us was thrilled with the prospect of camping high in the mountains in bad weather, so we scratched the idea of the Teton Crest Trail for good, at least on this trip. We reviewed our options and chose a day hike beginning at the top of Rendezvous Mountain on the south end of the Tetons. We would stay in Jenny Lake campground one more night, but only one more night. The campground was scheduled to close for the season the next day. We would have to leave, but where we would go for our last two nights was still undecided.

We piled into the two rental cars—Mike's and ours—and headed south toward the Jackson Hole Ski Area. We would cheat by riding the ski tram to the top of Rendezvous Mountain and then hike down Granite Canyon Trail. On the drive along the western edge of the valley, we spotted several cars pulled over on the shoulder. Passengers had climbed from their cars and were staring up at the slope, pointing toward something among the trees. Bobby spotted the object of their attention: a black bear maybe thirty yards up the hill. We pulled over and watched for a few minutes as it climbed higher up the slope. This was our second bear—the cub in Yosemite and this one—seen through the window of a rental car. If we had skipped the hiking altogether and toured the mountains by car, we probably would have seen more.

We dropped Mike's rental at the Granite Canyon trailhead and then continued on to Teton Village, the ski resort just south of the park. By the time we got there, the clouds had burned off and the sky was warm and sunny. We were wishing we had not given up on the Teton Crest Trail. Bobby found a restaurant, where we had omelets with the works. Then we climbed aboard the tram for the ride to the summit at 10,450 feet. When the door opened at the top, we found ourselves in a new climate. The landscape was rocky and barren; a cold wind blew. A few thousand feet does dramatic things to the weather. Climbing a mountain will often result in a greater drop in temperature than traveling hundreds of miles due north. The Indians of the West understood this well. Their seasonal migrations were often up and down rather than north and south. The same is true of many animals, including the elk of the Tetons.

Before we left the summit of Rendezvous Mountain to begin our hike, we admired the views in all directions. We could see the peak of the Grand Teton to the north. To the east were the Gros Ventres across Jackson Hole. The mountains to the west and south looked much different from the towering peaks in the center of the Tetons. The exposed rock of the smaller mountains is sedimentary—limestone and dolomite—not the far older granite, gneiss, and schist of the tallest of the Tetons.

We started down the trail, descending to the west, and soon crossed back into the park. The path wound along the east wall of a large cirque known as the Bowl. The spruces here were stunted because of the harsh growing conditions caused by winds funneling up the Bowl. We turned north and hiked through a grove of larger trees that are less exposed to the wind. Bobby was showing no ill effects from his fall the day before, though I noticed he didn't have his hands in his pockets. But there was no need. The sun was warming us; we were wishing we had worn shorts. The trail passed through stands of Engelmann spruce and subalpine fir en route to the Middle Fork Cutoff, three and a half miles from the tram. We walked through meadows that according to the trail guide are filled with wildflowers in the summer, but we were too late, just as we had been in Yosemite and Glacier. We missed the crowds by going in September, but we also missed the color.

After we reached the Middle Fork Cutoff, clouds returned. Soon it began to snow, the same popcorn snow that had fallen on us in Paintbrush Canyon. We were now glad we hadn't worn shorts. The weather here changes quickly and, because it comes from the west, from over the Tetons, there is no warning. The snowfall became heavier and began to accumulate. Our visibility was limited; a mist obscured the mountains. But the view up close was beautiful. The snow glistened on the evergreens and covered the ground.

We continued north, crossing footbridges over two forks of Granite Creek. A beautiful waterfall was just upstream from the first of the bridges. The constant spray from the cascade created a wet environment. Thick moss and ferns covered both banks, in stark contrast to the barren west slope of Rendezvous Mountain we had just left.

When we came to the Granite Canyon Trail, we turned east and started down the canyon. The vegetation in the canyon was much lusher than the one we'd hiked the day before. Granite Canyon runs due west from the valley. Paintbrush Canyon runs northwest, making it more vulnerable to severe weather coming down from Canada. We saw several mule deer on this section of the trail. Like the others, they were nonchalant. They glanced at us and twitched their ears but made no attempt to run for cover. Bobby spotted what he thought and thus declared was a golden eagle soaring far above.

As we descended, I was in my accustomed spot, hiking in the lead. There are risks as well as rewards in staking out this position. The lead hiker is the first to see wildlife, which is usually a good thing, but not always. In an area of dense vegetation, I came around a curve and spotted a large, dark brown rump directly ahead. The animal's legs were hidden from view by the brush. My initial thought was predictable: a bear. I froze, but before I could retreat, the beast lifted its head. It was a moose calf. I then spotted its mother in the brush nearby. As we approached, they crossed the trail no more than twenty feet in front of us. I don't know the best verb to describe their gait, but moose most assuredly do not caper.

The scenery as we descended the canyon was magnificent. The summit of Rendezvous Mountain dominated the view to the south. Below it, the face of the canyon revealed large avalanche chutes. As we walked down the trail, we occasionally heard the sound of running water. We stopped and searched the walls of the canyon until we spotted the source of the sound, water cascading over the face of the cliff and dropping hundreds of feet to the canyon floor. Although we were too late for the wildflowers, we passed red osier dogwoods with leaves of red and cottonwoods with leaves of gold.

As we continued down the trail, the granite walls that give the canyon its name became higher and steeper. We left the snow far behind. We spotted another moose cow, this one with twins. As we neared the mouth of the canyon, we walked through a forest of Douglas firs. The last section of the trail crossed a sage meadow filled with aspens. The aspens were just starting to turn yellow, but we were too early for peak fall color.

Riding the tram to the top was supposed to make this an easy day. The trail was downhill all the way. But in some ways, hiking downhill is harder on the body than uphill. Descending is not as physically exhausting, and you don't pay as stiff a price for being out of shape. But a long downhill hike is tough on the back, the knees, and the toes. It was a relief to walk across flat ground the last few hundred yards to the car.

We piled into Mike's car and drove the short distance south to Teton Village to get ours. It was nearly dark. We caucused to decide on a plan for the night and elected to stop at an Italian place on the road back to camp. Our sore backs, knees, and feet persuaded us to choose the soft chairs of a restaurant over a night by the campfire. I was the most reluctant to pick this option, but as we headed north up the valley after dinner, we saw that it had rained hard during the day. When we got back to the tents, our camp was soaked. There was not a dry place to sit, and all the wood was wet. We had done the right thing.

I did not sleep well that night. Tents are not soundproof, and Bobby's snoring from the one next to mine kept me awake. Whenever Bobby stopped snoring, as if on cue, bull elk started bugling. The bugle of a bull elk is a magical sound, but I wished they had a curfew.

We woke to more bad weather. The sky was again overcast; a light rain was falling. After little debate, we decided to declare a rest day and take a driving tour of Yellowstone. The four of us got into Mike's car and headed for the south entrance of the world's oldest national park. Along the way, we stopped and ate a big breakfast. The pancakes were good, but we were eating in restaurants far too often. This wasn't why we came.

The problem with a one-day driving tour of Yellowstone is that the park is just too big. We spent six hours in the car, which was too big a price to pay to see the sights. We didn't have enough time to get off the beaten track, and the beaten track, as usual, was crowded.

This was my first trip to Yellowstone since I turned eight there in the summer of 1965, a third of a century earlier. Near the southern border of the park, we drove past miles and miles of burned forest, all the victim of massive fires that swept through the park in the summer of 1988. We crossed the Continental Divide, turned northeast, and drove along the north shore of Yellowstone Lake. At twenty miles long, fourteen miles wide, and more than 7,700 feet above sea level, this is the largest high-altitude lake in North America. We stopped and enjoyed the view of the rugged mountains of the Absaroka Range to the southeast.

Our next stop was to walk among geysers and hot springs, mud pots and paint pots. It is little wonder that the Indians of the region feared the thermal wonders of the Yellowstone. To those who didn't know the cause, the unearthly sounds, the sulfurous smells, and the violent eruptions must have been terrifying. They must have thought the nether world was inhabited by fire-breathing monsters.

We stopped at the Grand Canyon of the Yellowstone and walked out to the overlook to see Yellowstone Falls. I remembered the falls from my visit here as a boy, but something was different. I could have sworn that we could see both the Upper and Lower Falls then, but now only the Upper Falls were visible. I came to a plaque that explained the change. An earthquake a few years after our trip had moved the rocks of the canyon and obscured the view of the Lower Falls.

We left the falls and drove along the Firehole River toward Old Faithful. Before we arrived, however, we got stuck in a traffic jam caused by a herd of bison. We stopped and got out to take pictures. Bobby got a good shot of an amorous, sniffing bull and a compliant cow, which Bobby said reminded him of a brown-noser and brown-nosee he worked with at the shipyard. We got to Old Faithful just after an eruption and decided we didn't have time to wait for the next one. The average time span between them is seventy-three minutes, and the day was growing late. We walked along a boardwalk that winds through thermal pools before returning to the car. I remembered my mother telling me she couldn't enjoy this on our trip here thirty-three years before this one. She was terrified I would fall off the boardwalk and be boiled alive.

Mike had been to Yellowstone more recently and more often than any of us. Throughout our six-hour driving tour, he provided detailed descriptions of every aspect of the park. The information was interesting, but after being stuck in the back seat most of the day, I was ready for a break from the cars and the tourists and the talk. John Muir wrote that "to sit in solitude, to think in solitude with only the music of the stream and the cedar to break the flow of silence, here lies the value of wilderness." At the end of a long day on crowded roads, I was ready for solitude and silence.

On the way back to the south entrance of Yellowstone, we crossed the Continental Divide three times—east to west, west to east, and east to west again. We left one national park and headed back toward another, driving south along the John D. Rockefeller, Jr. Memorial Parkway. We reentered Grand Teton National Park and stopped at Colter Bay Visitor Center to pick up a backcountry camping permit for our last two nights in the Tetons. The Jenny Lake campground was now closed; we had chosen Phelps Lake to spend our last two nights. After getting our permit, we drove south to Jenny Lake, where we parted ways with Mike, and then continued to the Phelps Lake trailhead.

The hike to the campsite beside Phelps Lake is only two and a half miles, but it was late afternoon by the time we parked the car and began loading our backpacks, so we needed to get going. I was packed and ready to go before Bobby and David and was concerned about getting to the lake in time to gather firewood before dark, so I set out ahead of them.

Phelps Lake is slightly lower than the trailhead, but the first mile of the walk to the lake climbs steadily to Phelps Lake Overlook before dropping down to the lake. The trail began in a lodgepole pine forest, then climbed through stands of Engelmann spruce along the moraine formed by Death Canyon Glacier. Hiking quietly by myself, I spotted two mule deer and several more of the ubiquitous moose as I walked through an aspen grove and among large Douglas firs. Then I reached the overlook, which provides a beautiful view of Phelps Lake. The lake was formed by moraines left behind by the glacier that descended Death Canyon during the Pinedale Period.

After resting briefly and admiring the lake and the mountains to the south and west, I began the walk down to the lake. The trail switched back down a meadow filled with dense vegetation. All alone, in the gathering dusk, I felt the presence of bears. No evidence supported my feeling, but I felt it just the same. I looked around for movement but saw nothing. I sang, and the bears, if there were any, stayed away. Before I reached the trail junction near the northwest corner of the lake, I heard Bobby and David talking on one of the switchbacks on the slope above me. They weren't far behind. Just before crossing Death Creek, which flows down the canyon to the lake, I turned on a side trail and walked along the lakeshore to the magnificent campsite, arriving shortly before dark.

The camp lay beneath towering Douglas firs on the north shore of the lake. In the waning light, I hurried to gather firewood. This late in the camping season, most of the wood near the designated tent sites had already been gathered and burned. The woods were thick, however, and a short distance up the hill I found plenty of wood on the ground. I made several trips up the slope to gather wood, then put up my tent. Everything that needed to be done before dark was now completed. I walked down to the lakeshore to admire the view.

The wind had died completely; the surface of the lake provided a perfect mirror image of the snow-capped mountains rising above the opposite shore. Trout were active, dimpling the surface as they fed. Each rise was followed by expanding concentric circles. I saw movement on the western shore of the lake and spotted three moose—a cow and two calves—wading in for a twilight dip. Just at dusk, bull elk east of the lake began bugling, filling the evening air with their calls. I thought back on the day. Only a few hours earlier, I had been stuck in the back seat of a car in a traffic jam of tourists. My life had improved dramatically since then. I watched the moose and trout for a few minutes and listened to the elk, thinking how lucky I was to be here.

But my reverie was soon interrupted by the realization that Bobby and David had not yet arrived. They should have been here long before now. My mind reeled with the possibilities. Bobby could have suffered another fall. In the fading light, perhaps David was again at work with his needle and thread. Or they could have missed the turn to the campsite. This seemed doubtful, because a sign in plain view marked the way. Or, perhaps, they had been attacked by a bear on the bearish slope above the lake, the bear whose presence I'd felt. Grizzlies are rare in the Tetons, but it takes just one to maul an unsuspecting hiker or two. I grabbed my flashlight and hurried back up the trail, expecting at any moment to come upon a big bruin feasting on my friends. I hustled the half mile or so back to the trail junction and then began climbing the switchbacks up the slope toward the overlook. I alternated between yelling for Bobby and David and singing. Before I had gotten far, I heard bear bells tinkling at the bottom of the slope below me. I called out, and Bobby answered. I turned around and jogged back down the trail, catching up with them just before they got to camp. In the midst of a deep conversation, the subject of which they could not recall, they had walked right past the sign pointing the way to the campsite. They had kept talking and walking along the western shore of Phelps Lake for half a mile before it occurred to them that they weren't where they were supposed to be.

Bobby and David were delighted with the campsite and my wood gathering. Bobby put up his tent, and we built a fire and cooked dinner: chicken soup, beef stroganoff, and lots of red wine. We then settled in for a perfect night. The temperature was ideal: cold enough for a campfire but not too cold. Bobby told several of the stories I've already recounted here. We drank a toast to Brian, wishing he was here, but cursed him for backing out by email. We finished the wine just as it started to sprinkle and then retired to the tents, pleased with our decision to come to Phelps Lake.

I don't know if it rained all night—I slept too well—but it was raining when I woke up. I lay in the warmth of my sleeping bag for two hours reading the last eighty pages of John Krakauer's *Into Thin Air*. As I finished the story of the tragic Everest expedition, I thought that people go to the wilderness for many different reasons. I go for the beauty—to see the mountains, to spend time in spectacular places. I go for the good times with my friends. These times have been some of the best of my life. And I go to get away, to escape for a while from the stress of everyday life and practicing law. I also enjoy the exercise and the sense of accomplishment after a hard day on the trail, but this is far down the list. And I don't go to take risks. I'm not seeking a notch in my belt. I go to the mountains to feel, not to prove.

I finished the book just as the rain stopped. When I emerged from the tent, there was Bobby, looking haggard. He reported that his tent had leaked and that he'd slept very little. He threatened to sue REI. He later withdrew the threat, confessed that he had not applied the seam sealer that came with the tent, and acknowledged that after he did the tent never leaked again. So he admits that getting wet in the Tetons was his fault, but he still claims that ramming the rock in Glacier was mine.

We cooked a disgusting dehydrated western omelet for breakfast. Its only value was that we learned never to do it again. I do not purport to know the perfect menu for a backpacking trip, but at least for me, dried eggs are out and instant oatmeal is in. Instant oatmeal is light, easy, warming, and filling. It tastes good. If you don't want to have the same thing for breakfast every day, you can buy a box of assorted flavors.

Our plan for the day was to hike up Death Canyon into the mountains. We would then return here for our last night in the Tetons. Before we could get started, however, Bobby declared himself a casualty of sleep deprivation. He decided to stay here, try to dry his sleeping bag and the inside of his tent, and maybe take a nap in mine.

Let me pause here for a product endorsement. My Walrus tent sleeps three comfortably. I have had it for many years and slept in it in Mississippi, Alabama, Tennessee, Georgia, South Carolina, North Carolina, Nevada, California, Montana, Wyoming, and Washington. It has never leaked, except at Washoe Lake in Nevada, but that was not the tent's fault.

The bad weather seemed to have finally departed. David and I had a beautiful day to hike up Death Canyon. The trail rose steeply from the northwest corner of Phelps Lake. We soon found ourselves between sheer granite cliffs guarding the entrance to the canyon. The steep walls rose hundreds of feet from the creek flowing along the bottom of the canyon. Waterfalls occasionally cascaded over the high ledges. After passing between the cliffs, the trail leveled off, and the floor of the canyon widened. The narrow entrance to the canyon makes this a natural fortress. In the late 1800s, horse thieves used the broad interior of the canyon as a way station for the horses they stole from nearby ranches. The entrance made it easy to keep horses in and pursuers out.

The trail crossed and recrossed Death Creek, which was lined with tall willows. About four miles from camp, we passed the Death Canyon patrol cabin. In the trees thirty yards from the trail was an enormous bull moose. A cow stood close beside him. We continued west, climbing through a forest of spruce and fir, finally coming to an open meadow strewn with enormous granite boulders. David and I climbed to the top of the largest boulder and decided it was a perfect spot for lunch. We were between five and six miles from camp and 2,000 feet above Phelps Lake. The sky was a brilliant blue for the first time since the day of our arrival. David and I ate our sandwiches and trail mix and stretched out on the rocks before heading back down the trail.

As we neared the patrol cabin on our descent, we again saw the huge bull moose we'd seen on the hike up, but now he was standing squarely in the trail. We looked around for an alternative route, but there wasn't one. Thick brush made leaving the trail to get around the moose impossible. We were at an impasse. From a distance of some twenty-five feet, I yelled at the big bull, urging him to clear the trail and let us pass. I called him names, but he didn't care. The only proof that he could hear was the fact that he occasionally looked over his shoulder and snorted. David and I backed off and discussed our options. It was mating season, bull moose can be quite aggressive during the rut, and we didn't want to pick a fight with an animal that weighed ten times as much as we did. David and I edged closer, ready to seek shelter behind one of the few nearby trees. I yelled louder. Finally, the moose strolled off the trail, looking back at us in disgust.

We made good time the rest of the way down the canyon. Both of us were ready to lounge at our beautiful camp beside Phelps Lake. We walked back through the towering canyon cliffs at the entrance to the canyon and arrived at camp at five o'clock. There we found Bobby in a much better frame of mind. David and I told him of the scenery in the canyon and the bull moose that had blocked our descent, but Bobby, like the moose, didn't care. He insisted he was glad he had stayed behind. He had taken a long nap, then sat in the sun by the lake, reading. He was reinvigorated. And soon enough, David and I were also glad that Bobby had stayed behind. In our haste to load our backpacks the previous day, we had left precious cargo at the car—tequila and cigars. During the day, Bobby had jogged back to the car and retrieved both. This was going to be our last night in the Tetons, and we started happy hour right away. David made faux margaritas with tequila and what I thought was Tang.

* * *

It turns out that I was right about the tequila but wrong about the Tang. After reading a draft of this chapter, Bobby wrote to correct me:

What's with the Tang? Tang? David made faux margaritas with tequila and Tang? Really? We were backpackers, not astronauts. This was the Tetons, not the moon. There was no Tang. The powder that David used for the margaritas was the green lime-flavored bug juice powder from an MRE I had brought. You made fun of my MREs in Glacier, but you sure drank the margaritas beside Phelps Lake. To make them, Doc set up a makeshift laboratory in camp with everything he needed: bug juice powder, tequila, filtered lake water, Nalgene bottle, drinking cup, and stick for stirring. He looked more like a pharmacist than the physician who had field-stitched my head a few days before. David sat there for fifteen minutes preparing samples of different proportions, testing them, and making adjustments. The formula he settled on wasn't half bad.

* * *

Before this trip, I had ordered a chair kit to go with my self-inflating sleeping pad. The pad folds into the kit, you tighten the straps, and you have an incredibly comfortable camp chair. When the kit arrived in the mail, I put it together at home. My wife sat down in it and promptly fell asleep. The chair kit has but one drawback, which caused me discomfort on our trip to the Cascades in 2000 and that will be revealed in a later chapter. But on this afternoon in the Tetons, the chair was perfect. Before starting the evening work of fire building and food preparing, I took my new chair down to the lakeshore. The scene from the previous afternoon repeated itself. I gazed across the lake to the mountains on the other side with a dusting of fresh snow on top. The rain that had soaked our camp had been snow at higher elevations. Trout again began to rise. Moose returned to the lake: this time a cow and just one calf. I wondered if these were different moose, or if the grizzly that had not attacked us the previous evening had made the calf now wading in the lake an only child. Bull elk from the massive Jackson Hole herd again began bugling. The magnificent scene was only an hour's walk from the car, and yet we had it all to ourselves. As I sipped my poor man's margarita, I thought to myself that I was a rich man indeed.

As the day turned to twilight, the temperature dropped quickly. I walked back to the tents to help build a fire and cook dinner. We had another good meal—chicken and rice soup, spaghetti, and peanut butter fudge pie, all washed down with more merlot. Just as the water for our last meal in the Tetons came to a boil, the flame on the stove went out. The propane we had bought at the beginning of the trip had just run out. Perfect timing. We settled in by the fire and lit cigars. The mood around the fire was alternatively rowdy and melancholy. Our trip was coming to an end. We knew we had to return to Mississippi, but we wished for more time here, especially now that the weather was finally cooperating. As usual, David turned in first, heading for the tent at a little after ten. Bobby and I stayed up for a while longer, letting the fire die. A little before eleven, Bobby left for his tent, leaving me alone in the dark. I stared at the coals for a time, then suddenly woke with a start. I had fallen asleep in my new chair. I retired to my tent and slept soundly on our last night in the Tetons.

I was awakened at first light by a loud bellow not far away: an alarm moose. David was already out of the tent. I pulled on my clothes and went in search of the bellowing moose. I found an adult cow standing in shallow water near the lakeshore a hundred yards west of our campsite. David was standing on the lakeshore watching her. He reported that she had bellowed and started to charge when she spotted him approaching her. We watched the cow for several minutes, but she did nothing entertaining. We walked back to camp, packed our sleeping bags and pads, and took down our tents. Having no propane, the only way to heat water for breakfast would have been to build a fire. We decided instead to hike out without eating and drive down to Teton Village for a repeat of the omelets we'd eaten there three days earlier. After inspecting the campsite to make sure we were leaving no trace, we began the short walk back to the car. It took us only an hour, but along the way, we counted eight more moose, including another huge bull and a yearling spike. They were no longer a novelty.

We got to the car by mid-morning, then drove the short distance to Teton Village. We were starving, but the restaurant in Teton Village, like Jenny Lake campground, had closed for the season. We drove on toward Jackson, crossing the Snake River near the tiny town of Wilson. Along the way, we spotted a coyote on the edge of a cow pasture. The coyote was crouched on its haunches, studying the cattle. It didn't look like much of a threat.

We soon found a place for breakfast. The waitress noticed how funky we looked and probably smelled and asked if we were hunters. When we told her we were hikers, not hunters—that we enjoyed seeing animals, not shooting them—she gave us a strange look. Many people have the same reaction. They don't understand the great joy of walking in the mountains. To those who haven't been there, it's hard to explain why we love to spend a day hiking up a steep trail and back down, ending where we started, exhausted and sore-footed. What we get to see is the main thing, but there's also the simple pleasure of walking; of traveling a distance by putting one foot in front of the other, one step at a time; of getting there on our own, without wheels or motors. In *Walking,* Edward Abbey wrote: "There are some good things to say about walking. Not many, but some. Walking takes longer, for example, than any other known form of locomotion except crawling. Thus it stretches time and prolongs life. Life is already too short to waste on speed. I have a friend who is always in a hurry; he never gets anywhere. Walking makes the world much bigger and therefore more interesting. You have time to observe the details."

After breakfast, we found a rent-a-shower place to which we would return later in the day. We then drove west toward Idaho, crossed Teton Pass, and stopped to hike up the Coal Creek Trail in the Jedediah Smith Wilderness south of the national park. The weather on this day, our last day, was perfect. There was not a cloud in the sky; the temperature was in the sixties. The dry weather made it easier to break camp but harder to leave the mountains.

* * *

Jedediah Smith was born in upstate New York in 1799. As a young man, he read a book about the Lewis and Clark Expedition and then headed to the West. After recovering from his near fatal encounter with a grizzly and the temporary loss of an ear, he formed his famous fur trapping partnership with Bill Sublette and David Jackson. Leaving Sublette and Jackson in charge, Smith set out in 1827 to explore lands beyond the outer boundary of the fur trade in search of more beaver. Smith went to Salt Lake and became the first white man to cross Utah. He was also the first to reach California over land from the East and the first to cross the Sierras.

He then turned north and explored Oregon and Washington, spending the winter of 1828 at Fort Vancouver. When the spring thaw came in 1829, Smith headed back east, returning to the Tetons in time for the annual rendezvous in August. He had been gone for two years.

The following year, Smith and his partners sold out to Jim Bridger and others for a handsome profit. Smith returned to St. Louis with more than $80,000 in furs and gave generously to his family and friends. But, like John Colter before him, the city life did not suit Smith. He once wrote: "But a few days of rest make the sailor forget the storm & embark again upon the perilous Ocean, & I suppose that like him I would soon become weary of rest." And so, before he could become a casualty of civilization, Smith signed on for a new expedition, this time bound for Santa Fe.

In the summer of 1831, Smith and the party he was accompanying found themselves in the dry wastelands between the Arkansas River and the forks of the Cimarron. They were desperate for water. Smith had gone out scouting in search of a stream to save the party and their horses. He found one of the branches of the Cimarron, and he stopped to drink and water his horse before returning with the good news. But exhausted and weak from thirst, Smith was not on his guard. A band of Comanche hunters ambushed him on the bank of the river and killed him. He was thirty-two years old.

* * *

As we walked up Coal Creek Trail into the wilderness named for Smith, we soon came upon two different sets of tracks, one much larger than the other. David identified the smaller tracks as those of a black bear, the larger as those of a grizzly. Henry Kelsey of the Hudson Bay Company was the first white man to record an encounter with a grizzly bear in America. In 1691, Kelsey killed a grizzly. He found the meat tasty but was discouraged by Indians from keeping the hide. They claimed it was God and that keeping it would lead to harm. Jedediah Smith evidently was not aware of this superstition, or else he chose to ignore it. He kept the hide of the grizzly that nearly bit off his head. And, a few years later, he was killed by Indians beside the Cimarron.

The Coal Creek Trail climbed gradually. The scenery here was much less spectacular than in the mountains in the center of the Tetons. The slopes were gentler, the peaks lower. There was none of the exposed granite that typifies the heart of the range. But the land through which we walked was beautiful in its own way, and the day was grand. We made about a five-mile round trip, walking through evergreens, aspens, and open meadows under a cloudless sky. We had seen a number of people on the trails in the Tetons, but we didn't see a soul on our hike on Coal Creek Trail. Along the way, Bobby speculated about what it would cost to run an air pipeline from here to Mississippi, to pump some of this air home to breathe and maybe to sell.

After returning to the car, we headed back into Jackson and took our rental shower. I made my annual tee shirt purchases for my family before we headed north to the airport. On the long flight home, we compared notes. All three of us agreed that hiking the canyons and camping beside Phelps Lake were the high points of our trip, the traffic in Yellowstone the low point. We regretted that the weather had deterred us from backpacking on the Teton Crest Trail. We wished for more time, time to follow the advice offered by John Muir in *Our National Parks*: "Wander here a whole summer, if you can, . . . panting in whole-souled exercise and rejoicing in deep, long-drawn breaths of pure wildness." But we couldn't stay a whole summer, and our six days in the Tetons were over. We landed in New Orleans at midnight. We collected our bags, and I bade farewell to Bobby and David. They headed east to the Mississippi coast; I drove north to Jackson, pulling into my driveway at 3:30 in the morning, exactly six days after I'd pulled out.

CHAPTER
9

Between Trips

In my early forties, I entered the mid-life crisis phase of my life. I suffered from a general malaise that came and went. I daydreamed, pondering radical change. I questioned whether I wanted to practice law for two more decades.

The cause of my predicament was the same, I suppose, as the cause of similar conditions suffered by millions when they reach middle age. My theory is this: Before a person turns forty, whatever dissatisfaction he feels with the state of his life seems temporary. When he reaches middle age, however, he comes to the realization that he is what he's going to be. Thoreau wrote that most men lead lives of quiet desperation. For the most part, I submit, the desperation takes hold when they reach middle age. When a man reaches his forties, he has obligations that make wholesale change difficult. For better or worse, he's stuck with what he's got. Some men shirk their obligations, leave their families, and flee. But most weigh the pros and cons, including the guilt they would suffer and pain they would cause, and choose to stay.

The strength of my connection to Bobby is based on many things. By now, you know that we both love the outdoors: hiking, camping, and campfires. We have similar tastes in music and books and similar senses of humor. We think the same things—and each other—are funny.

Our friendship, however, is also based on the disconnection from our surroundings that we've both felt. We are, in a sense, connected by our disconnection. As I have told Bobby, I often feel like a stranger in a strange land. Jackson is where my job happens to be, but I have never come to think of it as home. I have good friends in Jackson, but when the superficial is stripped away, we have little in common. Or maybe it just seems that way. Maybe, except in the wilderness, the superficial is never really stripped away. I try to summon up enthusiasm for what seems to interest my Jackson friends—golf and college football, for example—but I have little interest in either. I feel guilty for not contributing more to others. I look at what Daddy did, and I've done so little. And the clock ticks on.

Mississippi is often maligned, but there are many great things about my home state. The people are friendlier and more polite than in most places, and good manners are very important to me. We have more than our share of great authors and songwriters. Much of our state is beautiful. I love the rolling hills and bottomland hardwood forests, but it's not the mountains, and it's too hot. It's not just that it's too hot and humid to go outside in the summer, too miserable at seven in the morning to eat breakfast on my patio. It's also the missed opportunity. In Mississippi, the worst time of the year is when the days are longest, when it's still daylight after work.

In the long gaps between the trips Bobby and I take to the West, I get doses of wilderness too infrequently. Many of my friends and law partners are hunters. In the past, I thought about taking up the sport. Most everything about it appeals to me: escaping with the guys, sitting silently in the woods when the sun rises and the birds begin to sing, playing poker at the hunting camp, drinking beside the fire. All of it appeals to me except the killing. Don't get me wrong; I love a good cheeseburger. But all the same, I'll let other people do the killing. To me, shooting a deer would be like shooting a dog. If I had grown up hunting, maybe I would feel differently. But I didn't, and I don't.

I do have a special place in the woods that I love to go. I used to live no more than two miles from the Pearl River, which forms the eastern border of the City of Jackson. Along the river are deep woods filled with huge hardwoods: red oaks, water oaks, hickories and sycamores. My two favorites are white oaks, with their white, shaggy bark, and beeches, whose smooth, gray bark has attracted name carvers through the centuries. The woods are filled with white-tailed deer, squirrels, raccoons, and armadillos. I nearly always see egrets and great blue herons when I hike along the river. Beavers have built a large pond a mile downstream from the point where the trail enters the woods. At least one large alligator shares quarters with them.

I go to these woods in late afternoon, usually alone. This is when the deer are most active. I walk as quietly as I can, stepping softly, hoping to see the deer before they hear me, raise their tails in alarm, and go bounding away. Right at dusk, the barred owls begin calling to each other from across the river. I try to mimic their call to see if they will respond.

I have a favorite spot in these woods, a high point on the river surrounded by three large beeches and a huge red oak. In late November, when the beech leaves turn to gold, this is a beautiful place. The trail to the beech grove leads through a low spot filled with huge cypresses, surrounded by cypress knees pressing up through the ground like mushrooms. I camped several times beneath the beeches with my children, and I plan to return with my grandchildren.

One fall, many years ago, my older son Cliff and I hiked to this spot with my tent and our sleeping bags and food for dinner and breakfast. That night, with the aid of a flashlight balanced on my shoulder, I read the last fifty pages of Richard Adams' *Watership Down* to Cliff as he sat in my lap beside our campfire. I recommend that you read *Watership Down* to your children or to yourself. The St. Louis Dispatch gave the same advice about the book that I am now giving: "Astonishing . . . everyone who can read English should read it." The writer for the Times of London began his review with these words: "I announce with trembling pleasure the appearance of a great story." So read this great story. And if you can, if you're as lucky as I was, read it to a bright-eyed child on a beautiful fall night, under a golden canopy of beech leaves, beside a campfire, the two of you alone in the woods.

* * *

The trips Bobby and I take to the West, which I'm certain will continue as long as our health permits, are as much fun as I've ever had. But we also have a great time in the planning. First we have to pore over the options and pick a destination. The list of where we want to go just gets longer. There are too many places and too little time. After choosing a destination, we focus on an itinerary: where to camp, what trails to hike, what sights to see. Taking these trips in August and September also has another benefit as well. The date of our planned departure looms ahead on our calendars, a light at the end of the tunnel, the long, hot tunnel. It's a reward we give ourselves for making it through another Mississippi summer.

The effect our trips have on us, however, is not altogether good. The short time we get to spend in the mountains makes us long for more. Our trips increase our dissatisfaction with spending our careers in office buildings, with living out our lives in a state whose highest point is 806 feet above sea level. Only in Mississippi would this molehill be called a mountain: Woodall Mountain, in the northeast corner of the state. Bobby's case of wanderlust is even worse than mine. Through the years, he's seemed to have a new plan every time I've talked to him: teaching school and having the summers off; launching a career as a JAG officer and working only eight months a year; running a bar in a small town in Montana; becoming a forest ranger. Our trips make us dream of different lives. They make us focus on what's wrong—or what we think is wrong—with the lives we already have. They increase our quiet desperation.

My father, Paul Eason, who taught me to love camping

On the first of our travels - May Lake in
Yosemite, where I dreamed of bears

Yosemite Valley from the west end

Half Dome from Glacier Point

Half Dome from North Dome

Bobby and David Sawyer on the Highline Trail in Glacier

The Belly River in Glacier

Cosley Lake in Glacier

The Tetons from Jackson Hole

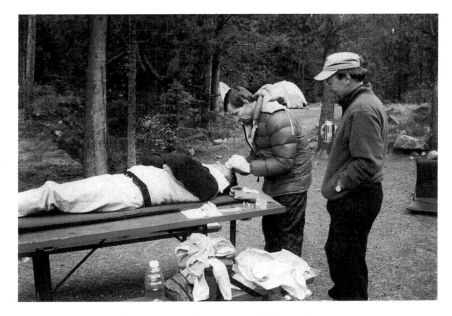

Bobby gets stitched after self-anesthetizing

The Cascades of Glacier Peak Wilderness

Bobby surveys the mountains

Shorts in a snowdrift in the Cascades

Campsite below Blue Lake in the Cascades

Our Wind River Range group other than
David Sawyer, who took the picture

Bobby trapped in his hammock

Campsite by Island Lake in the Winds

Taking a break in the Winds

With Brian high in the mountains

With Blake and Wilson on the cold last night in the Winds

The mountains of Glacier from the trail

Dawn Mist Falls in Glacier

A rare fish on our travels - grayling in Elizabeth Lake

Campfires without borders – Major Ariatti at Camp Sather in Baghdad

CHAPTER
10

1999 – Travels
Without Bobby

I have bragged on Bobby as a traveling companion, and with good reason. There is no one in the world I would rather go camping with than Bobby. Before our trips begin, however, he makes me nervous. There's always some contingency at work that could derail the trip. Bobby doesn't tell me about the contingency until our plans have been laid. He doesn't like confrontations. He doesn't want to tell me he might have to back out, and he doesn't want to tell his co-workers he's planned a trip he can't miss. So before our trips I wonder if I'll get a last-minute call from Bobby, cursing his job, muttering apologies, and urging me to go by myself and have a good time.

The only time Bobby actually bailed out was in 1999. We studied several options that year—the Grand Canyon, the Pecos Wilderness in New Mexico, and the Weminuche Wilderness in southwest Colorado. We settled on the Grand Canyon and began the annual review of the trail guide. Bobby bought a non-refundable plane ticket: a good sign, though not a sure sign, that he would go. Fortunately I had not yet booked my flight when Bobby called one morning. He was in a profane rage, in full-throated postal worker mode. Something had come up at work; he had to cancel. When Bobby cancelled, I made other plans.

I turned to another lawyer friend of mine who lives on the Mississippi coast, Bob Smith. Bob represented the plaintiff in the first case I had for the shipyard. In our work on that case, Bob and I discovered that we have a mutual interest in canoeing and camping. We have gone canoeing four or five times: to north Alabama, North Carolina, and Georgia. He's also taken me to Chandeleur Island off the Mississippi coast, where we've battled mosquitoes, fished for speckled trout, and watched the sun rise and set. When I called Bob in 1999, he had not backpacked in years, but he was game to try. In late October, we met in Birmingham and headed for the Joyce Kilmer-Slickrock Wilderness on the North Carolina/Tennessee border just south of Great Smoky Mountains National Park.

When Joyce Kilmer was a student at Rutgers University in New Jersey, he (yes, Joyce was a man) wrote the famous poem "Trees," which begins with the line "I think that I shall never see a poem as lovely as a tree." Kilmer, who was killed in World War I, never saw the wilderness that was later named for him. The connection between Kilmer and his wilderness is the trees. The Joyce Kilmer-Slickrock Wilderness has some of the most magnificent virgin forests that remain in the Eastern United States. The largest hemlock and the largest yellow poplar in North Carolina are within yards of each other on a short loop trail. They are ancient and enormous, but they are not sequoias. Compared to the giants in Mariposa Grove, these trees are infant matchsticks.

The name of this book is *Travels with Bobby*, not Travels with Bob, so I will not dwell on our weekend in the North Carolina woods, except to say this: Bob showed up with a backpack that was at least twenty years old and had no chest strap. After we hiked down the mountain from the trailhead, frequently clambering over deadfalls, Bob offered to walk out to the road and hitchhike rather than climb back up. I didn't argue. I went on a day hike by myself while he thumbed a ride to the trailhead, retrieved his truck, and brought it to the road near where we were camping.

I read an article several years ago in which two authors debated the merits and difficulty of Eastern hiking versus Western hiking. Bryson's book about hiking the Appalachian Trail was named *A Walk in the Woods* for good reason. The mountains in the East are covered with trees. The woods are beautiful, but sweeping, panoramic views are hard to come by. When you do get them, they don't measure up to the wondrous mountain scenery in the West. Because the forests in the East are thick, deadfalls blocking trails are far more prevalent than in the West. Scrambling over dead trees with a loaded backpack is exhausting. There is also far more precipitation in the Appalachians than in the Rockies. Afternoon thunderstorms are common in the mountains of the West, but a full day of unremitting rain is rare. On the other hand, there is no difficulty with altitude in the East. The highest point east of the Mississippi, the summit of Mount Mitchell in North Carolina, is only 6,684 feet above sea level. That is almost exactly the same elevation as the floor of Jackson Hole and lower than all but the lowest of the valleys in the Colorado Rockies. In some of Colorado's mountains—the San Juans in the Weminuche Wilderness, for example—the average elevation, including the valleys, exceeds 10,000 feet.

I live much closer to the Appalachians than to the Rockies, but it takes about as long to get to one as to the other. To go east, I drive; to go west, I fly. On balance, based on my experience hiking in both places, I'll buy the plane ticket. I love the woods, but there is nothing in the East that matches any of the places I've traveled with Bobby. Edward Abbey came to the same conclusion. In *Desert Solitaire,* he wrote that he would "rather go hungry in the West than flourish and fatten in the Siberian East."

CHAPTER

11

August 2000 –
Northern Cascades

And so to the West we returned. For our trip in 2000, however, Bobby and I believed a change was in order. In lieu of another hiking trip, we decided we would go canoeing. Both of us had read and enjoyed *Undaunted Courage*, Steven Ambrose's wonderful book about the Lewis and Clark Expedition. We had also read good things about the Wild and Scenic section of the upper Missouri River in central Montana, which was part of the Lewis and Clark route. This section of the river, which includes the White Cliffs, is little changed since the Corps of Discovery paddled up the river in 1805 and back down on their return from the Pacific the following year. We planned to take a copy of Lewis's and Clark's journals with us on the river and to camp where they camped nearly two centuries earlier.

My schedule for 2000, however, made it likely I would have to back out this time around. I was working on a case involving an explosion at a fertilizer plant on the bank of the same Missouri River, but in Iowa rather than Montana. The case was set for trial in mid-summer in Natchez, Mississippi. Estimates of its duration ranged from six weeks to four months. An article in the Natchez newspaper analyzed the boost for the local economy the trial was expected to have. Early in the summer, however, we settled. My schedule, which had looked awful, was now wide open. Not only that, but I had worked the equivalent of nine months in the first six months of the year. I had lots of vacation time coming.

Bobby and I decided to go for a whole week this time and picked a date in mid-September. He and I bought books about the river, surfed the Internet for information, and talked to outfitters about canoe rentals and shuttle services. One outfitter offered to buy our groceries if we would send him a list. We were undecided about two alternatives. We could spend the whole week paddling a long section of the river, or we could canoe a shorter section and then spend several days hiking in the Bob Marshall Wilderness south of Glacier.

* * *

You may have noticed that the Missouri River is not mentioned in the title of this chapter. That's because, about six weeks before our planned trip to Montana, work interfered with our plans. As a result, we wound up changing both the date and the destination.

The shipyard had a trial scheduled in late September in Virginia, and Bobby was the in-house lawyer responsible for the case. The Virginia lawyer handling the case was Fred Stant of Virginia Beach, a Harley-riding, ex-UVA basketball player who's as funny as Bobby. Because Bobby would not actually be trying the case, he figured he could send a younger lawyer to Virginia in his place. His boss, however, disagreed. If the case didn't settle, our mid-September date was out. Bobby's reaction was predictable. He called me in a profane rage. This is getting old, I thought as he vented. But all was not lost. I was still lazing about in the wake of the settlement of the explosion case—I had just returned from a two-week road trip to Colorado with my ten-year-old son Paul—and my schedule was still flexible. I could go most any time. I proposed that we back the trip up a week or two, but Bobby had problems then as well. He fumed and sputtered, and we hung up with the issue unresolved.

Several days later, when I got to work on a Friday morning, an email from Bobby awaited me. Like Brian two years before, he had chosen to be a wimp rather than call me. In his email, Bobby explained that David Sawyer and a friend were leaving in two weeks to spend three or four days mountain biking in Idaho. The week David and his friend were going was the only open week on Bobby's calendar, and he was not going to be denied a trip to the West for the second year in a row. So, Bobby wrote, he had driven to the Mobile airport that morning and bought a plane ticket to Spokane, leaving in two weeks and returning eight days later. According to Bobby, he planned to spend the first two or three days biking with David and his friend. Then, if I couldn't go, he would strike out on his own and camp and hike by himself.

I read the email a second time, feeling like a bride left at the altar. I typed part of a mean-spirited but entirely justified response, thought better of it, and called the bastard. After chewing him out, I studied my calendar. I was planning to be at the beach with my family until the day after Bobby was flying to Spokane. I told him I couldn't go on Friday but could fly out late Saturday. He felt guilty and promised to drive back to Spokane and pick me up.

We had only a week to finalize our plans before I left for the beach. We could still canoe the upper Missouri, but it was a long drive from Spokane. In addition, a number of forest fires were burning out of control in the northern Rockies in the summer of 2000, Montana was in the middle of a drought, and the governor had declared a statewide ban on campfires. We looked elsewhere.

Spokane is consistently ranked among the best places in America for outdoor enthusiasts and for good reason. Bobby and I studied the map and realized we could go in almost any direction—southeast to the mountains in Idaho, north to the Canadian Rockies, southwest to Oregon, or due west to the Cascades. We chose the last of these options in part because there were no wildfires in the Cascades. Also, my daughter Ann Lowrey had recently gone on a six-week backpacking/rafting/mountain climbing trip throughout the Pacific Northwest with an outfitter called Wilderness Ventures. I had quizzed the owner of Wilderness Ventures, and he highly recommended the Pacific Crest Trail in the Glacier Peak Wilderness south of North Cascades National Park. Bobby and I decided to take his advice.

* * *

So our trip was set. Bobby flew up on Friday and spent Saturday biking with David east of Spokane. At the end of his day in Idaho, Bobby left David and headed back to the airport in Spokane to pick me up. In the meantime, I left the beach in Florida on Saturday morning and drove west with my family. We parted ways in Mobile, where I had left my car on the way to the beach. They headed home to Jackson; I continued to New Orleans, where I dropped my car at a dealership to be serviced while I was gone. I took a cab to the airport and climbed aboard my 3:00 p.m. flight. As always, the first flight was to Salt Lake City. It was long after dark when the second leg to Spokane took off. As we flew north over the Bitterroots, I could see smoke and flames from the fires burning in the mountains below. My plane landed at nearly 11:00. I didn't spot Bobby at first and wondered what I would do if he wasn't there. He had no way to get in touch with me; I had no way to get in touch with him. I don't like to take my cell phone when I head for the mountains.

My worry was for naught. I spotted Bobby as I walked from the gate to baggage claim. He was grinning from ear to ear. We were both excited to be returning to the mountains. While we waited for my bags, Bobby told me about a man he'd met that day in Wallace, Idaho. The man told Bobby he had been working sixty hours a week as a computer programmer in the Bay Area in California, struggling to make ends meet because of the astronomical cost of living. One day, he decided he'd had enough and moved to Wallace, where he was working a third as much as he had in California and spending the rest of his time hiking and skiing. Bobby viewed his new friend as an inspiration and role model, much like John Colter.

Neither of us was especially tired, so we decided to drive west for an hour or two and find a hotel room. But our plan didn't work. As we soon discovered, the small towns along our route were too small to have hotels. We headed west on Highway 2, passing through Deep Creek and Reardan without finding a place to stay. In Davenport, as we both looked for some sign of a hotel, blue lights appeared behind us. By now, it was midnight. The temperature was in the forties. When the cop walked up to our car, however, I noticed he was wearing shorts. As if to make up for his adolescent attire, he struck a serious tone. He began lecturing Bobby about the danger of speeding, even though Bobby had been going only sixty on the flat, deserted highway. Bobby was humble and apologetic and employed a strategy he later told me had worked in the past. When the cop asked to see his license, Bobby made a point of flashing his military ID. The policeman's mood changed immediately, and he never gave another thought to writing a ticket. Fellow officers.

In the town of Wilbur, we came to the intersection with Highway 174. The turn to the northwest led to Grand Coulee Dam. A campground was promised. We made the same choice we'd made four years earlier in western Nevada, abandoned our search for a hotel room, and opted to camp. Along the way, we saw several mule deer on the side of the road as well as a lone coyote. We topped a hill, and Bobby nearly ran over a porcupine waddling across our lane. I wondered what damage its quills might do, but Bobby swerved and missed it. As it turned out, the wildlife we saw on the thirty-mile drive to the campground was more than we would see in forty-five miles on the trail in the next five days.

It was after two o'clock by the time we arrived at the crowded campground. We circled twice searching for an open site to pitch our tent before we found one. We put the tent up quickly—having learned our lesson beside Washoe Lake, we added the rain fly—and then crawled into our sleeping bags. It had been a long day. Surely I must have been the first person since the dawn of time to spend consecutive nights in Seagrove Beach, Florida, and beside the Grand Coulee Dam in Washington. I fell asleep quickly but woke up two hours later. With less than ten feet between tents, the campground was like a hotel without walls. Before I drifted back to sleep, I counted three snorers, and Bobby was not one of them.

We rose early, broke camp, and abandoned the tent city. We drove into town, ate a big breakfast, and then continued west toward the Cascades. The weather was made to order. Bobby had burned a new CD for the trip. We rolled the windows down and turned the volume up.

We arrived in Wenatchee in late morning and stopped to buy groceries. Our menu for the week was lacking in imagination. Every day, we would have instant oatmeal and coffee for breakfast, bagels with peanut butter and jelly or honey for lunch, and a dehydrated meal for dinner. Some dehydrated food is excellent; some is awful. Learning which is which has been a painful experience. Because we had to carry everything we would consume, there would be no cooler of beer on this trip. Our total supply of adult beverages consisted of a pint of Dewar's and an oversize bottle of Cabernet.

After shopping, we continued west through Cashmere into Leavenworth, a tourist town that might do better if it didn't have the same name as a federal prison. We then turned north and made our final stops at two small stores, where we bought fishing licenses, flies and leaders; fuel for my new ultralight backpacking stove; two Green Trails topographic maps to supplement the trail guide; and lunch, our last meal in civilization.

We then began our search for the trailhead, relying on the directions provided by the author of the trail guide. His directions, however, didn't get us there. This was not the first time we've had this problem. Authors of trail guides are better at explaining where to walk than where to drive. We got lost, had to retrace our route, and ultimately flagged down a kind woman who pointed the way. We finally made it to the trailhead at Little Wenatchee Ford Campground just after three o'clock. There were seven or eight cars in the dusty parking area, but not a soul in sight. When we got out to divvy up the food and pack our backpacks, however, we immediately had company. Lots of company.

The company consisted of flies. Black flies. At first, there were just a few—a minor nuisance—but news of the presence of two warm-blooded mammals spread fast. Soon there were hundreds, then thousands, all with a lust for blood. I had read that no spray is effective on black flies, and it turned out to be true. We sprayed ourselves with Deet, but the flies kept coming. All we could do was swat. And though the flies were relentless, they weren't elusive. By the time we finished packing, hundreds of tiny carcasses littered the ground around the car. They were fighting a war of attrition and dying for the cause.

Many flies died in the assault, but they achieved a victory of sorts as well. While Bobby was trying to pour the red wine into a lightweight plastic container, he reached to slap a fly and knocked over the bottle, spilling nearly half the wine into the trunk of the car. I shook my head. The flies had reinforcements; we had no more wine. The author of our trail guide had warned that the uphill climb into the Cascades "may require courage and fortitude in the heat of the afternoon sun in fly season." The way things were starting out, we were going to need some liquid courage to fortify our fortitude. We needed more wine, not less.

Bobby and I finally shouldered our packs. He had a sick look on his face. I'm sure I did too. We were both thinking the same thing: What are we doing here? We hurried up the trail, as if we could escape, as if the flies couldn't fly.

The situation did improve somewhat once we were underway. The first part of the trail was through dense vegetation, which protected our legs. Also, now that our hands weren't occupied with packing, we were less defenseless. Each of us was carrying a fly rod in one hand, but the other hand was free to be a full-time fly swatter. But the kamikaze flies were fearless, and there seemed no end of them. Neither of us wanted to be the one to say it, but the truth was undeniable: If the flies didn't let up, they were going to ruin our trip. Half a mile up the trail, a garter snake slithered across the path in front of us. Bobby offered a sad assessment: "We've got snakes and flies in Mississippi."

* * *

The name of the trail we had chosen was Cady Creek Trail. The creek and the mountain pass to which we were climbing are named for E. F. Cady, who explored the region in 1860. Our hike began in the Henry M. Jackson Wilderness, which bears the name of the late Washington senator. We planned to walk a little over five miles to Cady Pass, climbing some 1,400 feet. Then we would turn north on the Pacific Crest Trail, continue to climb, and ultimately cross into the Glacier Peak Wilderness. Both wilderness areas are part of the Mt. Baker-Snoqualmie National Forest, which lies south of North Cascades National Park. After exploring the PCT for several days, we would return to the car via either the Cady Ridge Trail or the Little Wenatchee River Trail. We were also considering a side trip to Blue Lake, which a ranger had recommended for trout fishing.

One of the benefits of hiking in the Cascades is the spectacular alpine meadows with magnificent views at moderate elevations. You can have the scenery without giving up the oxygen. The trail we were on, however, didn't start out in an alpine meadow. The trailhead was at only 3,000 feet. After marching through boggy weeds, we climbed into a beautiful, dense, old-growth forest of cedar, fir, spruce, and hemlock. The trail ran beside tiny Cady Creek. The forest and creek were beautiful; we had the trail all to ourselves. Just us and the flies. We pressed on without resting. Searching for hope, fighting despair, I told Bobby I'd read that flies are worse at lower altitudes. Our only hope was to escape them by climbing.

We were nearing the spot where we planned to camp. I wondered if we were going to have to throw up the tent and dive in, trapped like caged animals. I paused briefly to check the map. The name of a nearby mountain proved that we were not the first to suffer this fate. Two miles to the southeast stood a peak named Shoofly Mountain. I held the map and the fly rod with one hand and swatted the back of my neck with the other. Flies were here when Shoofly Mountain was named, and their descendants were here now.

Then, suddenly, the flies disappeared. One minute they were swarming around us by the hundreds; the next they were gone. I stopped walking and held out my arms; I had to be sure before I celebrated. I saw no flies and heard no buzz. Then I turned around and looked at Bobby to make sure the swarm of flies that had been tormenting me hadn't turned on him. He was grinning and said, "We outlasted the bastards." Bobby thumped two final fly carcasses from his arm with satisfaction. All we could figure is that the temperature had dropped below their comfort level. We didn't know what the future held but, at least for now, we had peace.

Because my entire focus had been on the flies, I had not yet studied Bobby's pack. Now I had time to do so. Under siege from the flies, Bobby had done a terrible job packing. It looked like there was more gear dangling from the outside of his pack than there could have been on the inside. I told Bobby he looked like Mr. Haney and his truck from the old Eddie Albert show, *Green Acres*. Bobby responded, "Who you think you are? Eva frickin Gabor?"

When we picked out a spot to camp a few minutes later, we discovered the red wine was not the only casualty of the fly attack. With the flies as his focus, Bobby had not tied his tennis shoes securely to his pack. At some point along the three and a half miles we'd covered, they had fallen off. And because I was hiking in front, we had no idea how far back they were. I offered to set up camp, build a fire, and cook dinner while Bobby jogged back down the trail to look for them. But Bobby was exhausted after the snorers at Grand Coulee Dam and the black flies along the trail. He said screw it, they were old tennis shoes anyway. He gathered wood while I put up the tent.

We weren't ready to cook yet, so Bobby fixed us both a Scotch and water. I rigged up my chair kit and collapsed beside the fire. We were flyless

171

and happy. The Scotch gave us a second wind, and we cooked freeze-dried spaghetti—one of the good ones—and drank all the red wine Bobby hadn't spilled. We decided it made more sense to concentrate the effect of the wine rather than ration it out at a pitiful half cup a night. The strategy was logical, but watching the last drops drip from the container on our very first night was sad.

* * *

The next morning dawned clear and cool. We emerged from the tent with trepidation, listened for the telltale buzz, but heard nothing. No flies, at least not yet. We heated water and had our morning oatmeal and coffee. My new stove was performing perfectly. Bobby had a chance to pack in peace this time, but he did little better. Everything imaginable—everything except tennis shoes—was hanging from his backpack. When he walked, the attachments swung in rhythm. He had the look of a peddler, prepared to hawk his wares to other hikers.

The path this morning was steeper and continued nearly two miles up to Cady Pass. I noticed that Bobby seemed to be struggling, which surprised me. Bobby's four years older than I am, but he's always in much better shape. With his regimen of diet and exercise, he'll probably live to be a hundred, if a bear doesn't get him. But if a bear chases us, Bobby reminds me, he'll only have to outrun me.

We reached Cady Pass at 4,400 feet at mid-morning and turned north on the Pacific Crest Trail. The trees grew thinner as we climbed above 5,000 feet, giving us magnificent views in all directions as we crossed and recrossed the ridgeline. To the west, the Pass Creek drainage led down to Skykomish River. Across the river valley was Bald Eagle Mountain. To the east, across Cady Ridge, were the summits of Longfellow Mountain and Whittier Peak. The view to the north was dominated by Skykomish Peak in the foreground. In the distance to the northeast, we caught glimpses of Glacier Peak, at 10,541 feet the highest mountain in the region and the fourth highest in Washington. Its face is dotted with the glaciers that give the mountain its name.

The beauty we had fought through the flies to reach was not limited to the mountains in the distance. At close range, we were surrounded by wildflowers with beautiful blooms of every color. On our previous trips, we had been too late for the wildflower display, but not this time. In the alpine meadows, the flowers formed a solid carpet of color, all achieved without the aid of any earthly gardener. The sinister buzz of black flies was replaced by the harmless buzz of a thousand bees. Their mission was nectar, not blood.

Around eleven o'clock, we stopped to rest in a sloping meadow just west of the ridgeline. As we were lounging among the flowers, I scanned the view and spotted an impossibly large mountain looming all alone on the horizon in the distance to the southwest. It was so huge and so alone that at first I thought it must be a mountain-shaped cloud, like the cloud Baptiste had seen. I squinted and shaded my eyes. It was clearly a mountain. It had to be Mount Rainier. From our vantage point, its peak seemed to be level with us. But this was an illusion; we were actually 9,000 feet below its summit of 14,410 feet. I wondered how far away we were. When we returned to the car later in the week, I studied the Washington road map and estimated that the meadow from which Bobby and I had spotted Rainier was a hundred miles from its summit.

We had seen a few hikers just north of Cady Pass but none in the last hour or so. As we lay in the meadow staring at Mount Rainier, however, two backpackers stopped for a visit. They said they were from Sedro-Wooley, Washington, and confirmed that the peak in the distance was Rainier. The view of the mountain, however, was not what held their interest. As Bobby and I stared at Rainier, the two men stared at Bobby's pack. They were clearly amused, and curious. They saw what was on the outside and asked what was on the inside. Bobby refused to provide details: "Just camping stuff. You know, stuff I need." The two hikers soon continued down the trail. As they passed from view, I heard them laughing.

We continued north and began passing through sizeable snow fields. I walked across them with no problem, but Bobby, with his stork-like legs and high center of gravity, struggled on the steeper slopes. Not only did Bobby have no walking sticks, but he carried a fly rod that occupied one of our hands and would make catching himself difficult if he fell. He looked exhausted.

The snow on these slopes was left over from the previous winter. The Cascades receive enormous amounts of snow from the moisture-laden

clouds that come across Puget Sound from the Pacific. In the winter of
1998-99, the Mount Baker ski area near here broke the world record for
measured snowfall in a single location in a single winter. The new record
annual snowfall, the last flakes of which fell on May 12, 1999, was 1,140
inches—exactly 95 feet. The old world record, 1,112.5 inches, was recorded
on Mount Rainier.

In a patch of snow alongside the trail, Bobby and I noticed a spot where
the snow was reddish pink in color. Our first thought was that some animal
had met a violent end here. We studied the view in all directions, looking for
bears. As we continued up the trail, we realized that the stain in the snow
wasn't what we thought it was. The pink spots in the snow became more
numerous and much larger. They couldn't be blood. After we got home,
Bobby faxed me a magazine article that solved the mystery. The article
described something called "watermelon snow," a kind of algae that grows
in near-constant freezing temperatures. The reddish pigment is created
by the algae to defend itself against ultraviolet radiation that bombards
snow fields. Watermelon snow traps radiation. This was discovered, the
article said, when a uranium miner's coffee pot made his Geiger counter
click after he melted watermelon snow. Watermelon snow also produces
antioxidants that may protect humans from cancer but, consumed in
large quantities, it causes diarrhea. The article closed by advising that "you
shouldn't eat yellow snow either, but that's a different story."

We stopped for our bagel-sandwich lunch at tiny Lake Sally Ann,
which had attracted several other hikers. This was our first lake on the
trip. Though we had not received any fishing report about Sally Ann, we
had high hopes. But the lake was too high, too glacial, and too frozen too
much of the year. No trout. We struck up a conversation with two girls.
Two more days on the trail (for us, not them), and they would have looked
much more attractive. Four more days, and we would have followed them
anywhere. We asked about their route, and they told us they had camped
at Blue Lake. They weren't fishermen (fisherwomen?), so they had no trout
report, but they highly recommended the lake as a campsite, though they
also warned us that the trail from the lake up June Mountain was very
steep, painful to ascend and dangerous to descend.

We dawdled a good while at Lake Sally Ann. Bobby seemed especially
reluctant to hoist his pack again. When he finally did, he set out at a snail's

pace. He was obviously suffering. We decided to make camp to rest and regroup in a saddle just below the Cady Ridge Trail junction. When we stopped, Bobby heaved his pack from his shoulders, dropped it in a heap, and turned and stared at it in disgust. To satisfy my curiosity, I grabbed his pack and picked it up. We had attempted to split the food and gear that was for both of us evenly, but his pack weighed at least ten pounds more than mine. I fastened the belt and chest strap and tried to walk. The pack was not only heavy, but the swinging items caused the weight to shift with every step. Just staying upright must have been a constant struggle for Bobby. I knew Bobby had done a poor job packing during the fly attack, but I was concerned that I wasn't carrying my share of the load. After Bobby and I rested a bit, I suggested that he unpack and start over. In the unpacking process, Bobby produced a veritable cornucopia of useless crap. Some of the useless items he'd actually meant to bring: for example, his three-pound Bowie knife/ machete. But Bobby and I discovered that he'd also brought things he'd meant to leave in the car, stuff he'd accidentally stuck in his pack in the midst of the fly attack. Bobby let fly a string of profanities when he discovered two toiletry kits in the bottom of his pack, not only his small camping kit with the bare essentials—toothbrush, toothpaste, and deodorant—but also his heavy leather one. The big one contained a full bottle of shampoo, contact solution, an electric razor, and a full bottle of Williams Lectric Shave. I posed a question: "Bobby, can I borrow your Norelco and Lectric Shave? I seem to have forgotten mine." He answered with a one-finger salute.

We studied the map and decided we would hike out on our last day down Cady Ridge Trail instead of down the Little Wenatchee River drainage. This would keep us at a higher elevation longer and hopefully cut down on the time we would spend communing with black flies. This also meant we would be coming back this way. Bobby separated the useful from the useless, put the latter in a plastic bag, and hid it in a tree. We would reclaim it when we returned later in the week. With my assistance, Bobby also did a much better job of packing. He put the heaviest stuff in the main compartment closest to him. His pack was no longer top-heavy, and there were no longer items on the outside swinging from side to side. From then on, Bobby was a new man.

* * *

Six months after our trip to the Cascades, Bobby sent me Rick Bass's *The Lost Grizzlies*, which he'd just finished and greatly enjoyed. On page thirty-six of the book, Bass had written the following passage:

> I try desperately, each time I go into the mountains, to carry as heavy a pack as I can, because I know I will be old any year now, and unable to carry such loads. I want to do everything, see everything, taste and smell and imagine everything . . . . There'll be plenty of time for a light pack when I get older.

When I got to this point in the book, I saw that Bobby had underlined the passage. I didn't ask him why, because I knew. In the Cascades, Bobby had made himself miserable, and thought himself foolish, for taking a pack that was far heavier than necessary. I had piled on, making fun of his electric razor, spatula-size Bowie knife, and Williams Lectric Shave. Bobby had continued to think he was foolish in the months since our trip. But here, in the middle of Bass's book, Bobby had found his justification. Bobby had shouldered the ridiculously heavy pack, he could now claim, simply because he could, because doing so proved he was still a young man, and because he wouldn't be able to do so in the coming years. But at the end of our second day in the Cascades, Bobby didn't look like a young man. He grimaced every time he tried to move.

* * *

The saddle below the trail junction was a great campsite. We had excellent views of the mountains to the south and Glacier Peak to the north. Firewood on the slope that rose to Cady Ridge was plentiful. There was only one drawback, though it was a big one: no water. The trail guide promised water within a quarter mile along the Cady Ridge Trail, but we walked at least twice that far and couldn't find it. I remembered we had crossed several streams en route from Lake Sally Ann, so we headed back south with our water filters and bottles. All the streams, however, were runoff from the mysterious pink snow. We didn't chance it. Instead, we wound up hiking all the way back to Lake Sally Ann and filling up there.

The next morning, when we continued north on the PCT, we passed a stream almost immediately that would have spared us two tired miles of walking the previous afternoon.

With plenty of firewood and enough water for dinner and breakfast, we put up the tent and spent the last hour before sunset relaxing. I always take a book when I go camping. This time I had Moby Dick, which I found too heavy, both literally and figuratively. I sat and read, wondering how long it would be before Ahab and the white whale finally squared off. We finished off the Scotch and would be teetotalers for the rest of the trip. As the sun dropped over the mountains, we settled in by the fire and cooked dinner. Bobby, who was beaten down from carrying his top-heavy peddler's pack, sneaked off to the tent as soon as we finished.

I stayed up by the fire, staring north toward the summit of Glacier Peak. The setting sun illuminated its western slope. The glaciers on that side of the mountain glowed a bright pink. The sunset gradually faded, and for a time the mountain was in darkness. One by one, the stars popped out above its peak. For a while, the sky was filled with them. But then the eastern slope of the mountain began to glow. The glow grew brighter, and the stars disappeared one by one. I stirred the fire, determined to stay up until the source of the light on the eastern slope of Glacier Peak appeared. The full moon finally showed itself, rising above the mountain that had blocked my view. All of Glacier Peak was now aglow. The stars had gone into hiding; they could not compete.

The full moon woke me a time or two during the night, but otherwise I slept well. Bobby slept like the dead and awoke rejuvenated. After breakfast, we studied the map and decided to set out for Blue Lake. Troutless Lake Sally Ann had whetted our appetite for fish, and we wanted to justify bringing our fly rods all the way across America and toting them through the wilderness. It was another beautiful day. In comparison to the first two days, Bobby said his pack weighed nothing at all. Even discovering the stream from which we could have gotten water the afternoon before didn't dampen his spirits.

The trail climbed along the northeastern slope of Skykomish Peak to Wards Pass. Waterfalls cascaded down the slope above us to the west. The Little Wenatchee River drainage fell away to the east. As we climbed toward the ridgeline, we discussed how difficult it would be for somebody to find us if there were an emergency at home. I had given my family only a rough itinerary, which we were about to abandon by heading to Blue Lake. Looking for us would be like searching for a needle in a wilderness area. We decided the best hope would be for whoever needed us to hire a small plane to crisscross the mountains, pulling a banner commanding us to hike out and phone home.

When we reached the ridgeline, the Skykomish River came into view far below. Soon we came to a flat saddle called Dishpan Gap, where two trails led to the west. One dropped steeply down to the river; the other followed a level course along the slope of June Mountain. We took the high road.

The views from this trail were spectacular. The river valley lay thousands of feet below us. Across it was the north face of Skykomish Peak. Streams cascaded down the mountain, occasionally dropping in waterfalls. The combination of the scenery and his lightened load had energized Bobby. He wasn't going to collapse after all.

We soon came to another trail junction and had to decide which path to take to Blue Lake. We could hang a right and take the short, steep route, about which the girls at Lake Sally Ann had warned us. The steep route headed up 750 feet to the crest of the ridge, then straight down nearly 1,000 feet to Blue Lake, all in little more than a mile. The other option was to continue hiking west on this trail for nearly two more miles. We would then swing back to the north, drop down to Little Blue Lake, and then climb nearly 500 feet up to Blue Lake. We had plenty of time, so we chose the longer, safer route.

The trail continued through wildflower fields with splendid views. We crossed several more steep snow fields. I tromped across first, kicking boot prints into the snow for Bobby to follow. But he still struggled. His pack was lighter, but it was still perched atop his stork legs. Every few steps, he had to drop to all fours to avoid sliding down the mountain.

Just before reaching the turn to the north, we spotted a mule deer on the slope above us. The doe stared at us warily and then trotted over the ridge and out of sight. She was nothing like the tame national park deer. Hunting is legal here, and she acted like she knew it. Not counting other hikers, the deer was the only large mammal we saw in five days in the Cascades.

Bobby suggested we stop for lunch at the trail junction in a saddle on the western edge of the ridge. We now had our first unobstructed view to the north since leaving the PCT. Bobby scanned the terrain with his binoculars and spotted Blue Lake. It was only slightly below us, but the trail from here to there was anything but level. Bobby looked below us into the canyon we would have to climb down and then up to get to the lake. The girls had not come this way and had not warned us about this route. Still looking through the binoculars, Bobby said we needed a zip line. I suggested a helicopter.

We lay down to rest with our heads on our packs before beginning the descent. Before we rose, two hikers—a man and a woman—appeared. The woman was gorgeous. As they passed by, she spoke to us in a French accent. Exquisite. Time spent by a man in the wilderness, like beer, improves the appearance of women. My theory is that each day in the wilderness has the same effect as two beers. On an empty stomach. The French hiker, however, would have been beautiful if we'd been stone cold sober and passed her on a sidewalk on the Champs Élysées.

The trail that led down to the valley was gorgeous as well. We crossed beautiful rock gardens. Tiny streams flanked by lush ferns led down to Sloan Creek. Much snow remained in the valley, which was protected by high ridges and mountains on three sides. Several times we had difficulty spotting the lightly traveled trail exiting from the opposite side of a snow field.

We finally reached the bottom and stopped at a tiny pond below Little Blue Lake. Bobby dropped his pack and walked around the pond, scanning it for fish. He spotted a flash of movement in the water and immediately declared it a trout. If so, it must have been a lonely fish. Or maybe Bobby was fantasizing. We both searched the clear waters of the pond thoroughly and saw no other signs of life.

We then began the steep climb to Blue Lake. We trudged up the difficult incline, the afternoon sun beating down on us. Sweat poured down my face and ran into my eyes. After struggling across the snow fields on the descent, we were already tired, but our exhaustion created a spark of creativity. As we climbed the last hundred feet, we swapped ideas for inventions that would make backpacking more enjoyable. I suggested the first: a bicycle tire attached to the bottom of your pack frame to bear the weight of the pack. Bobby then had an even better idea: dehydrated vodka. I proposed freeze-dried Cabernet.

* * *

A number of months after our return from the Cascades, Bobby called me at the office, excited. He'd just received the new issue of *Backpacker* magazine, which identified an outdoor food company touting powdered wine. Hopeful but skeptical, I sent an email to the company seeking details. The next day, I had a response. The powdered wine was for flavoring food, not drinking. The alcohol content, if there was any alcohol at all, was so tiny the FDA did not even require it to be disclosed. I called Bobby with the bad news, but he was upbeat. "Look at it this way," he said, "we can still be the ones to invent the real thing. We'll get rich and leave these offices for good."

* * *

Blue Lake is magnificent. It lies in a cirque with steep cliffs towering above it on three sides. A beautiful grove of evergreens and a sloping green meadow dotted with boulders line the rest of the shoreline. A stream easily crossed by rock-hopping bisects the meadow. The stream meanders a hundred feet or so down a gentle grade before plummeting in a waterfall to Little Blue Lake nearly five hundred feet below. Snow-capped peaks of the Cascades dominate the horizon to the west. The girls at Lake Sally Ann had given us sound advice. The meadow at Blue Lake was the most beautiful campsite Bobby and I had ever seen. We dropped our packs beside the creek and walked the short distance to the lakeshore with our fly rods. We were ready for action. Trout for dinner; we could taste it.

As we surveyed Blue Lake from the shoreline, however, we began to suspect that the forest ranger had led us astray. The water in an alpine lake, even one many fathoms deep, has a clarity that is difficult to fathom. Blue Lake was no exception. Even where the water was deep, we could see the bottom clearly. And if there had been any trout, we could have seen them. We squinted and shaded our eyes, but we saw no movement, no fish. We walked up and down the shore, repeating the process, cursing the ranger and our luck. Like Lake Sally Ann, Blue Lake appeared to be barren. Hoping my eyes had deceived me, I rigged my rod, tied on a fly, and cast half-heartedly, hoping to summon hidden trout from the depths. Bobby looked on. My fly drew no takers. I walked around the steep eastern side of the lake, where the water was deepest. The rocky bottom was perfectly clear even at these depths. Still no trout. To gauge the depth, I picked up a rock and tossed it in, counting the seconds until it settled on the bottom. The rock came to rest just after I reached a thousand eleven.

Bobby and I cursed the ranger. He had recommended we come here because of the trout, but there were no trout. Perhaps the ranger made an honest mistake. On the other hand, maybe he took secret pleasure in sending us to a lake he knew was barren. Maybe he was sadistic, like the imaginary ranger who turned on the sprinklers at Washoe Lake.

We gave up on fishing and returned to the meadow beside the creek. We still had several hours before dark, so instead of catching small fish, I read about a huge one (actually a mammal). I rigged my chair kit and climbed atop a large boulder in the creek just above the waterfall. At long last, on page 574, Captain Ahab spotted Moby Dick, and the chase began. In the end, Ahab got his, as did all but one of the crew of the Pequod. Ishmael alone survived. Melville had to spare one of the crew to tell the story. I hoped I wouldn't have to write 574 pages about my travels with Bobby before I caught a trout.

After Ahab met his end, I walked over to my pack, removed the tent, and put it up beside the creek. Bobby gathered firewood, and we built a fire to ward off the growing chill. This would be the coldest night of the trip. I moved my chair to the fireside. Bobby and I watched the sun drop over the snow-capped peaks. We had the lake, the creek, the waterfall, and the sunset all to ourselves.

Bobby and I cooked dehydrated beef stroganoff, cleaned our plates, and added wood to the fire. On this night, Bobby told me for the first time about Jake and Jasmine and his decision to abandon private practice to become a corporate lawyer. When I told Bobby I couldn't believe he hadn't told me this story before now, Bobby winked and said, "There's a lot of stories I haven't told you."

After a few seconds of silence, I returned to the point in the story when Bobby had asked Jasmine whether she had given Jake what he wanted. I asked: "Legs up? That's really how you asked her?"

Bobby was defensive: "I thought she was going to say no, OK? I mean it was a frickin traffic ticket. And it wasn't even *her* ticket. If I'd known she'd gone legs up, I would have been more diplomatic."

"Yeah, right," I responded.

We then sat in silence for a minute or two staring at the flames. The wine and whiskey long gone, I raised my cup of Kool-Aid toward Bobby and proposed a toast: "To Jake." I wasn't toasting Jake's philandering, but his role in bringing us here. But for Jake's misconduct, Bobby would never have applied for the job at the shipyard, he and I never would have met, and we wouldn't be camping by the shore of Blue Lake. I didn't have to explain any of this to Bobby. He understood, and he raised his cup to mine. "To Jake," he repeated.

* * *

Months after our trip, I was drinking a beer while reading *The Lost Grizzlies*. Bass was writing of his great fondness for Doug Peacock, with whom he was hiking in the San Juans of southwest Colorado in search of grizzly bears. Bass had written: "One good friendship in life is more than many of us ever come away with. I have been blessed with a few, and have been given another, Peacock."

While reading the book before sending it to me, Bobby had scratched out Peacock's name and penciled in mine. I smiled and raised my beer toward Bobby, two hundred miles away on the Mississippi coast. I took a sip, thought back on our night at Blue Lake, then raised my beer again. "To Jake," I said, this time just to myself.

* * *

The night by Blue Lake was perfect. All was right with the world. But all things must pass, both good and bad, and so the bubble burst.

Our conversation had moved to Bobby's latest scheme to leave the shipyard, where Jake's indiscretions had led him. Bobby's dream, as always,

182

was to reorder his life so he could spend more time in places like this. The scheme involved a new position in the National Guard. I was too tired to follow the details. Just as I was dozing off, Bobby shouted for me to get up. At the same time, I felt something hot on my backside. I hopped up and saw a spark glowing on my Therm-a-Rest pad, which was folded into my chair kit. The spark had popped out of the fire while I was admiring the moonlight on the mountains. I brushed the spark off, then stared down at the pad in fear. Neither of us had brought a repair kit. A hole in the pad would mean no chair to sit in and no pad to sleep on for the rest of our time in the mountains. Bobby produced a flashlight, and we inspected the pad together. We found no damage, and I breathed a sigh of relief. I sat back down, feeling lucky.

I didn't feel lucky for long. A few seconds after I returned to my chair, I again felt something on my backside. This time it wasn't hot. It was air, and the air was blowing. I hopped back up and grabbed Bobby's flashlight again. I felt the pad with my hand and peered at it intensely with the light. And there it was: a tiny pinhole, almost too small for the eye to see, so small that Bobby and I had missed it with our first inspection. But the hole was big enough for air to escape. After all, air molecules are small.

I was riding high at 9:00, shot down at 9:15. We tried covering the pinhole with moleskin, knowing it would never work. I sat back down. Still the air spilled out. I remembered the hiker who came to Bobby's rescue in the Tetons, the kind soul from Phoenix with the ancient first aid kit. I imagined that he would come to our rescue again, appearing out of the darkness, bearing a repair kit, excited at the prospect of using it for the first time after carrying it through the mountains for decades. Where was he now? He had come to Bobby's rescue. Why not mine?

Long after our trip, I learned from Bobby that I didn't need the good Samaritan from Phoenix. All I needed was for Bobby to look in the bag in which he'd packed his own Therm-a-Rest. Had he looked, he would have found the repair kit that came with it. But he didn't look, the moleskin didn't work, and my pad was flat. Bobby, my dear friend, suggested we hike all the way out the next day. We could drive into town, get the pad fixed or get a new one, and return to the mountains for our last two days. I thanked Bobby, but his proposal seemed drastic. We agreed to play it by ear, to see how I fared during the night with an airless pad. I sat back down in my damaged chair. The air slowly seeped out; my ass settled onto the cold ground. After a minute or two, I laughed. I thought back on Bobby's rock problems on our last two trips—hitting a big one with the rental car in Glacier and a small one with his head in the Tetons—and I thought of the razor and the Williams Lectric Shave. "I guess I'm the dumbass this time." Bobby was staring at the flames. After a few seconds, he started to nod. He looked up at me and smiled.

When it was time to turn in, I had an idea. The hole in my pad was minuscule; the leak was slow. I removed the pad from the chair kit. Though the pad is self-inflating, it can be blown up by mouth as well. I blew it up as full as I could get it, closed the valve, and put it in the tent. I put my sleeping bag on top and hurried to crawl in. Then the race began. My goal was to be asleep before the pad went flat. It would be hard to fall asleep on the hard ground with a deflated pad, but the ground might not wake me up if I fell asleep before all the air leaked out. The pressure to fall asleep was on, but I won the race. I dozed off immediately.

But I didn't sleep through the night. At 2:30, I woke up. The full moon was directly overhead, brighter than any streetlight. The pad was deflated, the ground hard. I was not only uncomfortable, but I was cold too. The cold part of my discomfort surprised me. I was in my twenty-degree goose-down bag, and we were in my snug Walrus tent, the fly on. I put on my fleece top and pants that I'd been using for a pillow. After an hour or so of miserable tossing and turning on the hard ground, I drifted back to sleep.

I awoke again shortly after dawn. Even covered with fleece and surrounded by down, I was cold again. When I tried to move, I discovered I was stiff as well. There was no such thing as a self-inflating pad when I was a Boy Scout, and I never bothered to take an air mattress on campouts. But I was thirty years younger then.

Shivering in the early morning chill, I hurried to build a fire. After I'd warmed myself front and back, I decided to walk around to unkink my sore muscles. I climbed up to the lakeshore and discovered why I was so cold. It was mid-August, but the entire lake was covered by a sheet of ice. I stared at the surface and pondered just how uninhabitable this place must be in the winter. The prospect made me start shivering again. I returned to the fire, rewarmed myself, then lit my stove to heat water for our coffee and oatmeal. Bobby soon emerged from the tent. I sent him up the hill to see the frozen lake. He returned, excited. "Holy shit, a frozen frickin lake in August."

* * *

As usual, I was suffering from gastrointestinal shutdown in the mountains. Also as usual, Bobby's system was working like clockwork. After his second cup of coffee, he announced that it was time for his morning stroll. "You don't need to go?" he asked with mock concern. I didn't, but I still followed him. I pursued at a safe distance as Bobby searched for the perfect spot. I was stalking him. When Bobby took a few steps, so did I. When he stopped to search for potential sites, I stopped. Once, when he turned nearly all the way around, I took cover behind a boulder. I was sneaky, grouse-like. He never knew I was there, until it was too late.

Bobby finally picked out a spot and, like a cat, began making preparations. He used his boot to kick out a hole, then dropped his pants. When I was sure he was committed to the task, that there was no turning back, I rushed forward with my camera. Bobby squatted, defenseless, as I snapped pictures to record the event for posterity. All he could do was grin and wave. I trotted back to the fire, pleased with my ploy.

* * *

We cleaned the breakfast dishes and took down the tent. After making sure the campsite was clean, we headed up the trail. We were going up the steep route this morning. The trail rose abruptly as it climbed the slope south of Blue Lake. Before we had gone far, we stopped to catch our breath and looked back down on our spectacular campsite. John Hart wrote that "your camps, after all, are the spots in the wilderness of which you have special knowledge; it is your campsites that you particularly remember." I will remember our beautiful camp at Blue Lake all my years: the lake, the meadow, the creek, the view; the hole in my pad; the photos of Bobby's bare, skinny ass. I am grateful for the ranger who misled us. (Note: I considered including in the book one of the photos I took while stalking Bobby, but my wife Carrie, after seeing the photos, persuaded me to spare you.)

We turned and faced the trail leading up the mountain. The route was steep; the crest was nearly a thousand feet above us. The task looked daunting, but our condition had improved as a result of three days hiking in the mountains. We climbed with less difficulty than we expected. On one of the switchbacks that led to the crest, we looked back down to the surface of Blue Lake, now more than five hundred feet below us. We saw boulders that at first we thought lay on the bottom of the lake. But as we studied the scene, we realized that what we saw was actually a reflection of the boulders on the opposite shore. Even in shorts, we were sweating as we climbed, but the surface of Blue Lake was still frozen.

We reached the crest just before ten. This was the highest point on our trip, 6,562 feet according to the map. We were high in the mountains, but elevation is relative. In comparison to our last trip, we were actually lower than the floor of Jackson Hole.

It was another clear, cloudless day, and the views to both east and west were spectacular. The snow-capped peaks of the Cascades stretched away in both directions as far as the eye could see. Mount Rainier rose from the horizon far to the southwest. I'm usually the one who sings, but now it was Bobby's turn. He sang about standing on a mountain top and staring out at the Great Divide, about seeing a hawk and his soul beginning to rise. I recognized it as the song we played on our first trip as we drove south from Reno, Bob Seger's "Roll Me Away," and I joined in. When we stopped singing, Bobby offered the ultimate compliment, Brian's compliment: "This is the shit."

We rested, took pictures, then started down the slope to the east. The going was easy, and we soon reached the junction where we'd taken the low road the previous day. We retraced our steps to the Pacific Crest Trail at Dishpan Gap. This was our point of decision. We could turn south here, hike out to the car, get my damaged pad repaired, and return to the mountains the next day. Or we could turn left and continue north on the PCT toward Glacier Peak. I refused to let Bobby let me be a candy-ass. I recalled John Colter's two-hundred-mile trek across Montana after escaping the Blackfeet. Colter had no Therm-a-Rest pad; he didn't even have shoes. We turned north.

The trail wound to the northeast and hugged the ridgeline, with spectacular views of Kodak Peak in the foreground and Glacier Peak in the distance. Just beyond Sauk Pass, we reached the junction with the Little Wenatchee River Trail. A gentle slope covered with wildflowers lay below us to the east. Someone in years past had given this lovely spot a lovely, alliterative name, Meander Meadow.

We swung around the eastern slope of Kodak Peak. The trail guide encouraged a climb to Kodak's modest summit to—guess what?—take photographs. We had already completed one steep climb, however, and a gentler one loomed ahead on the PCT. We skipped the climb to Kodak Peak, crossed into Glacier Peak Wilderness, and began the mile-long descent down to Indian Pass at 5,000 feet.

* * *

I first got the notion that I might want to write about my trips with Bobby at some point between the Tetons and this one. As we descended toward Indian Pass, I was considering what I should include. I imagined enthusiastic readers heading for the wilderness after reading my bestseller. And so, as I followed my fantasy to its logical end, I thought it would be helpful to the converts to include advice about the proper array of equipment for a backpacking trip.

As I was making a mental list of gear to recommend, we came upon a couple who looked to be in their fifties resting in the shade beside the trail. The woman said they were from Corvallis, Oregon, but were about to move to Asheville, North Carolina. They were amused that we had come here all the way from Mississippi. As we spoke, I studied their appearance, comparing them to us. Both looked as if they had just been helicoptered in. Bobby and I were greasy and dirty, our clothes a mess. They couple beside the trail looked as fresh as daisies. They were clean; their clothes looked freshly laundered. Bobby and I had on heavy backpacking boots. The man and woman were wearing "approach" shoes, little more than tennis shoes. Our loaded external-frame packs, even with Bobby's offload on the second evening, had to weigh fifty pounds apiece, maybe more. The man and woman from Oregon had small, mesh, frameless packs that couldn't have weighed more than twenty pounds. Bobby and I both assumed they were out for no more than two or three days in the mountains. After discussing our itinerary, we asked about theirs. The man said they were on day five of a seven-day, hundred-mile hike on the PCT. I stifled a groan. We asked how they could possibly complete a week-long hike with what looked like day packs. The man responded by recommending a book called *Beyond Backpacking* by Ray Jardines. Jardines had tired of carrying heavy packs into the wilderness, set out on a mission to minimize the weight of what he carried, and then wrote a book about it.

The man and woman explained some of their secrets. Their packs themselves weighed almost nothing. They used their sleeping pads to create frames of sorts inside the mesh packs. They had no tent, only a lightweight tarp. They shared a single, oversize sleeping bag. Bobby and I spoke up simultaneously, vetoing that idea for us. The woman showed us a featherweight jacket she had made that doubled as a rain top and windbreaker. The net results of their efforts were packs that weighed twenty-five pounds each at the start of the trip, half of which was food. The idea, according to the man, was to live like a monk, to give up all non-essentials, to avoid the burden of a heavy pack. After all, he said, the joy is in the walking.

I'm not sure I completely agree with him. To me, the joy is in the walking *and* the camping. Creating a good camp by a clear mountain stream, sitting on a boulder and reading a good book as the day slips away, enjoying a campfire with a good friend: All of these, to me, are at least as enjoyable as the walking. I believe that carrying a little extra to add to the creature comforts at camp—a book, libations—is worth the price. But with that one exception, I couldn't argue with anything the couple from Oregon said. With thanks for their advice, we parted ways. They headed up the trail; we headed down. When we got out of earshot, I said I bet they didn't have a Bowie knife or Williams Lectric Shave. Bobby noted that he didn't see any fly rods either.

I decided then that maybe I shouldn't be the one to offer advice on backpacking gear. So if you're reading this, and you've decided that backpacking sounds like fun, and you're thinking you might just give it a try, read *Beyond Backpacking*. And get a subscription to *Backpacker* magazine, which is filled with tips for lightening your load.

Our trip had now been fly-free for three days. We'd almost forgotten the miserable start. But we'd also been above 5,000 feet since the morning of the second day. As we descended to Indian Pass, the flies found us again.

There was a beautiful, grassy meadow there. I longed to lie down in it, to rest my weary soles. But because of the flies, the damnable flies, we pressed on. As we climbed up the trail through the forest north of the pass, we again left them behind. They must have been acrophobic.

We were now almost due west of Indian Head Peak, whose summit is at 7,442 feet. On the western face of the mountain is an unusual rock outcropping that gave the mountain its name. Bobby and I studied the outcropping from different angles as we passed by. It didn't look much like an Indian to us, but the Tetons didn't look like tetons either. Maybe we're just lacking in imagination.

I pulled out our second Green Trails map. We had just crossed from the north end of one to the south end of the next one, and we congratulated ourselves on the accomplishment. Just up ahead, I pointed out to Bobby, we would reach tiny Kid Pond. This would be our last, best hope for trout. We picked up our pace in anticipation. But Kid Pond, which lies in a grassy meadow just east of the trail, was another disappointment. The stagnant water was brown and murky. A self-respecting trout would never live in it.

As we continued north, I looked down at the fly rod in my hand. Maybe it was a curse, I concluded. I shared the thought with Bobby, telling him that perhaps there was a lesson to be learned from our fourth consecutive trout-free trip. Like Jacob Marley in *A Christmas Carol*, I pointed out, we had lived wicked lives. Our fly rods were like Marley's chains. Our fate was to carry them through the mountains of the West, on trip after trip, never to catch a trout. Bobby stared down at his fly rod in disgust. "Marley's frickin chains," he muttered.

We decided to make camp in another half mile at the junction with White River Trail. Our plan was to continue north on the PCT two or three miles beyond the junction to see what the trail guide described as the "climax meadows," whatever that means. There was no stream on the map there, however, and the trail guide didn't mention any. Our first thought was to gather wood, set up camp, and hike north in the morning. But this was the warmest day of the trip, following the coldest night. Even though we were at nearly 5,400 feet, black flies descended on us when we stopped. The key factor was temperature, not elevation. After a few bites, we decided to leave our packs and walk up the PCT to White Pass, just south of Glacier Peak. This would allow the day to cool and the flies to relent. We would get to take an evening, pack-less stroll on what some say is the most beautiful segment of the entire Pacific Crest National Scenic Trail. After our evening hike, we couldn't disagree. The PCT spans more than 2,600 miles from Mexico to Canada, but it is hard to imagine a more beautiful stretch than this one.

There was no water where we dropped our packs, so we took our water bottles and filters with us as we headed north. Depending on what we found, we would either take water back to our packs or return for our packs if we found a better campsite. Within two hundred yards, we discovered a creek winding down from a large snowbank on the east side of the ridge. We studied the snow—no pink—but there was no flat spot for a tent. We left our bottles and filters beside the creek. We would fill the bottles on the way back and return to our packs to set up camp.

Around the next curve in the trail was another pond. This one was called Reflection Pond. It was tiny, and trout seemed unlikely. But the water was clear; our hopes rose. We decided there might be trout here, primarily because we had left Marley's chains with our packs. Our lack of fishing gear might be just the thing to fill this lake with fish. We stared at the surface, searching for movement, more than willing to jog back down the trail for the rods if we spotted anything. But we didn't, and so moved on.

The trail then wound around the east side of the ridge. The next two miles of the PCT were through one of the most gorgeous sights I have ever seen in my life. The temperature had dropped into the fifties. Without packs, we were liberated. We walked through acres and acres of magnificent wildflowers. These were the climax meadows, an alpine Garden of Eden. There were too many colors to count. The White River valley dropped thousands of feet below us to the east. Five miles north was the towering summit of Glacier Peak. Enormous glaciers spread across its southern face. We stopped and stared. For the second time on this day, Bobby issued the ultimate pronouncement: "This is the shit." I more than agreed: "This," I said, "is the no-shit shit."

The trail led toward White Pass at 5,900 feet. It stayed just east of the ridgeline, except once, when it topped the crest. This point gave us views of the North Fork of the Sauk River 3,000 feet below and the mountains that rose high above it to the west. The trail crossed the ridge again at

White Pass and turned northwest. We continued on for half a mile beyond the pass, then stopped and turned around at 7:00 so we could make camp before dark.

As we retraced our steps on the PCT, we heard a whistling noise on the slope above us. We peered toward the crest, searching for the source. Finally, we spotted it: a fat, round, golden-throated marmot. Then we saw a second, then a third. We stared at them; they stared back. We knew what they were. I don't know if they knew what we were.

* * *

While reviewing my trail guides and other references before writing about my trips with Bobby, I ran across something called Bergmann's Rule. I have no idea who Bergmann is or was, but his rule is that warm-blooded animals of a given group tend to be larger in colder climates. The rule is based on a surface-to-volume analysis. If two objects have the same shape—say a basketball and a baseball or a big bear and a small one—the larger one has a lower surface-to-volume ratio. In the case of animals, the lower ratio results in less loss of body heat. For this reason, animals grow larger in colder climates to stay warmer. Or so Bergmann says.

When I read about Bergmann's Rule, I was reminded of the marmots that had gazed down at us from above the Pacific Crest Trail. The memory led me to propose a corollary to Bergmann's Rule. My corollary holds that animals of a given group tend to be *rounder* in colder climates because a spherical object has a lower surface-to-volume ratio than any other object of different shape but comparable size. And the furry animals we had spotted on the slope above us looked almost perfectly round as they squatted and stared at the intruders.

* * *

Bobby and I made it back to our water bottles and filter just before dusk and stared at the creek bed they lay beside. It was dry. There had to be some mistake. We couldn't have dropped our bottles and filters at the wrong place, but why would someone have moved them? We looked around for clues to help us solve the mystery. But this was the right place;

the bottles and filter were right where we had left them. Then we realized what had happened. The location had not changed, but the conditions had. When the sun had dipped below the ridgeline, the snowbank that fed the creek had quit melting. And when the snowbank quit melting, the creek quit running. Nature had turned off her faucet.

We began a search and found another stream not far away that hadn't yet shut down for the night. We pumped the bottles full with our filters and hurried back to our packs to set up camp. We had experienced a grand day, hiking more than twelve miles in a spectacular place in glorious weather. Our feet were sore, but we weren't nearly as tired as we had been after hiking eight miles two days earlier. Bobby and I were feeling the benefits of healthy living. With every day we spent on the trail, our condition improved.

By now, the temperature had dropped into the forties, and the flies were long gone. We put the tent up and gathered wood in the growing darkness. I heated water for our dehydrated meal du jour. Our menu called for some kind of Mexican chicken dish. I wish I could remember the name, but not because it was good. To the contrary, I want to make sure I never eat it again the rest of my life. It was chicken ranchero or something like that. Pointing down at his plate, Bobby complained about the food and the name: "Why can't they just call it what it is? This isn't chicken ranchero; this is chicken shit." These were strong words coming from Bobby, the man who eats MREs and claims to like them.

As hungry as we were, we wound up hiking over the ridge and flinging most of the chicken shit down the mountain toward the North Fork of the Sauk River. I told Bobby we needed to make sure we got rid of it a long way from camp to avoid attracting bears. Bobby disagreed: "Bullshit. That crap ain't attracting nothing. Rub some on your chest; you'll be safe for life."

Even if Bobby was right, I decided I would rather risk being eaten by a bear than smell the chicken shit all night. I also remembered the putrid smell of what we thought was a bear below Piegan Pass in Glacier. As nasty as the chicken shit was, I was unwilling to assume that a bear would agree with my assessment. I washed my plate with extra vigor and brushed my teeth a full two minutes.

When I was ready to go to sleep, I used the same routine I had the night before. I blew up the pad as tight as possible right before turning in. And, once again, I won the race. It was much warmer this night, and I slept until after daybreak without interruption. When I finally woke up, my pad was flat and my back was stiff, but I was well rested.

Just after breakfast, Bobby took his morning stroll. I noticed he looked over his shoulder every few seconds to make sure I wasn't stalking him with the camera. But I already had my pictures. I sat by the tent and sipped my coffee.

When Bobby returned in five minutes, he spoke: "I just had an idea. We still got the package that chicken shit came in? I was thinking I might go scrape up what I just deposited in the woods and put it back in the package. We could let it dry and then return it for credit to those bastards that sold it to us."

"You don't think they'd be able to tell the difference?" I asked.

"I don't see how," Bobby said. "They look the same; they smell the same. I didn't taste both, but I bet you couldn't tell them apart."

Our disgusting meal did have one benefit. As I was finishing my second cup of coffee, my body decided that it refused to co-exist with the chicken shit another minute. I, too, took a morning stroll. And to keep Bobby from seeking revenge, I took the camera with me.

We broke camp and headed back south on the PCT. Our plan was for an easy day. We would camp in the same spot we had stayed three nights earlier—just below the junction with Cady Ridge Trail. We had only six miles to cover, so we could dawdle and take a couple of side trips, perhaps along Wenatchee Ridge or maybe down the Little Wenatchee River Trail through Meander Meadow. Once again, the weather was perfect—five days in a row.

After two miles, we dropped back down to Indian Pass. Unlike the previous afternoon, it was cool when we got there and thus fly-free. We then climbed back up to the eastern slope of Kodak Peak. Bobby and I considered climbing it and should have, but instead we kept walking. The Wenatchee Ridge Trail looked uninteresting, so we passed it by as well. When we got to the next trail junction, however, we veered off the PCT, turned east, and began walking down toward the Little Wenatchee River. Meander Meadow was on our left. We walked maybe half a mile and then stopped. The view was getting worse instead of better, and we were undoubtedly headed for Flyland. We turned around, hiked back up the hill, and continued south.

There was much more traffic on the PCT than on any of the side trails. We first passed a happy Australian having an animated conversation with himself. A few minutes later, just south of Sauk Pass, we came upon a young hiker sitting beside the trail. We stopped to talk. He was in the midst of a long trek by himself—more than 300 miles to Canada. His long blonde hair was tied in a ponytail. Each of his sentences ended with "man." He was the picture of contentment. I noticed a strange contraption strapped to the side of his pack. It was shaped like an hourglass, maybe ten inches wide and sixteen inches long. My first thought was that it was an elaborate bong—that the solitary hiker's contentment was chemically induced, at least in part. But I wasn't sure, so I asked. I was wrong, but only by one letter. Our new friend explained that the contraption was a bongo drum. He entertained himself at night by playing it.

We wished him luck and continued on our way. After we were out of earshot, I remarked, "What about that guy? Can you imagine hauling a bongo drum up the Pacific Crest Trail?"

Bobby defended the happy hiker: "What are you talking about? He's probably asking himself right now, 'Can you imagine hauling a fly rod down the Pacific Crest Trail?' He thinks we're the dumbasses."

I said, "And that guy doesn't even know that one of the dumbasses— the really dumb one—brought an electric razor. I may be dumb, but you're dumber. Maybe I'm Jeff Daniels, but you're Jim Carrey."

Bobby invited me to kiss his ass, but he was laughing. Life was good.

After a few minutes, I said, "You know, it really does seem like most of the people we see on the trail are a little bit goofy. Some more than a little bit. What do you think?"

"I know what you mean," Bobby responded, "I wonder what that says about us. We're on the trail too. You think we're goofy?"

"Not me," I said. "I'm perfectly normal. But I'm not the one who brought the Bowie knife."

"Kiss my ass again," Bobby said.

Between Dishpan Gap and Wards Pass, our string of talk wound through a number of subjects and somehow made its way to country singer David Allen Coe and a trip to the horse races in Hot Springs, Arkansas, that I took years ago. On our one day at the races, a snowstorm hit between the last two races. It snowed so hard we couldn't see the horses across the track. I was ahead for the day and bet all my winnings on the long shots in the last race, figuring the snow would serve as a great equalizer. But I was wrong; the favorites finished one-two-three. Our top choice trotted home a distant last, rider-less, his jockey having fallen off in the blizzard. I asked a track veteran if I could get my money back, if the loss of the jockey cancelled the bet. He just smiled.

We were supposed to leave town after the races, but the roads were closed because of the snowstorm. We had to pay a bribe/tip just to get a room. That night, my friends and I wound up in a bar listening to a country band. I told Bobby I remembered the band's playing Coe's biggest hit, "You Never Even Called Me By My Name," and singing along. As we neared Wards Pass, I sang the verse that was added to make it the perfect country and western song, then closed with the final lines of the chorus. "You don't have to call me darlin', darlin', but you never even called me by my name."

Just as I finished belting out the last words, we rounded a blind curve in the trail. Three college-age hikers—two guys and a girl—were coming toward us. All three were grinning from ear to ear. We asked about their trip; they asked about ours. My singing, which undoubtedly was the reason for their smiles, wasn't mentioned. They looked at our fly rods and asked if we had caught any. "Nope," I admitted, "haven't seen any either. But we're ready just in case." They grinned again.

We parted ways, and Bobby and I resumed our hike. After rounding the next curve, both of us broke out laughing. We were thinking the same thing.

"Think maybe they think we're a tad goofy?" I asked.

"What you mean 'we,' kemosabe?" Bobby asked. "You were the one singing."

"You're just lucky they don't know about that electric razor and Williams Lectric Shave," I countered. "Plus you've got a fly rod too."

Bobby contemplated the fly rods. "Marley's frickin chains," he mumbled. We continued down the trail, laughing and telling stories.

* * *

The late Supreme Court Justice William O. Douglas, who grew up here in Washington, wrote that "those who love the wildness of the land and who find exhilaration in backpacking and sleeping on the ground may be idiosyncratic; but they represent important values in a free society." The reason backpackers are considered idiosyncratic, I submit, is because of modern man's aversion to discomfort. As Aldo Leopold noted, comfort at any cost is the modern dogma. And so it is for most Americans. But not for Bobby and me. People may think we're nuts for walking all day and sleeping on the ground, but we wouldn't trade our trips to the mountains for anything in the world. If we must suffer some discomfort, so be it. All the same, I planned to patch my sleeping pad before our next trip.

* * *

Our physical condition and pace had improved by the day. We made good time, much better than we needed to make, and made it to the junction with Cady Ridge Trail far ahead of schedule. This was where we had planned to camp, but it was only a little after noon. We made lunch, studied the map, and discussed our options. There was no place nearby to hike that we hadn't already hiked. It was only six and a half miles to the trailhead, and I didn't relish another night trying to race my leaking pad to sleep. The straw that broke the camel's back was the chicken ranchero. The memory was fresh. We couldn't face another dehydrated meal. After a short debate, Bobby and I agreed to hike down to the trailhead, drive back to civilization, and find some beer and cheeseburgers.

Before we started down Cady Ridge, Bobby had to recover the gear he'd hidden in a tree near the trail. Everything he'd left was still there, with one exception—a large, cheap, plastic water container. We preferred not to think that another hiker had stolen it—after all, nothing else was missing—but there was no other explanation. The container cost only three bucks, but Bobby still felt violated.

The first half of the Cady Ridge Trail was relatively level and remained above 5,000 feet. The walk along the ridge provided more grand views of Glacier Peak to the north and the summits of the Cascades stretching away to the south. Just after the halfway point, the trail dropped sharply. Over the last two and a half miles, we descended from over 5,200 feet to the trailhead at 3,000. We went from heaven to hell and walked through purgatory to get there. The descent was the backpacker's equivalent of the Bataan Death March. The trail was steep, hot, and dusty, devoid of views but filled with flies. Ah, the flies. They were worse than on our first day, or at least seemed like it. Bobby and I killed them by the hundreds. We moved fast, as fast as the steep trail would permit. With my low center of gravity and better balance, I pulled ahead. In the midst of the fly attack, I wasn't waiting for Bobby. Every few minutes, I scraped from my arms the dead flies I'd killed. Both arms were covered with blood. From the profanity raining down from the trail above me, I knew Bobby was suffering the same fate. We were desperate to make it to the car, but the trail just kept dropping. It seemed endless. We finally reached the junction with Cady Creek Trail and hustled the last half mile to the car. I looked for Bobby's missing shoes as I retraced our steps on this section of the trail, but I didn't look hard. Escaping from the flies was a higher priority. I beat Bobby to the car by a minute or two, fished out the keys, opened the trunk, and threw in my pack. Before I closed the trunk, I detected the strong odor of stale red wine. The spilling of the Cabernet seemed like something that had happened weeks ago. As the flies continued their onslaught, I opened the driver's door and jumped in, cranked the engine, and flipped the AC to max. Only a couple of flies managed to get in with me. I killed them in short order.

Bobby soon appeared at the car with a stricken look on his face. He tossed his pack into the backseat and climbed into the front seat beside me. "Unfrickinbelievable" was all he said.

"How many you think you killed?" I asked.

"Eight hundred frickin thousand," he said.

We had walked more than thirteen miles, the most of any day of the trip. I looked at my watch; it was not even three o'clock. I backed up, turned around, and headed into civilization. Our goals were beer, a room, showers, more beer, and burgers, in that order.

We decided to stay in Leavenworth, which had a quaint alpine look. After picking up a Heineken for the ride, we drove to the edge of town and got a room at a motel on the banks of the Wenatchee River, whose headwaters we had walked past earlier in the day. We flipped a coin; I lost. While Bobby took a shower, I read a brochure about the town and learned that the alpine look was faux. Leavenworth had been a mining town, but the economy had fallen on hard times. The city's leaders commissioned the marketing department at the University of Washington to help find a solution. The marketing gurus suggested a transformation from mining center to tourist mecca. The change required a strict building and zoning code. If the transformation was to be a success, there could be no double-wides downtown. So it was that a mining town became a Swiss mountain village. I shook my head at the realization that the whole place was contrived. In the wilderness, everything is real. There are no gimmicks.

After taking a shower, I studied myself in the mirror. At least temporarily, my waist was thinner, my chest bigger. I didn't have a six pack, but I didn't have a keg. We bought a literal six pack and sat beside the river watching a mother duck leading her ducklings through an eddy. Bobby wondered if there were any trout in the river. I studied the water. It looked like a river trout would like, but neither of us made a move to retrieve our rods from the car. We had neither the energy to get them nor the heart to face more failure.

After two or three beers, we drove back downtown in search of the perfect cheeseburger. We found a place where we could dine al fresco. A lovely blonde waitress brought menus. After we had downed a couple of draft IPAs, Bobby insisted that our waitress was flirting with me. I was on the cusp of a beer buzz, but my judgment was still intact. "She just wants a big tip." Her friendliness continued, and another beer improved both my mood and her appearance. When she brought the check, she got what I'd said she wanted: a handsome tip. Bobby and I then returned to the motel, cranked down the AC, and crawled into our beds. The real bed was better than the leaky pad.

The next morning, we drove back to downtown Leavenworth. After breakfast, we wandered the streets, looking at the useless bric-a-brac and trinkets in the windows of tourist-trap gift shops. Bobby wondered aloud why people would buy any of what the shops were selling. I was thinking the same thing but said something different: "I don't know. I figured you were going to get that miniature carved accordion player to take on our next trip."

Amongst the tourist traps, we found one place worth entering: an outdoor shop. Bobby bought a capilene shirt, and I got a Therm-a-Rest repair kit. I vowed that I would never go padless again. We looked for tee shirts to commemorate our trip and take home to our families. We wanted shirts that said Glacier Peak Wilderness or Henry M. Jackson Wilderness, but they weren't to be found.

The non-existent tee shirts underscored the differences between national parks and wilderness areas. National parks occupy some of the most spectacular places in America. Hunting is prohibited, which makes the wildlife approachable. National parks also offer conveniences that wilderness areas do not, such as visitor centers and cabins, even tee shirts. Access is easy; trails are likely to be of the highest quality. The trails in wilderness areas are not as well maintained. The Forest Service does not have the staffing to give the same attention to trails that is provided by the Park Service in national parks. And clearing trails in wilderness areas is hard work. Internal combustion engines are prohibited. The absence of chainsaws reduces noise pollution, but it means that trail-clearing (and dog-burying too, I suppose) must be done the old-fashioned way. The difference in trail quality, however, is offset by other factors. In wilderness areas, there are fewer people, fewer rules, and more freedom. Because they attract more visitors, national parks must restrict where hikers can camp and build fires. Wilderness areas are more lenient. Because the time we spend by campfires is one of the great joys of our trips—perhaps the greatest—Bobby and I will think twice before going anywhere in the years to come that won't let us have a campfire.

We left the Cascades and headed back across the plains of eastern Washington toward Spokane. To see country we hadn't already seen, we took a more southerly route. Central Washington was indistinguishable from northwest Texas, which I had driven across six weeks earlier with my son Paul while driving home from Colorado.

Bobby and I stopped and gorged at a Mexican restaurant in Moses Lake, a town on a lake of the same name in south central Washington. Our waiter appeared to be a recent immigrant; he spoke no English. I wondered what drew him here, to the middle of the Washington plain, to what some would regard as the middle of nowhere. He was more than twelve hundred miles from the border of his native country. When the waiter returned to the kitchen, Bobby spoke up: "No hablo Inglés, my ass."

"What do you mean?" I asked.

Bobby said the waiter was faking it—that he'd adopted the recent-immigrant routine to lend authenticity to the Tex-Mex cuisine. Bobby said he figured the waiter had walked into the kitchen and told the cook, "Gimme a number three, hold the refried beans, and a number five with extra hot sauce. Come look at these yahoos from the South; they're buying it."

Since the night before, when I suggested that the gorgeous waitress was flirting with me to get a bigger tip, Bobby and I had swapped roles. He was now the cynic. Maybe they were both acts, but I preferred to think they were both sincere—that the waiter had just arrived here to pursue the American dream and the waitress had gone home and dreamed of me.

We arrived in Spokane in mid-afternoon. Our flight didn't leave until first thing the next morning, so we had time to explore. We stopped at a park beside the Spokane River in the middle of town and walked down to the bank. The water was clear and the current fast. We studied the rapids and wondered whether the river was canoeable. The day was hot; we no longer had elevation to shield us from the heat. Spokane is less than 2,000 feet above sea level. We walked a few hundred yards along the bank and then returned to the car.

We drove west to Fairchild Air Force Base. Bobby's position in the Reserve allowed him to get us a place to stay there. When we pulled up to the gate, the guard was nonchalant, but his respect and deference increased instantly when he saw on Bobby's ID that he was a major. This was the second time on the trip the ID had come in handy. I still find it hard to conceive of Bobby as a military man, at least one who gives orders.

After we checked in, we went to the BX and renewed our search for tee shirts to take home to our families. There were still no shirts with either of the wilderness areas inscribed on them. We left the base for more exploring. We drove north of town and hiked a short nature trail, then stopped at a bridge that crossed the narrow Little Spokane River. A boy of no more than eight or nine was standing on the bridge, fishing for trout. He reminded me of myself, thirty-five years earlier, fishing for bream and bass and catfish in the creek next to the house in Tupelo where I grew up. I asked the boy the question posed to fishermen of all ages, everywhere: "Any luck?" He'd caught two or three and proudly lifted them for us to see.

* * *

On the drive back to the base, we saw several mule deer in fields beside the road. We were again proving that we were better at spotting wildlife from the car than from the trail. There was a spectacular sunset, the entire western sky aglow with shades of pink and red and orange. The colors slowly faded to blues and grays and then, finally, to black. A fitting metaphor. The day, like our trip, had come to an end. We drove along in silence. Our return-to-real-life melancholy had set in.

As we walked down the aisle of the plane the next morning, I noticed that Bobby's fly rod was still taped together with the same Delta Airlines tape he'd used on the trip out. A long trip for nothing, I thought, just like the can of GAZ Bobby had mailed to and from Montana. We again saw smoke as we flew over the fires burning out of control in the Bitterroots. On the long flight from Salt Lake to New Orleans, we compared notes on the trip, as we always do.

In terms of wildlife, our five days hiking in the Cascades had been a dismal failure. The land was spectacular and yet bereft of animals, at least animals that were willing to let themselves be seen. In terms of fauna, there was none of what we wanted—large mammals capering across the meadows, cutthroat trout rising to inhale our flies—and far too much of what we didn't—legions of black flies that assaulted us at the beginning and end of our hike.

But other than the fauna failure, the trip was a spectacular success. The scenery was magnificent, the weather perfect, the campsites unsurpassed. And though we just had each other, the company was grand. I have told you stories about Bobby that are hardly flattering, but you should not think ill of him. Like my daddy, Bobby is the most modest of men. He does not have it in him to brag. He does not tell stories to make himself look good. Just the opposite. And the unflattering stories he's told me are the same stories I've told you. But make no mistake; Bobby is a fine person and a loyal friend, and he's one of the funniest people I've ever known. For a host of reasons, he is the absolute best of camping companions.

We had enjoyed a great trip, and we had also learned a valuable lesson. Before now, Bobby and I had been reluctant to take a true backpacking trip. We both feared that carrying packs on a long hike would make us miserable. Although there had been times on this trip when we—especially Bobby— were temporarily miserable, we now knew that we could backpack and enjoy it. We looked forward to making our packs lighter so we could enjoy it more.

* * *

Our reentry to the real world was our worst yet. It was August, not September as it had been in the past, and we landed in the heat of the day, not at night. We then had to carry all our gear for half a mile to Bobby's car, which was broiling in the sun. We climbed into the oven-like car and started broiling too. An obnoxious woman gave us trouble when Bobby tried to pay the ransom to free his car from the parking lot. On a New Orleans street, a car stopped in front of us in the middle of the street, halting our progress. Two slouching teenagers walked out from the sidewalk and leaned into the windows of the car. Money and something else changed hands.

"One of these years," Bobby muttered. "One of these years, I'm not coming back. One of these years, I swear I'm going to stay in the mountains." The air conditioner in the car was on high, but it was fighting a losing battle.

When Bobby dropped me off at the dealership to get my car, I was immediately accosted by a pushy, threatening panhandler. I gave him two dollars in change from my pocket; he shuffled away without a word of thanks. I stood there and watched him, disgusted. People should be civil in civilization, I thought. But they're not. In fact, there's little about civilization that's civilized. I'll take the mountains any day. Turn me loose, set me free, as Merle Haggard sang. Bobby's right; we shouldn't come back.

Of course, we always do. Our families are here, our jobs, our responsibilities. Our friends. And life here is not always hundred-degree days in August, drug dealers, and panhandlers. Just as life in the mountains is not always hiking through fields of wildflowers in perfect weather. I needed to remind myself of these truths, and I did. After this pep talk, I felt better—more balanced and less desperate. I loaded my six-disc changer with CDs, climbed behind the wheel, and headed north to Jackson.

CHAPTER
12

The Six Hundredth
Campout

Nearly a year after our trip to the Cascades, I attended Troop 12's 600th consecutive monthly campout in July 2001. Sensible people do not camp in Mississippi in July, but in 2001, Troop 12 did it for the fiftieth year in a row.

The Mississippi summer through the end of June had been more moderate than usual that year. In early July, however, both the temperature and the humidity rose to their customary levels. The weekend of the 600th campout was the hottest of the summer.

My son Paul, who's named for his granddaddy, was at summer camp in Alabama and missed the campout weekend, but the rest of us headed north on the Natchez Trace to Tupelo on Friday afternoon. The weekend itinerary called for the troop to gather on Saturday morning on the lawn of the First United Methodist Church, which had sponsored Troop 12 since its formation seventy-five years earlier. The Scouts planned to set up camp on the church lawn and build a rope bridge to entertain themselves and passersby. The Scouts would be joined by any former troop members foolish enough to camp in the stifling heat. There would be a banquet on Saturday night, followed by a gathering of present and former Scouts of all ages. The early church service on Sunday morning would honor the troop, and three members of the troop would become Eagle Scouts.

On Friday night, we went to dinner with Daddy and two of his childhood friends, Harwell Dabbs and his younger brother Bill, who had come to Tupelo for the weekend's events. Harwell and Daddy were best friends growing up in Tupelo in the twenties and thirties. Harwell was the fourth Eagle Scout in Troop 12, Daddy the fifth, and Bill the seventh.

Harwell brought an old newspaper with him to dinner, an issue of the Tupelo Daily Journal from early 1939. A front-page article, complete with picture, announced that Harwell Dabbs had achieved the highest rank in Scouting, the Eagle. I expressed surprise that becoming an Eagle Scout was front-page news, even then. Harwell said he got special treatment because he had an after-school job at the paper. I scanned the old newspaper, marveling at the prices in the ads, studying the news of the day, pondering all that had happened in the six decades since then, all that had changed. When Bill received his Eagle two and a half years later, he didn't get the same royal treatment from the Daily Journal. His accomplishment was overshadowed by other news. Bill became an Eagle Scout in December of 1941, the same month Japan bombed Pearl Harbor.

I questioned the Dabbs brothers about growing up with Daddy, seeking any hint that he had engaged in normal childhood misbehavior. I was disappointed. The best they could offer was a tale of building a canoe from a kit in an upstairs room of the church. Once completed, the canoe was too big to take down the stairs. They had to remove a window, lower the canoe, then replace the window. My perception of my father as a near-perfect man remained intact. It still is.

Right after breakfast on Saturday morning, Daddy went downtown to the church to help put up tents and organize the Scouts. I stalled, occasionally checking the thermometer just outside the kitchen door. By 10:30, the temperature had reached ninety. Guilt finally got the best of me, and I drove downtown. The tents were up. Half a dozen men and boys huddled in a tiny square of shade under a tarp that had been put up in the center of the church lawn. The heat was oppressive, the air damp and still. We talked about miserable summer campouts from years past. This promised to be another one. I left the shelter of the tarp and wandered back to the Scout hut, the troop headquarters located behind the church.

I found Daddy in the un-air-conditioned hut, organizing a service project. As he wiped the sweat from his face, I offered him a philosophical silver lining. The miserable weather, I suggested, underscored the extraordinary nature of the troop's campout record: 600 months in a row, fifty years without a miss, in every kind of weather imaginable. Because the troop's achievement was first and foremost *his* achievement, Daddy didn't see my point. In all his years, and with all his accolades, he never managed to be impressed with himself.

Soon I was rescued from the heat by an old friend, Dan Purnell, who was in the troop with me thirty years earlier and in the canoe with me on Bear Creek when I was unable to paddle because of a broken arm. Dan and I took a break from the heat and went to lunch, where we talked about old times.

The banquet Saturday night was the highlight of the weekend. Several hundred friends and former Scouts gathered to celebrate the troop's achievement and honor Daddy. Jack Reed, a longtime community leader and former candidate for governor, served as master of ceremonies. A troop alumnus cooked barbecue. Many old friends were there. Daddy spoke about the history of Troop 12. His talk was long on facts and short on sentimentality, as I knew it would be.

Former troop members gave speeches that were longer on sentimentality. Lewis Whitfield was a young Scout in the early fifties. He and his family lived around the corner from Mama and Daddy when they were newlyweds. At the banquet, Lewis spoke of watching for Daddy to come home from work, accosting him before he could make it inside to his bride, pressing him for aid and advice about knots and merit badges. According to Lewis, Daddy always had time for him. In 1957, the year I was born, Lewis became Troop 12's forty-third Eagle Scout. Twelve years after speaking at the 600th campout, almost to the day, Lewis delivered a beautiful eulogy at Daddy's funeral.

Ken Kirk was the senior patrol leader in the troop in the summer of 1951. It was Ken who originated the idea a half century earlier for the troop to go camping every month. At the banquet, Ken gave an emotional speech in which he thanked Daddy for everything he had done for three generations of boys in Tupelo.

Before the campout, I had considered asking to be put on the program so I could give a speech of my own. I would have talked of what it has meant to have a man like Paul Eason as my father, of the long shadow he has cast over my life. I would have shared my earliest memories of the smell of campfire smoke and the feel of Daddy's whiskers on my neck when he returned from a weekend in the woods with the troop. I would have spoken of my own time in the troop. But I also would have talked about my travels with Bobby, of the magnificent places we've seen, to remind all the troop members, young and old, that camping doesn't have to end when childhood does. I decided not to speak, primarily because I feared I would become too emotional. After listening to Lewis Whitfield and Ken Kirk talk about Daddy, I knew I had made the right decision.

After the banquet, we all gathered in front of the Scout hut for a group portrait. The oldest men in the photograph were Daddy and the Dabbs brothers and Jack Reed, all of whom were Scouts in the thirties. The youngest were the eleven-year-olds who had just joined the troop. The age difference was nearly seventy years. I took a picture of Daddy and three men who were in the troop when he became the leader in 1947. You couldn't tell which of the four old men was the leader and which were the Scouts. I'm sure Daddy was the only one who was still camping. He was four months away from his eightieth birthday.

Ann Lowrey visited with a young man who had rafted the Middle Fork of the Salmon with us in 1994. They were ten and eleven then, seventeen and eighteen at the time of the banquet. Several former Scouts with whom I spoke made a point of thanking me for sharing Daddy with them. The notion that I had missed out on anything because of the time Daddy devoted to the troop had never occurred to me.

At about 9:30, when the festivities ended, it was still ninety degrees. Ann Lowrey and her mother planned to head back to Daddy's for the night. I convened my son Cliff and Daddy to decide on a plan. I asked Cliff whether he wanted to camp. "Y'all must be crazy," he said, "I'm going to Big Paul's." I couldn't argue. I turned to Daddy and asked him the same question, hoping he would see the wisdom in Cliff's decision. I tried to make it easy. I suggested we could stay on the church lawn until everybody turned in, drive home and sleep there, then return early in the morning. Nobody would know we didn't sleep in the tent. Daddy would have none of it; I could leave, but he was staying. I decided to play it by ear, hoping it would get cool enough for staying to become bearable or remain hot enough for Daddy to become reasonable.

At about eleven, Daddy retired to our tent. It was still far too hot for me to try to sleep. I stayed up with two old friends, Jim Leake and Scott Reed, who had also stubbornly refused to call it quits. Jim told a story from college days about four of our Tupelo friends. They had gone water skiing at Pickwick, an impoundment lake on the Tennessee River northeast of Tupelo. Over the course of the day, they had drunk a case of beer and smoked half a bag of pot. In their altered state, three of them decided to play a joke on the fourth. As they were clipping along in the ski boat at twenty-five miles an hour, the three simultaneously leaped out, leaving the fourth behind. One of the jumpers bobbed up, a grin on his face. Then the second appeared, then the third. They were delighted: drunk, stoned, and pleased with themselves. Until the fourth head bobbed up. The victim of the prank, his judgment also impaired, had also abandoned ship. When the three demanded an explanation, he said he figured the boat was on fire or something. This was before the era of kill switches, and the boat didn't stop just because nobody was driving it. The four peered into the distance as the pilotless boat raced toward the horizon. Even in the shape they were in, they knew the story would have no happy ending. The boat went straight; the river curved. After a few minutes, a good Samaritan plucked the four from the water and took them up the river. Soon they spotted smoldering wreckage on the shore, but they weren't the first to spot it. Adding insult to injury, a group of vandals had descended like vultures on road kill. As the rescue boat approached, the thieves scattered. Not only was the boat totaled, it was empty as well. The skis and ski jackets were gone. So was the cooler. Even what was left of the pot.

I finally crawled into the tent with Daddy at 12:30. The temperature was still in the eighties. Cars rumbled by, playing rap music at high volume. I was sorely tempted to sneak out, drive to Daddy's house, and return in the morning. But guilt, and sweat, kept me glued to the top of my sleeping bag. To help me fall asleep, I tried to summon up pleasant thoughts. Soon I had one: In less than two months, I would be camping with Bobby beside a clear, trout-filled lake in the Wind River Range in Wyoming. There would be no heat, there would be no humidity, and there would be no rap music. I fell asleep and dreamed of the mountains.

CHAPTER
13

September 2001 –
Wind River Range

The Wind River Range holds no allure for car-bound tourists. Unlike Yosemite and Glacier, no scenic drive bisects the Winds. Unlike the Tetons, foothills obscure the Winds' highest peaks. Because of their relative inaccessibility, the Winds are the least known of the mountains in which Bobby and I have hiked. Among backpackers, climbers, and fishermen, however, the Wind River Range is a mecca. The range draws thousands of all three every year, many of whom return year after year.

The Wind River Range stretches for 110 miles in west central Wyoming, running southeast to northwest. The range is thirty-five to forty miles wide and covers more than 2,000,000 acres. The Continental Divide follows its spine. Among its mountains are more than forty peaks rising above 13,000 feet, including Wyoming's tallest mountain, Gannett Peak. At 13,804 feet, Gannett is thirty-four feet taller than the far more famous Grand Teton. Of the twenty-four highest mountains in Wyoming, the Grand Teton is the only one that is not in the Wind River Range.

The slopes of the highest mountains in the Winds are dotted with glaciers, including seven of the ten largest glaciers in the lower forty-eight states. The range also contains more than 1,600 lakes. Many are filled with trout.

The ancestors of the trout in the range arrived courtesy of the Great Depression and a man named Finis Mitchell. Mitchell was a baby when his family arrived in Wyoming in 1906 in a mule-drawn wagon. In 1923, he took a job with the railroad in Rock Springs, a settlement south of the Winds. Life was good until the Depression struck and Mitchell lost his job. To feed his family, Mitchell became a fishing guide. He and his wife, Emma, built a fishing camp in the Winds. But there was a basic flaw in their plan: With few exceptions, there were no trout in the Winds. Trout were present in some of the larger lakes at lower elevations, but waterfalls and steep cascades had deterred them from migrating to the many lakes in the high country. Unlike the trout, Mitchell was not deterred. He set out to take the trout to lakes they couldn't reach on their own.

Mitchell's method of stocking the lakes of the Winds was simple but effective. He filled five-gallon milk cans with water and fingerling trout and covered the cans with burlap to keep the trout from sloshing out. Mitchell strapped the cans to the sides of pack horses and climbed into the mountains, where he released the trout. The pristine lakes were ready-made for trout; they were filled with all manner of things trout like to eat. When Mitchell released the fingerlings, they took to the lakes like, well, fish to water. The trout and Mitchell's guide service flourished. Mitchell ultimately stocked more than 300 lakes with cutthroat, golden, brook, and brown trout. He estimated that he hauled 2.5 million fingerling trout into the mountains. Thanks to Mitchell, the Wind River Range is now one of the finest backcountry trout fisheries in America.

* * *

Our unquenched quest for trout was a key factor in our decision to go to the Winds. Bobby and I were determined that we would not go fishless for a fifth straight trip. After picking the Winds, we issued invitations. David Sawyer committed immediately. To create a complete reunion from our Glacier trip, we asked Brian Drake, who was still in school but now living in Dallas. We decided to give Brian a reprieve in spite of his cowardice in cancelling on the Tetons at the last minute via email. We also invited two friends of mine, Blake Teller and Wilson Carroll, with whom I had been on several canoe trips. Blake used to work with me until his father talked him into returning to his hometown so the two of them could practice law together. Blake is a delightful camping companion, always happy, always smiling, never complaining. He showed only two faults on our previous trips. First, he had little if any decent camping equipment. When I called to invite him to go to Wyoming, Blake promised he had upgraded. As the trip approached, however, it became apparent that none of his new gear was light enough to take backpacking. He wound up mooching and buying at the last minute. His second fault was more serious: On our prior trips, he habitually drank more than his share of the beer. When I discovered an empty cooler on the last night of a canoe trip with Blake and two others to the Locust Fork in Alabama, I demanded an accounting of the two six packs that had been there an hour earlier. Three of us together had consumed just five of the beers. I looked at Blake; I was thirsty, and incredulous. "Seven? You drank seven of our beers?" He grinned and shrugged. A few minutes later, he was gulping down a Zima he'd bummed off some people camping nearby.

Wilson and I also worked together many years ago. On our canoe trips, Wilson was always the person most likely to do something crazy and get himself killed. In the early 1990s, we canoed the Chattooga, one of the rivers on which *Deliverance* was filmed. Wilson, who was spouseless and childless at the time, insisted on running Bull Sluice at the end of Section III of the river. The rest of us, all married with children, planned to run it too until we saw the plaque memorializing the paddlers killed while attempting to do so. Wilson ran the rapid alone, but not successfully. His canoe flipped at the top, and he was swept through the rapid, his head narrowly missing the aptly named Decapitation Rock. The rest of us held our breath until Wilson bobbed up in the pool downstream, a smile on his face. By the time of our trip to the Winds, Wilson was married and had two young children, Gus and Grace. I wondered if he had changed.

So the lineup was set—six men from four cities, ranging in age from twenty-six (Brian) to forty-nine (David). We had only to pick a date. July or August would give us wildflowers, but the trails would be more crowded. Even more important, wildflower season coincided with bug season. Still licking our black fly wounds from the Cascades, Bobby and

I settled on the first week of September. One of the trail guides promised that the weather can be stable for days at a time in September. It can be unstable too, as we discovered.

* * *

As I have noted, Bobby has often conjured up schemes to escape his daily grind as a corporate lawyer, to spend more time outside. He called me in the early summer of 2001 to report his latest. He was applying to be a contestant on *Survivor*. Even if he didn't ultimately win, being selected would get him out of the office for six weeks.

The *Survivor* application process required a short video as well as a written submission. Bobby shot his video in two sites: his pier on the Wolf River and his office at the shipyard. In the first half of the video, Bobby filmed himself on the pier talking about all the time he'd spent on the river and in the surrounding swamps and forests. The goal was to sell the judges on his survival skills. The second half of the video consisted of a plea rather than a pitch. With his camera, Bobby slowly panned the stacks of papers on his desk, then the four walls of his windowless office. At the end, in a desperate tone, Bobby begged the judges to "get me out of this frickin place."

But the begging didn't work. The time for selecting contestants came and went; Bobby heard nothing. I told him he should have gotten me to write a letter of recommendation. I would have told them that Bobby would be a star.

* * *

After Bobby failed to make the *Survivor* cut, his focus returned to our upcoming trip to the mountains. He and I went through the usual ritual of studying and restudying trail guides. As for food, Bobby and I decided that we would all be on our own for breakfast and lunch. David volunteered to handle dinner the first night, and I put myself in charge of buying dehydrated dinners for the group for the other nights. While I was planning meals, an issue of *Backpacker* magazine arrived in the mail. It contained an article ranking dehydrated food. I followed its advice, and we were not disappointed. Our meals on the trip were excellent. No more chicken ranchero. We were learning by trial and error, improving at the craft of backpacking.

I also took a more serious approach to exercise than I had in the past. I walked and jogged far more miles than we would cover on our trip. I even lifted weights. I didn't want to suffer in the mountains.

During the summer, while on a camping trip with my son Paul and his Boy Scout troop, I mentioned our upcoming trip to the Winds to another of the fathers. He told me he had a friend named David Hardy who backpacked in the Winds every year. I called David, and he generously offered his advice. He told me he had backpacked in the Winds twenty-three of the last twenty-five years. I couldn't imagine a more persuasive endorsement.

In early August, I learned that Bobby was still hawking his disgusting MREs. He said he'd gotten some from his Reserve base, put them in a box, and mailed them to Brian with neither a note nor a return address. Several days later, Brian called me, laughing. He assumed correctly that the anonymous package had not come from his brother Jonny, who was then stationed in Germany, but instead had come from Bobby. I confirmed Brian's suspicions, assured him we would have plenty of civilian food, and prohibited him from taking the MREs to Wyoming.

A couple of weeks before the trip, all of us except Brian gathered at my house on a Friday night to eat, drink, and plan. Bobby and David drove up from the coast, and Blake drove the fifty miles from Vicksburg, where he lives. Blake and Wilson met Bobby and David for the first time. I was the only one who already knew everybody. David prepared a sumptuous meal while the rest of us reviewed maps and equipment lists. Everyone was set except Blake, who had virtually nothing. I loaned him Ann Lowrey's backpack and self-inflating pad; Wilson promised him a sleeping bag. Bobby and David were going out a day early to get used to the altitude. I proposed that we authorize them to spend thirty bucks for each of us on flies and other fishing gear. Wilson objected that this was excessive. The issue remained unresolved.

The next morning, we met with David Hardy. He offered advice about where to stay the first and last nights of the trip—the Half Moon Lodge in Pinedale, Wyoming—and where to buy fishing gear—the Great Outdoor

Shop, also in Pinedale. His advice on where to hike, however, was of little use. David, we learned, never bothered with trails. Instead, armed with topo maps and a GPS, his practice was to take off cross-country. He and his companions rarely saw another soul on any of their trips. We were still pondering a number of routes, but all were on trails. David had never set foot on any of them.

During our visit, David pulled out his worn topo maps, and we discovered that he had a treasure. A number of backcountry, off-trail routes had been drawn on the maps in red pencil. On one of his first trips to the Winds a quarter century earlier, David said he had looked up an elderly gentleman in Rock Springs, seeking advice on hiking in the Winds. The gentleman was Finis Mitchell, the man responsible for stocking the lakes we planned to fish. The red markings on David's maps were Mitchell's.

The next two weeks, I focused more on the trip than on work. Our plan was to fly to Salt Lake City on Saturday, September 1, and then drive northeast to Pinedale. We would hike into the mountains the next morning, spend five nights on the trail, then reemerge on Friday. After a final night in Pinedale, we would drive back to Salt Lake and fly home.

About a week before our departure, I sent Bobby an email reporting on my state of preparation. I was ready, I wrote. I was pumped. Bobby responded in Bobby fashion:

> Amen. I'm frickin ready too. Find myself thinking about the trip about 80% of the time. Go to sleep thinking about sleeping outside. Drive to work thinking about the wilderness. Sit at my desk and think about ordering some shit. Read catalogs in the john.

At last, the time arrived. Bobby and David flew out a day early, on Friday. Blake drove over from Vicksburg early Saturday morning, picked up Wilson and me, and we headed to the Jackson airport. We flew to Dallas, then to Salt Lake City. Along the way, Blake read what I had written so far about our first four trips. Several times during our week in the Winds, I started to tell Blake about one of our previous trips but realized he had already read what I was about to say.

We rendezvoused with Brian at the Salt Lake City airport, then rode the shuttle to pick up our rental car. When we got to the car rental place, however, we realized we had a problem. We stared at our enormous pile of gear and at the Chevy Malibu I had reserved. It was a mismatch. Our only option for an increase in size was a slightly larger Lumina, but it had no CD player. I had burned seven or eight new CDs especially for the trip and stood firm in favor of the Malibu. We put as much as we could into the trunk, but much of the pile still remained. We squeezed what was left into the front, then squeezed ourselves in with it. Before cranking the engine, I looked around. I couldn't see any of my passengers, so I called roll. All three confirmed that they couldn't see anybody else either but were in the car and ready to go. I popped a homemade Steve Earle disc into the CD player, and we were underway.

The route to Pinedale first took us east across the Wasatch Mountains past Park City. We made a beer stop and continued northeast into Wyoming. I drove so I didn't drink. We left the interstate just past Evanston and turned north. The land was dry, desolate, and empty. The only signs of civilization were the road we were on and the snow fences alongside it. Wyoming is the least populous state in America, with fewer than half a million people spread among nearly 100,000 square miles. With five people per square mile, Wyoming is even emptier than Montana. By way of comparison, New Jersey, the most crowded state, has nearly 1,100 people per square mile. You can get lost in Wyoming, but if you really want solitude, go to Alaska. Its total population is slightly more than Wyoming's, but there's much more room for the people to spread out. It has just over one person for each of its 570,000 square miles.

My new CDs were a hit. We listened to Steve Earle and Lucinda Williams and then, at Blake's request, Jerry Jeff Walker. Track one of the disc was "LA Freeway," written by Guy Clark, which has been one of my favorites since college. Jerry Jeff and I sang together. "Adios to all this concrete. Gonna get me some dirt road back street." Just as he and I sang these words, the song's wish came true. The pavement abruptly ended; we bounced along over a rough, rocky road. A sign declared that the road was under construction, but destruction seemed more like it. After several miles at twenty miles an hour, I no longer agreed with Jerry Jeff. I was ready to get back on the freeway. My wish again came true. The construction/ destruction ended, and the pavement resumed.

We stopped for another six pack in Big Piney, which bills itself, according to a sign at the city limits, as the icebox of America. We asked the man at the counter about the icebox sign. He explained that the winters here are bitter, the temperature sometimes dropping to fifty below. When we returned to the car, I questioned the wisdom of those who erected the sign. The city where I live touts itself as the Bold New City. It does not mention its humidity, mosquitoes, or crime, though it has lots of all three.

As we drove north, the highest peaks in the Winds loomed in the distance. Just north of Daniel, we turned east and drove straight toward the mountains on our way to Pinedale. As we approached the town, the mountains disappeared, concealed by a high plateau between us and them. We found the Half Moon Lodge and found David. Bobby had gone to afternoon Mass, presumably to pray for us and a trip with no black flies, free-range cows, or rogue sprinklers. Bobby soon returned and greeted Brian. It was the first time the two had seen each other since Brian dropped us at the airport after our trip to Glacier four years earlier. Since the Glacier trip, Brian had graduated from college, gotten married, and moved from Montana to Texas. Bobby's life was little changed, except that he was no longer a captain in the Reserve as he had been in Glacier. He was now Major Ariatti, on his way to becoming a lieutenant colonel before he retired.

Several of us made a trip to another liquor store and stocked up on Scotch for our five nights in the mountains. We then headed to the Great Outdoor Shop for fishing provisions. Bobby had already gotten his. Brian and David didn't plan to fish, so just Blake, Wilson, and I were buying. Wilson, who had opposed budgeting thirty dollars apiece for fishing gear as excessive, promptly went on a spending spree. He selected flies, leaders, spinners, licenses, extra maps, and other assorted gear, some useful and some not. He had become expansive, almost manic, and it showed at the cash register. The total was $255, which came to eighty-five bucks apiece for the three of us. This didn't include Blake's last-minute purchases of camping gear. As we started down the trail the next day, Blake looked like Minnie Pearl, with price tags still dangling.

After paying the tab at the Great Outdoor Shop, we returned to the Half Moon and gathered in the parking lot to divvy up food and gear. It soon became apparent that Wilson, David, and Brian had brought much more than Bobby, Blake, and I had. Even without any team gear, their packs were bulging. I had thought that having six backpackers instead of two as we'd had in the Cascades would give us economies of scale and lighten our loads, but when we finished distributing everything, I had more stuff than the previous year and my pack was unquestionably heavier. David and Brian picked up the six loaded packs in the Half Moon parking lot and declared that they weighed at least sixty pounds apiece. I had failed to achieve my goal of a lighter pack. Brian and I planned to stay in my tent. Brian is eighteen years younger than I am and built like Arnold Schwarzenegger. After all the loading was completed, however, the tent wound up strapped to my pack. Even so, Brian's pack was just as heavy as mine. Only later did I discover the cause: Brian had smuggled the MREs Bobby had sent him.

We put our packs in our rooms and headed for dinner at a combination restaurant and bar. The restaurant in the back was called Calamity Jane's. In the front was the Corral Bar. We had burgers and pizza and several pitchers of Fat Tire beer. Wilson remained effusive. At least three or four times he stared at his mug, smiled, and pronounced to the rest of us, "This is great beer." He was exactly where he wanted to be, doing exactly what he wanted to do.

We rose early the next morning and walked back down the main drag for breakfast. Brian, Blake, and Wilson ate like it was their last meal, which in a way it was. We had arranged for the owner of the Half Moon to take us to the trailhead at Green River Lakes. We planned to hike the Highline Trail from the northwest end of the range back to Elkhart Park, the trailhead near Pinedale. Before heading for Green River Lakes, two of us and the Half Moon owner ferried our two rental cars to Elkhart Park, where, hopefully, they would be waiting for us at the end of the week. We saw mule deer on the edge of the road on the twenty-minute drive.

After dropping off the cars, we returned to the Half Moon and loaded our packs and ourselves into the owner's old Suburban. We were nearly as crowded as we had been in the Malibu. He drove us northwest up the Green River valley to the trailhead, deposited us, and went on his way. We shouldered our heavy packs and headed up the trail. The day was clear, the temperature in the seventies.

I had chosen this route in part because the hike the first day would be level and at relatively low elevation, at least for the Winds, and would give us a chance to get acclimated. The trailhead was at 8,000 feet, and we wouldn't start climbing until the next day. We started our hike along the north shores of the two Green River Lakes, with Big Sheep Mountain looming across the larger of the lakes to the southwest. The top of Osborn Mountain rose to the northeast. David Hardy and his son had climbed this peak on their trip to the Winds earlier in the summer. The day grew warmer, and sweat ran into my eyes. I stopped in the shade of a pine and wondered: Do we really need all this stuff? Along the lakeshores, we passed a number of day hikers, but as we put some distance between us and the trailhead, the crowd, as always, grew thinner. A pair of hikers reported seeing moose and a black bear, but we saw neither. We were headed southeast, straight for Squaretop Mountain, the most photographed landmark in the Winds. Unlike the Tetons, its name describes it well.

At one o'clock, we stopped for our first meal on the trail, a picnic on the banks of the Green River, which feeds the two lakes. We had our fly rods and all our tackle, but there are no trout in this section of the Green. The water is a milky turquoise, choked with glacial silt carried down from the high peaks on the west side of the Continental Divide, and is not hospitable to trout. I pulled off my boots and socks and dipped a foot into the water. It was frigid; I could stand it only a second or two. I heard a splash upstream and then saw a head pop up in the middle of the river. The head screamed. It was Wilson, being Wilson.

We continued on our way, hiking through Engelmann spruce, lodgepole pine, and open meadows. We passed Squaretop and Granite Peak, which rose nearly 2,000 feet straight up from the south bank of the river, crossed two creeks coming down from the high country, Elbow and Pixley, and soon reached Beaver Park. There were no beavers in Beaver Park, but to our surprise there were llamas. The llamas, the first of several species of pack animals we saw on the trip, were tethered to trees near a campsite. After a long day on the trail, the idea of pack llamas seemed tempting, until we spoke to the men in the campsite. They reported that the llamas were of surly disposition, that one in particular had caused major problems. When their heads were turned, the llama had broken and run. The llama retrieval had taken hours and forced them to change plans. They peered at the rogue beast with contempt and asked if we'd ever eaten grilled llama.

After leaving the llamas, we started scouting for a campsite. It was our first day on the trail, we had covered right at ten miles, and we were ready to shed the overweight packs and put our feet up. We crossed the river on a wooden bridge and found a perfect spot on the south bank. Brian and I put up our tent and then walked to the river to fill up our water bottles. I got out my water filter and began pumping, but my efforts accomplished nothing. I tried several times, but the pump wouldn't pump. Brian suggested that maybe the filter on the inside was clogged.

I looked up at him. First I thought it, then I said it. "What filter on the inside?" Brian unscrewed the device. I didn't even know you could unscrew it. There was no filter at all on the inside, much less a clogged one. This is where the filter is supposed to be, he explained.

After Brian broke this news, I was silent for a minute or two as I reconstructed the history of my filterless filter. It was two years old. I had bought it on my trip to North Carolina with Bob Smith in the fall of 1999. The clerk in the outdoor store hadn't said a word about adding an internal filter, and I sure didn't know any better. I had used the filter on that trip, on the trip to the Cascades with Bobby the following year, on the trip my son Paul and I went on to Colorado, and on a two-night trip to the Sipsey Wilderness in Alabama. On all four trips, I had pumped away, blissfully ignorant, and I had suffered no ill effects. I looked down at the small tube through which I had pumped all that water. Searching for some benefit from all that pumping, I said that at least it kept out sticks and small animals. "Big animals too," Brian added, patting me on the shoulder. We borrowed Wilson's filter and finished the job, then walked back to report the discovery. I knew Bobby would be pleased that I was taking another turn as the dumbass.

But soon he regained the title. Before our trip to the Winds, Bobby bought some new camping gear, including a backpacking hammock. Bobby had called me, excited, the day the hammock arrived in the mail, and again the day after he tried it out in the woods behind his house. He planned to use it in the Winds in lieu of a tent. It was comfortable, and he would hang it some distance from our tents and spare the rest of us from his snoring and spare himself from our snoring as well.

Just before the trip, however, something happened that gave Bobby second thoughts. Surfing the Internet, I discovered a report of grizzly activity on the Highline Trail near Green River Lakes, the very trail we were on now. One bear had made such a pest of itself that rangers had been forced to euthanize it. I dutifully passed the report on to Bobby and the others.

When I next spoke to Bobby, I asked if he really intended to sleep in a hammock amongst the grizzlies. He didn't see any cause for concern, or at least claimed he didn't. "Y'all are gonna be right there in tents. There's no' difference."

"Maybe so," I acknowledged, "but maybe not." I offered an analogy. "Let's say a bear walks into your kitchen. There are two candy bars. It's the same kind of candy. There's only one difference. One of the candy bars is in a cabinet. The other is sitting on the counter."

"Bullshit," Bobby said, "the bear would eat both frickin candy bars." But he obviously saw my point. "You really think I ought to be concerned?" he asked.

"Who knows?" I responded. "But I think I'd rather be in the cabinet."

By the time of the trip, however, Bobby had put his concerns aside. He was committed to the hammock. It turned out Wilson had brought one too, though his was far less elaborate than Bobby's high-tech, high-priced model. As the rest of us began working on dinner, Bobby rigged his hammock between two trees. Then he climbed in to test it. Then we heard a loud crash. Then a high-pitched cry for help. Then another. We leaped to our feet and went running.

We got to the scene and surveyed Bobby's predicament. He was on the ground in his hammock, trapped but unhurt. The hammock was still tied to the two trees, but one of them was no longer standing. The trunk of the tree was lying on the ground alongside Bobby, its limbs pinning him to the ground. When Bobby had climbed into the hammock, the tree's root system had given way. The tree had toppled over on top of him, its trunk missing him by inches. I instructed Bobby not to move, as if he had a choice, while the others retrieved their cameras. Bobby lay patiently as we recorded the incident for posterity. After Bobby finished posing, I told him the rest of us were leaving him now, going back to work on dinner. Bobby was in no position to be abusive, but that didn't stop him. Disregarding his invitations to have intimate relations, we took pity and freed him from his trap. I studied the tree. It was no sapling. It was six to eight inches in diameter at the base and twenty feet tall (now twenty feet long). I couldn't understand why it had fallen so easily. After the trip, I found an explanation while reviewing one of our trail guides. In the Winds, the author reported, the soils are "generally thin." Bobby had been undone by skinny dirt. But he was undaunted. He found a bigger tree and rehung his hammock.

Among the luxuries David had brought was a small bag of charcoal. He grilled shish kebab—steak, tomatoes, onions, and mushrooms—which he served over wild rice. It was delicious. For the rest of the trip, our dinners would be dehydrated meals or, we dared to hope, trout. Choosing optimism, Wilson had brought almonds. He'd brought everything he'd thought of, and he'd thought of everything,

We turned in early after dinner. It had been abnormally dry in the West, and we decided a fire would be risky. The night grew cold quickly, and we were exhausted after ten miles on the trail. Before we turned in, however, another task remained. Mindful of the grizzly activity, I reminded the others that we needed to hang bear bags at least ten feet off the ground and at least four feet from the trunk of any tree. But the evergreens around our campsite proved unsuitable to satisfy these requirements. There were no sturdy limbs of a suitable height to throw a rope over. And the trees all had numerous bushy low limbs that made climbing them virtually impossible. After several failed attempts, Brian and I managed to get our food eight or nine feet up a tree, but it was no more than a foot from the trunk. We were disappointed in the results until we saw Wilson's. His bear bag was no more than six feet off the ground, and no more than ten feet from where Wilson lay in his hammock. Before heading to his own hammock, Bobby sized up the situation and offered an assessment. "That's not a bear bag. That's a frickin bear piñata." But Wilson had a theory. "If it's easy for the bear to eat my food, I figure the bear will be less likely to eat me." The theory had superficial logic, but it defied conventional wisdom.

I slept well, awoke refreshed, and surveyed our camp; the bear piñatas were all intact. All of us were present except Blake, who'd gone wandering. He returned shortly and reported that he'd been following an animal—either an elk or a large mule deer—that had come through our campsite. As I sat sipping my coffee, another animal appeared, this one coming right toward me at a dead run. It got within ten feet, then stopped on a dime. The animal, a snowshoe hare, paused briefly, twitched its nose, and then sped off in another direction.

Breakfast highlighted the different approaches of Wilson and Blake to the subjects of preparation and supplies. Instant oatmeal wasn't good enough for Wilson. He had regular oatmeal, with raisins and nuts and brown sugar to add flavor. Blake had little to eat and had forgotten to bring coffee. In a practice that was repeated five straight mornings, he mooched my used coffee bag to make a watered-down cup for himself.

After breakfast, everybody was rested and ready to hit the trail. Everybody except Bobby. He looked haggard. When I asked how he'd slept, Bobby shook his head. "Not worth a shit. Froze my ass off in that frickin hammock." David checked his thermometer. It was thirty-eight degrees.

* * *

Bobby is not a material guy, with one exception. He is the Imelda Marcos of camping gear. If he sees some fancy new equipment, he's got to have it, even though he'll rarely get to use it and already has something that will work nearly as well. He became intrigued with the hammock before our 2001 trip because it was fully enclosed in mosquito netting, had a waterproof roof, and could be entered and exited via the bottom. The lack of insulation that resulted in his miserable first night in the Winds was not highlighted in the sales brochure.

The failure of the hammock in its debut was followed by another problem several years later. Bobby often tacks a few days on to a business trip to hike and camp, and in 2004 he used such an opportunity to hike the Narrows, which follows the course of the Virgin River in Zion National Park in Utah. Bobby reserved a spot for the night before his hike at the Zion Campground and, planning to use his hammock, asked if there were trees. The ranger assured him there were plenty of cottonwood trees. It turned out there was tree, not trees. Bobby managed by tying the rope on one end of the hammock to the one tree and putting the other end of the rope through the sunroof of his rental car. This meant the bottom of the hammock was nearly five feet off the ground, which made getting in and out hard for Bobby to do but entertaining for the other campers to watch. Bobby was supposed to camp the next night at the halfway point on the eighteen-mile hike, but to avoid yet another misfortune he left the hammock in the car and did the hike in one day. I don't know whether Bobby has ever used the hammock again, but he hasn't brought it on any more of our trips.

Bobby attributes his fascination with sleeping off the ground in a hammock to time he spent in a treehouse in New Orleans. Until the early 1960s, the levee along Bayou St. John was buffered from St. Bernard Avenue by woods for more than a mile. Bobby and his buddies spent many an afternoon there fighting Indians, harassing redcoats, and pushing the Germans back to Berlin. Bobby always had his Bowie knife with him. But all good things must come to an end, and so it was with Bobby's sanctuary. Developers came, the trees were cleared, and roads were graded. It was just like what happened to Paradise, Kentucky, where John Prine's parents grew up. The third verse of Prine's "Paradise" describes it:

> The coal company came with the world's largest shovel.
> They tortured the timber and they stripped all the land.
> They dug for the coal till the land was forsaken.
> And they wrote it all down as the progress of man.

When their land in New Orleans was stripped and forsaken, Bobby and his friends vowed revenge. Houses started going up in the new subdivision, and the juveniles became delinquents. They were ten years old and thus did not have cars, so ingenuity was required. The boys travelled by water, not by land. After the construction workers left for the day, the gang would assemble on the bayou in a flotilla of canoes and pirogues. From there, they would paddle across the bayou to the construction sites and begin "shopping." Lumber of all lengths and widths was gathered, along with anything else that could prove useful. There were no plans, no blueprints, no material list. Not even a rough idea. The gang engaged in reverse engineering, pilfering building materials and then figuring out what to do with them. The lumber was tied together and towed behind the armada back across the bayou. Carpet, nails, and other items were loaded topside. Once back in their neighborhood, the boys dragged their loot to the bottom of three closely spaced trees on a vacant lot. Over the course of the weeks that followed, a treehouse took shape. Thicker boards were used for joists and thinner ones for decking. When they ran out of lumber and accessible tree limbs, the treehouse was three stories tall. The first floor was the least aesthetic but most weatherproof. It had walls and a ceiling. Above it were two larger decks from which the boys launched attacks on intruders. All was right with the world again but, again, progress intervened. The lot was sold, and a new home was built. The treehouse met the same fate as Bobby's Baghdad Tiki Bar forty years later, though both were great while they lasted. Not long after the treehouse came down, Bobby and his parents moved to the Wolf River in Mississippi, where the land was neither stripped nor forsaken and Bobby's hideouts remained undisturbed.

* * *

Though we covered only seven miles on our second day in the Winds, for me it was far and away the hardest day of our trip. Not only did we climb nearly 2,400 feet at high elevation, but along the way I developed blisters on both heels. My broken-in boots had performed well while preparing for the trip and while hiking on level terrain the first day, but on the long ascent the second day, they failed me. The climb caused rubbing, then hot spots, then blisters, which then popped. I suffered the rest of the trip.

Our walk that morning continued along the Green River, with two or three more bridge crossings. The trail remained relatively level for the first hour or so, but we knew from the topo map that a steep climb awaited. The first landmark we passed was Three Forks Park, a meadow east of the trail where Wells Creek and Tourist Creek converge with the Green River. Sheer cliffs rose more than 3,000 feet on the east side of the meadow. The boggy meadow looked to me like a perfect place for moose, but no moose agreed with me.

At the south end of Three Forks Park, we left the Green River for good, turned southwest, and climbed through a forest of spruce and lodgepole pines, gaining more than 800 feet in the next mile and a half. After climbing a series of switchbacks, we took our first break in a shady spot along Trail Creek. As we rested, three men from Pennsylvania came up the trail and stopped to talk. Like us, they were on their annual backpacking trip to the West. Over the course of the rest of the day, we passed each other several times and compared notes about our trips. They said they'd never been to Glacier because they thought there was no airport nearby. I told them they were mistaken, that major airlines fly to Kalispell. They said they would check it out. I hoped that they would, that they would go to Glacier, hike through Ptarmigan Tunnel, and look down on Elizabeth Lake.

At about noon, we reached a rock-hop crossing of Trail Creek. Bouncing along on his approach/tennis shoes, the shoes I now wished I was wearing, Blake had pulled ahead of us. He missed the turn, continuing up the steep canyon rather than crossing the creek. The rest of us arrived just as he disappeared into the forest above us. We checked the map and spotted where the trail emerged from the creek on the other side. We yelled, but Blake was out of earshot. I stared up at the steep canyon. "Should somebody go get him?" My question was met with silence. Nobody volunteered, and my blisters and I sure weren't going. We decided to wait at the creek and let Blake figure out his mistake by himself. He soon reappeared.

After crossing the creek, we continued our steady climb through the forest. One at a time, I felt my blisters pop. We stopped for lunch in the shade beside the creek. After eating my peanut butter and jelly bagel sandwich, I took off my boots and socks and surveyed the damage. David, our only doctor, was in charge of medical supplies, but just as he didn't have the anesthetic Bobby needed in the Tetons, he didn't have the moleskin I needed now. I dressed the blisters with band-aids and duct tape as I did for the rest of the trip. We rested for another half hour; no one seemed in a rush to resume the climb. I didn't want to put my boots back on, much less start walking again. Wilson and I, with occasional help from Blake and Brian, sang for the group: Jimmy Buffet's "Come Monday" and Prine's "Angel from Montgomery." Nobody booed, but Bobby threw pine cones. Finally we rose and began to stir. I put on the two sources of my pain—boots and pack—and trudged up the trail.

We continued to climb, crossing the contour lines of the topo on the way up to 10,000 feet. The trees became sparse and stunted. I noticed that we were hiking in the order of our ages, youngest to oldest. Brian (twenty-six) led, followed by Blake (thirty-five) and then Wilson (forty-two). I (forty-four) was a distant fourth, then Bobby (forty-eight), and finally David (forty-nine). But David was bringing up the rear just to keep Bobby and me company. Several times I stopped to catch my breath at the end of a steep switchback and waited for David and Bobby to join me. I noticed with some irritation that David was neither panting nor sweating despite perhaps the heaviest pack in the group. For reasons I never fully understood, David had brought an ice axe. He said he thought it could double as a walking stick, but it was only two feet long. It would have worked only as a crawling stick.

To buy more time for my breathing and heart rate to return to normal, I frequently asked David to check his GPS. We were now above 10,000 feet and also above tree line. The views to the north, from where we had come, were spectacular. Bobby, in contrast, looked awful. Not only had he gone sleepless, but his jaw on one side was severely swollen. He never complained, but the problem plagued him the whole trip. Every night after the first one, he turned in early. He was neither lively nor amusing, and the rest of us were deprived.

At the end of the steep climb, we came to a beautiful open meadow surrounded by rocky peaks. We passed a lake named for its elevation, Lake 10,362, and crossed over into the Pine Creek Drainage. As we reached the shore of Summit Lake, our first fishing opportunity, we passed four young campers carrying fly rods. Blake and Wilson were already at the lake, rigging rods and getting ready to cast. Brian, the first to arrive, was lying in the meadow with his head resting on his pack. The four fishermen reported that they'd been camping at Summit Lake for four or five days, fishing there and in the surrounding lakes. A hailstorm two days earlier had blanketed the meadow with ice, and the fish had quit biting. Blake and Wilson didn't last long. The day had grown cold, the wind had risen, and fishing from the lake's exposed shore was difficult. Plus we were no more than a mile from our destination for the night—lower Twin Lake, which had been recommended by the salesman at the Great Outdoor Shop—and we were ready to get there. We left Summit Lake, our fishless streak intact, and continued south on the Highline Trail.

Lower Twin Lake is only twenty-five feet higher than Summit Lake, but the route there was anything but level. We dropped, then climbed, then did something dangerous and stupid. After Blake and Wilson had repacked their fishing gear, we swung around the south shore of Summit Lake and descended to a crossing of Pine Creek. We climbed due south in search of Elbow Creek, the second Elbow Creek of our trip. The map showed the creek winding down from Lower Twin Lake to the east and crossing the trail. We had to find the creek because the trail itself didn't go to our planned campsite. We would have to walk up the creek to get there.

The first small creek we passed turned out to be the wrong one. We nominated Brian, our youngest and strongest, for a scouting mission. He returned shortly and reported failure. Soon we came to a much larger creek bed. This late in the season, the creek carried little water, but this had to be it. We began climbing along the edge, Brian in the lead. The route became steeper, and we found ourselves on a narrow ledge with a sheer thirty-foot drop down to the rock-strewn creek bed. We soon reached what looked like an impasse, at least to me. The ledge disappeared, replaced by a rock face that angled away from the creek at forty-five degrees. One slip on this face, and the unlucky hiker would wind up in the creek bed far below. It looked far too dangerous; I proposed that we turn back and find another route. But Wilson, the reckless Wilson of Bull Sluice at the Chattooga, disagreed. He also volunteered to serve as scout. He took off his pack, dropped to all fours, and scrambled up the slope.

One of my law partners went on a sailing trip years ago with David. During their time together, my partner reported that David acquired a nickname—Superman—because he could do anything and do it better than anybody. To this point on our trip, David had been more like Clark Kent, meandering along at the back of the pack with Bobby and me. Now he took off his disguise, but he acted more like Spiderman than Superman. He didn't wait for Wilson's report, and he didn't bother to take off his pack. As if he had suctions on his boots and hands, he climbed effortlessly up the slope. Brian looked at us, shrugged, and followed David. I held my breath, waiting for one of them to slide down the slope and fall to his death, but it didn't happen. They reached the top, turned around, and encouraged us to follow.

Three of us remained at the bottom, along with Wilson's pack. We refused to bow to peer pressure. I tested the slope. Almost immediately, one foot started to slip. "No way," I declared. "No frickin way," Bobby agreed. Blake just shook his head. The three of us retreated a few feet and found another way up. It was nearly as steep, but we wouldn't fall nearly as far. We passed the four packs up, fireman style. At the top of the climb, we had to cross over the slope the other three had climbed. The prospect was daunting.

As I sat on the edge, trying to balance the weight of a pack without being pulled down the rock face to my death, I looked up. Brian and David stood there with their cameras, memorializing our peril, ready to take pictures, but not to help, if one of us fell. I imagined what would happen if I was the one. I raced forward in my mind to the day when Brian and David would sit down with my family to show them the pictures. After all, my family would want to know how it happened; they would have the right to know. Brian and David would show them the photos in chronological order, with a running explanation. "Here's Brooks sitting on the edge of the slope. He looks fine. But in this next picture, you can see he's starting to lose his balance. Now look at this one; he's really starting to slide. Look at the expression on his face; he knows he's in deep shit. And the blur you see in this next picture, that's him. This last one—well, you really don't want to look at it."

I didn't fall, but I nearly suffered a different tragedy. The side compartment of my pack was unzipped, and my Nalgene bottle filled with Scotch fell out near the top of the slope. Bobby spotted it, replaced it, and rezipped my pack. I rewarded him with a Chivas and water when we got to camp. Bobby, to our great loss, had not made it to the liquor store in Pinedale to buy his own.

We scrambled over the last ledge and dropped down on the other side, reshouldered our packs, and walked the last 200 yards up to the lake. David found an ideal campsite in a protected area beside the creek just below the lake. The site came equipped with a huge flat boulder to serve as our camp table. We were not the first to pick this spot. There was a fire ring on one side of the boulder table. We looked around for tent sites and found room for our three tents. There were stunted trees from which to hang hammocks as well, but Bobby's romance with his hammock was over. Wilson hung his but only for lounging. He agreed that it was too cold to sleep in it. I picked a place for my tent, dropped my pack, and dropped down beside it. It was Labor Day, and we had spent the day laboring. I was all done in.

Blake pointed up to the slope to the north. A yearling bull moose and cow stared at us. We were the intruders, but the two moose seemed neither angry nor scared. To help kill the pain from my blisters, I poured myself a drink. Brian "borrowed" my Scotch and mixed one for himself. As compensation, he promised to share some of his bourbon with me later. I tried to explain that I have despised bourbon since a very unpleasant experience in my youth, but he was already pouring. A few minutes later, I noticed that Bobby was unrolling his sleeping bag in David's tent. "No hammock tonight?" I asked. Bobby responded with a string of profanities. He offered to give me the hammock if I would carry it the rest of the way. Not only had it proved unsuitable for cold nights, but Bobby was ill-prepared for Plan B. The only pad he had was, like him, wafer-thin. He would be nearly as padless as I had been in the Cascades.

The difficult climb generated another debate about the weight of our packs. I was ready to believe they weighed two hundred pounds apiece, but in truth I thought they didn't weigh more than fifty. Brian and David, however, still insisted they weighed at least sixty. Brian said he did curls with sixty pound dumbbells, and the packs weighed at least that much.

I thought about this for a minute. "Sixty-pound dumbbells?" I asked. Brian nodded. "That's with one arm, right?" He nodded again. "And I'm carrying our tent?" Brian offered to take it the rest of the way, but I didn't give it to him until the last day, after he no longer had the MREs. After dinner, Bobby, David, and Wilson crashed early, but Blake and Brian and I stayed up by the campfire, sipping after-dinner drinks and swapping stories. Brian and Blake each told a memorable one.

* * *

Brian told of a friend of his named Jason who had a romantic interlude with a girl in Birmingham during his college years. Their inhibitions and judgment washed away by alcohol, the two of them wound up in her bed in her parents' house. Her bedroom, it so happened, was right next door to theirs. But young love is oblivious, especially when intoxicated. Jason said he intended to leave, he really did, but the combination of alcohol and amorous activity put him right to sleep. When he woke up, the sun was already high in the sky. Jason took a few seconds to realize he wasn't where he was supposed to be. He knew he needed to escape, but he needed to pee even more. Quiet as a mouse, and wearing the same clothes a mouse wears, he tiptoed into his date's bathroom. As he stood facing the toilet, he heard footsteps coming into the bedroom. He then heard a voice; it belonged to his date's mother. The voice got louder; she was pissed. Footsteps then came toward the bathroom. In a desperate attempt to hide himself, Jason stepped into the bathtub. He reached for the shower door, but there wasn't one. He looked for a shower curtain; still no luck. He thought, Who takes a bath anymore? There Jason stood, only his feet and ankles hidden from view. And they weren't what most needed hiding. When he saw the doorknob start to turn, he knew it was all over. He covered what needed hiding with his hands, turned his face to the side, and closed his eyes, squeezing them tight.

When Jason got to this point in the story, Brian said he interrupted him. "Why'd you close your eyes? You know, just because you couldn't see her doesn't mean she couldn't see you." Jason responded that he figured nothing good could come from eye contact. Brian said he had a point. Blake and I agreed.

According to Brian, Jason said he stood there, perfectly still, and nothing happened for four or five seconds—long enough for him to start thinking he was invisible. Then a blood-curdling scream broke the silence, followed by rapidly receding footsteps. Jason opened his eyes when he couldn't hear them anymore. The coast was clear. He returned to the bedroom, threw on his clothes, kissed his date on the cheek, sprinted down the stairs, and made his escape. And he never saw the girl or her mother again.

* * *

Several weeks before our trip, I had played in a charity golf tournament in Jackson. I was assigned to a foursome with three younger men I had never met, one of whom turned out to be Blake's roommate from Ole Miss. I knew Blake's nickname was Blade, but I didn't know why. His old roommate told me. Beside our campfire below Lower Twin Lake, I asked

Blake for his version of the story. Like Brian's tale, Blake's involved the inverse relationship between drinking and judgment.

Along with another couple, Blake and his future wife Stacy were in Jackson for an Ole Miss football game. It was only their second date. The two couples closed down a bar on Friday night and then went looking for more beer. Making his first bad decision, Blake stopped at a convenience store in a bad part of town. He stayed in the car with the two girls while his buddy went in to get a twelve pack. A group of young thugs were loitering in the parking lot. One of them said something Blake found offensive. Making his second bad decision, Blake responded with a comment of his own. The group then sauntered over and surrounded Blake's car. Blake made it a trifecta by getting out—to calm the situation, he said. As he was taking off his jacket—a calming gesture if ever there was one—one of the members of the gang slugged him in the face. Blake grabbed his attacker by the shoulders and rammed him headfirst into another car. In a fair fight, Blake would have been fine, but he was outnumbered, and outweaponed as well. As Blake turned to face the group, another gang member hit him over the head with a beer bottle. He taunted Blake and threatened him with the bottle's jagged remains. At this point, Blake said, he came to his senses. The bottle had gotten his attention, and his desire to impress the girls was now outweighed by his will to live. His thoughts turned to flight. Blake's buddy came out of the store, and other members of the gang fell upon him. The beer, however, was a priority. Rather than drop it to defend himself, Blake's buddy raced to the car and threw the twelve pack into the window. The four were about to make their escape when the original attacker—the one whose head Blake had rammed into the car—pulled a knife. Blake saw the knife and decided to offer the thug advice. "You don't really want to do that." But Blake was wrong. As Blake tried to pull his leg into the car, he saw, and felt, the knife blade plunge into his thigh. After withdrawing it, the young tough added insult to injury and stabbed Blake's left front tire. But Blake now had a weapon of his own. As the assailant walked in front of the car, Blake hit the gas. The thug rolled up on the hood, his face mashed flat against the windshield. Blake shifted to reverse, punched it again, and the thug rolled off.

The tire had now gone flat, but Blake's brush with death had improved his decision-making skills dramatically. He decided to risk damage to the rim rather than change the tire then and there. He pulled out of the parking lot and drove away. But he didn't go far. The pain was overwhelming. Blake pulled over, and his buddy took the wheel and chauffeured Blake to the hospital, where he got treated and stitched and the tire got changed. By the next day, he was back in form, attending the Ole Miss game, walking with only a slight limp, and drinking the beer for which he'd paid so dearly. And that, he concluded, is how he got to be Blade.

After Blake finished his tale, I stirred the fire and offered an assessment. "No wonder Stacy married you."

Blake didn't understand. "Why? What do you mean?"

"She could see how smart you were," I explained. "She knew you would be a good provider."

* * *

I slept well. Brian reported the next morning that I had snored like a chainsaw. After breakfast, Blake rigged his fly rod and headed for the lake. The rest of us lolled about in our campsite, in no hurry to do anything. The talk turned to old Westerns. Wilson spoke of spending his formative years lusting for Linda Evans on *The Big Valley*. I observed that there was no comparable beauty on *Bonanza*. Bobby corrected me. "You're forgetting Hop Sing," he said.

Our itinerary called for us to spend two nights in one spot, either here or at Island Lake, our next destination. We decided to fish a while and then decide, but it was clear what the decision would be. It was another beautiful day. We had a perfect campsite next to a beautiful lake that we'd been promised was filled with trout. We were still tired from the hard climb the previous day. My blisters needed a day to rest and heal. We would devote the day to fishing and spend a second night here.

At 10:00, Bobby, Wilson, and I finally got our rods and hiked up to the lake. We found Blake on the north shore with a grin on his face. He lifted his stringer; he had one small trout, either a golden or a golden/cutthroat hybrid. Golden trout are the Holy Grail for the Wind River angler. They are wary, elusive, hard to catch. Cutthroats have the opposite reputation. Blake reported that he'd been approached by a bull moose—perhaps the same one we saw the day before—as he was casting from the shoreline.

The moose came too close for comfort. Just as Blake yelled at the moose to scare him off, a trout inhaled Blake's fly. The moose waited for Blake to reel in the trout before ambling away. Blake had been fishing all his life in Mississippi, but this was his first trout ever. The troutless streak on our trips had come to an end, though neither Bobby nor I could take credit for breaking it.

The four of us worked our way around to fish the mouth of the stream coming down from upper Twin Lake. The action was slow, but we had occasional strikes and landed a few. I broke my personal troutless streak by snagging one in the side and then caught a second one the conventional way. By late morning, Blake and I had each caught four or five, but none more than twelve inches long. Bobby and Wilson had been shut out. Shortly before noon, we returned with our bounty to camp. Blake cleaned the trout, and I pan-fried them. Delicious.

While the four of us were fishing, Brian and David had gone exploring. Brian had climbed to the rim overlooking the lake, where he'd found several small ponds as well as bear tracks. David had gone back down the slope in search of an easier way out. He'd found a gently sloping game trail that wound down to the Highline Trail just south of Elbow Creek. If we had walked another fifty yards on the Highline Trail the afternoon before, we would have come to the game trail and avoided our death-defying rock climb. The two moose at our campsite when we arrived must have wondered why we came the hard way.

After his fishless morning, Wilson decided to take an afternoon romp to the slopes north of the lake. Brian borrowed Wilson's rod and took his place on the lakeshore. Brian had brought no gear and didn't plan to fish, but the spinning tackle he used was more successful than our fly rods, if not as fashionable. He caught seven or eight, though two of them were no bigger than fish sticks. Blake caught four or five. I landed a couple, but the largest one I hooked escaped. The big one, as always, got away. Bobby caught one. Just one, but it was enough for him to shed Marley's chains.

Having caught no fish in the morning, Wilson had been surly at noon. When he returned from his afternoon ramble, however, he'd undergone another mood swing and was in high spirits again. He carried on at length about the views of the peaks of the Continental Divide to the north and east. He'd found the same ponds Brian had seen in the morning. Like a dog marking its territory, Wilson had stripped down and dived into each of them. While Blake cleaned the fish, Brian and I took Wilson's filter down to the creek to replenish our water supply. I held the containers while Brian pumped. He started laughing and pointed upstream. Fifty feet from us, Wilson stood in the middle of the creek, naked, bathing. "Pump fast," I commanded. David still had some charcoal, and we grilled the trout for dinner. I lifted my cup and proposed a toast to Finis Mitchell.

By now, Wilson's mood swings had become a running joke. He was the happiest and the saddest, the most excited and the biggest whiner, the camp poet and the camp bitch. He could have been any of the four French Canadian fur trappers who were present when Baptiste named the Tetons. As the six of us ate dinner, I posed a question: "Y'all think Wilson needs to be on medication?"

Bobby answered my question with one of his own: "Which one?"

"I don't know," I said. "Lithium, I guess. Maybe Prozac."

Bobby shook his head. "Not which medicine, which Wilson." Still in the middle of a happy phase, Wilson laughed with the rest of us.

In the Cascades, Bobby and I had discussed how difficult it would be to find us in the event of a family emergency. We had heard a helicopter on our second day in the Winds, presumably rescuing an injured hiker, and the subject of dealing with a family emergency came up again after dinner. I told the others what I'd come up with the previous year: that the best way to find us would be to rent a plane and tow a message banner behind it back and forth across the mountains. Bobby said he'd considered the problem after our trip to Washington and implemented a plan. If a loved one died while he was gone, he'd told Stephanie to "put 'em on ice and wait till I get home."

* * *

The section of the Highline Trail we hiked on Wednesday was billed by one author as the most spectacular walk in the entire range. It did not disappoint, but the weather was another matter.

After we broke camp and put on our packs, David led us down the game trail he'd found the day before. We reached the intersection with the Highline Trail after a short stroll and laughed at ourselves for having scaled the rocks to get to our campsite two days earlier. Bobby pointed out that the animals who made the game trail were smarter than we were.

We headed south a short distance, then turned east and started to climb. The views as we rose far above tree line were spectacular. As Brian and I stood resting and gazing back to the west, Bobby joined us. "I think this qualifies as the shit," Bobby said. Brian and I smiled, remembering our hike over Piegan Pass in Glacier four years earlier.

The weather had changed. It was cold, overcast, and windy, and it was getting more of all three by the minute. At 10,800 feet, the trail leveled off. We crossed a broad, beautiful meadow dotted with lakes. The meadow was filled with dead wildflowers. It must have been spectacular a month earlier. My blisters were no better, but after a couple of miles they became numb. As we passed above the north shore of Elbow Lake, hail began to fall. At first, the hail was light, and we kept hiking. But it soon got heavier, the hailstones bigger and more painful. Bobby and I ducked under the ledge of a large boulder and looked at each other. We had already burned up our one rest day and needed to reach our destination, Island Lake, before dark. As we were pondering our predicament, Wilson came around a curve in the trail and joined us. I awaited his comments on the weather; I knew they would be extreme, one way or the other. Wilson was grinning. He stared out at the scene—the hailstones pounding the desolate tundra—with a look of absolute bliss. It was the same expression as when he'd stared at his Fat Tire beer in Calamity Jane's. "Isn't this great?" he asked Bobby and me. I checked the map. The mountain just to the north, its peak encircled by storm clouds, was named Brimstone Mountain. But bolts of fire did not come shooting down at us from the summit, the hail abated, and we continued our hike.

Patches of blue soon appeared in the sky. We climbed to a broad saddle overlooking another lake. David checked his GPS. We were at 11,050 feet, the highest point on our trip. The trail then wound down to the shore of magnificent Upper Jean Lake at 10,800 feet, where we stopped for lunch. The sun was now out, but the chill remained. Wilson, never one to cut corners, unpacked his pack, took out his stove, and made soup. I made do with my bagel. The food was nothing special, but the setting was. The water in the lake was crystal clear, its surface as smooth as glass. Henderson Peak and Titcomb Needles towered more than 2,000 feet above the lake's eastern shore. We wanted to linger, but the weather began to change again. A new wave of clouds rolled in, and it began to sprinkle. As we continued down the trail along the side of Fremont Creek, the sprinkle turned into a downpour. With the hard rain came lightning. We spotted shelter under a boulder ledge on the other side of the creek and rock-hopped across. There the six of us crouched, wet and shivering. Because he'd had to repack his pack, Wilson was the last to arrive at the shelter. He had been enthralled by the hailstorm, but this was different. He glared at me. I had planned the trip; the bad weather was my fault. "I thought this was supposed to be a [series of expletives deleted] fishing trip."

David's the doctor, but Bobby offered Wilson medical advice. "Calm yourself. Take five deep breaths. Close your eyes. Stick a pill under your tongue. In just a little while, things will be all better. You'll see." Wilson grinned. He was just playing his role.

As we watched the lightning and listened to the thunder, David provided an interesting statistic. "More Mississippians get struck by lightning than residents of any other state. Wouldn't it be ironic if one of us got struck by lightning up here?" he asked.

Bobby turned and looked at him. "Yeah. That would be really cool. That would make for a great story." But it didn't happen. The thunderstorm, like the hailstorm, passed quickly, and we continued on our way.

The path followed the bank of Fremont Creek, a beautiful mountain stream freshened by the hard rain. Small waterfalls fell from the slope to the east. Earlier in the day, Blake had asked me about the elevation of Elkhart Park, where we would leave the trail in two days. When I told him it was 9,400 feet, he came as close to complaining as he ever does. He asked, "Didn't we start at 8,000 feet?" I said yes. "So we're hiking uphill?" I confirmed that as well. From the expression on Blake's face, I could see that he thought this was foolish, that we should have hiked in the opposite direction. Without waiting for him to ask, I explained why. We needed a day at 8,000 feet to acclimate, I told him, and a level hike to start out. Beginning at Elkhart Park would have given us neither. Blake nodded, but I could tell he wasn't buying it. Now, as we continued toward Lower Jean Lake, Blake had further evidence for his position. We passed several groups of hikers headed northwest on the Highline toward our point of origin. After the last group was out of earshot, Blake turned around and offered his proof. "You know, it seems like everybody we pass on the trail is headed the other way."

I couldn't let this veiled challenge pass without comment. "So I guess you think that means there are more people going that way than this way?" Blake shrugged. I continued: "Did it ever occur to you that we never see most of the people going the same way we are? That the only ones we see are going either real slow or real fast?" Blake thought about this for a second and decided not to put up a fight. He smiled, turned around, and continued up the trail.

We rock-hopped across the inlet creek at the northwest corner of mile-long Lower Jean Lake and rested on a rock outcropping, enjoying the view of the mountains to the east. The trail remained level for the next mile before dipping several hundred feet back down to tree line as we approached Fremont Crossing, where a wooden bridge spanned the creek fed by huge Island Lake. As we came down the wooded slope, we spotted several mule deer on the trail ahead of us. We saw them twice more as we rounded curves in the trail, but they had four legs and no packs and soon outdistanced us.

Before reaching the bridge, a side trail headed back west to a thundering waterfall on Fremont Creek called Big Water Slide. One of our trail guides recommended taking this half mile side trip if time and energy allow. We had neither, so we followed the advice in our other trail guide, which suggested a shortcut to the south shore of Island Lake on an unmaintained trail. To reach the shortcut, called Fremont Cutoff, we left the Highline Trail before reaching the bridge and walked to the side of the creek. The creek was wide at this point, and the rock-hop crossing was the longest and most difficult of the trip. Brian led the way and made it look easy. The rest of us followed, with Bobby bringing up the rear. Five of us stood on the south bank and rooted for Bobby to make it across. It was painful to watch. I figured the top three feet of Bobby, including his pack, weighed 180 pounds, the bottom three feet a tenth as much. Each time he hopped from one rock to another, he teetered precariously before regaining his balance. When he finally made it across, the rest of us cheered.

Fremont Cutoff parallels the creek we had just crossed and leads to the shore of the lake that feeds it. We assumed the trail was level, but we were wrong. We climbed, then climbed some more. We were at the end of a long day and were ready for relief. Before long, however, relief was in sight. We topped a rise, and Island Lake appeared far below. We could see and hear Lower Titcomb Falls on the far shore, a beautiful waterfall fed by the lakes of Titcomb Basin to the north. We sent Brian down to the lake to scout for campsites. He soon motioned for us to follow. He'd found a spectacular spot on a cliff overlooking the lake with a huge boulder for a table, a sheltered spot for a campfire, and several tent sites with magnificent views, all accompanied by the music of the falls. The campsite rivaled Blue Lake in the Cascades for beauty. We dropped our packs and flopped down on the ground. We'd covered ten miles, hiking in hail, rain, and sunshine. We'd climbed and dropped more than a thousand feet, but our net elevation change was a grand total of two feet. The elevation of Lower Twin Lake is 10,348 feet, Island Lake 10,346. Blake should have been pleased; we had gone downhill.

After putting up the tents and gathering firewood, we decided some hygiene was in order. Wilson did his usual and dove headfirst into the frigid water without testing it. I tiptoed in; it was unbearable. I edged forward to thigh depth, bent over, and washed my face and hair with camp soap. I then returned to camp, semi-clean, but as clean as I was willing to get.

Before dark, Bobby and I studied the view to the north, using our map to help pick out the features. The huge mountain directly across the lake was Fremont Peak. At 13,745 feet, it is the third highest in Wyoming. The mountain is named for John C. Fremont, who climbed it in the course of a mapping survey in 1842. In a report to Congress, Fremont declared that the mountain was "the highest peak of the Rocky Mountains." He was wrong. Not only does Colorado alone have more than fifty mountains that exceed 14,000 feet, but Gannett Peak, which is taller than Fremont, is less than five miles away. Just northwest of Fremont Peak, we could see an enormous glacier. I looked at the map. From its shape and orientation, I concluded that it was Helen Glacier and said so to Bobby. "Frigid bitch," he muttered.

Before dinner, several of us mixed a toddy. I was running low, and we had another night to go. I was going to have to ration myself. But Blake came to my rescue; he said he still had plenty and told me not to skimp. So I didn't. And neither did Brian. Two hours later, as we sat by the fire, I told a story I found greatly amusing, as did Brian, though I noticed that he and I were the only ones laughing. Their loss, I decided. Brian and I also outlasted the others by the fire, staying up until the weather changed again. A magnificent thunderstorm moved in. Before the rain began, we watched as the lightning bolts illuminated Fremont Peak and the surrounding mountains of the Divide. We enjoyed the show until the rains came and then retreated to the safety of my tent. Or the purported safety, I should say.

I wrote the first draft of the chapter about our trip to the Tetons before going on our trip to the Winds. In that chapter, I bragged on my Walrus tent and its performance in the rain. I should have known better. My bragging served as a curse; my tent leaked in the rainstorm beside Island Lake. I don't blame the tent. I should have pulled the rain fly tighter, but I didn't and water puddled on top and dripped through. It rained hard for hours. At one point, I woke up and wondered if we might wash off the edge of the cliff. In the morning, the inside floor of the tent was soaked. I was saved from a soaked sleeping bag by my wet pad, but Brian didn't fare as well. We climbed out of the tent and checked on the others. They'd managed all right, but Bobby had again slept little. He was wishing he'd left the damnable hammock at home and brought a decent pad. Not only was Bobby exhausted, but the side of his face now looked like a gourd, and David had no way to fix him. I suggested stitches, but there was no cut to sew up. David said he was game; he even had a bigger needle. I knew Bobby felt bad when he let this pass without response. The storm was gone; the sun was out. We made coffee and breakfast and waited for the tents to dry. Wilson made his gourmet oatmeal. Blake perched on the edge of the boulder like a vulture, waiting for my used coffee bag.

We broke camp and headed southeast along the lakeshore. Our plan called for us to camp our last night at Seneca Lake, only five miles away. We also had an important side trip on the itinerary, to Titcomb Basin. Along with the Cirque of the Towers in the southern end of the range, Titcomb Basin is one of the two most famous and most spectacular destinations in the Winds. The basin is named for brothers Harold and Charles Titcomb, who made the second ascent of Fremont Peak nearly sixty years after John Fremont made the first. The broad basin that bears their name is filled with beautiful alpine lakes. It is surrounded on three sides by towering peaks. To the west are mountains we had seen from the other side the previous day. To the east and north are the magnificent summits of the Continental Divide. The eastern slopes of these mountains, all of which exceed 13,000 feet, are covered with enormous glaciers. Our walk into Titcomb Basin was to be one of the highlights of our trip. In the end, however, only half of us decided to go.

When we reached the east end of Island Lake, it was time to decide. Three of us chose to head north into the basin. My blisters were bad, but I had come this close to one of the most beautiful settings in the Rockies, and I wasn't going to miss it. David and Brian weren't going to miss it either. The others had different ideas. Blake and Wilson wanted more fishing. Seneca Lake was reported to be the best rainbow trout fishery in the Winds; they wanted to get there early. Bobby was torn. He was tempted to go with us, but his sleep deficit had taken a toll. He looked like death warmed over. He was also determined to catch more than one fish on our trip. It was cold and windy—a better day to hike than fish—but we couldn't persuade the three of them to go with the three of us. "I paid forty dollars for this frickin fishing license," Bobby said, "and I'm gonna use it."

David, Brian, and I hid our packs in rocks above the trail on the east end of Island Lake. Without them, we were liberated. Even with blisters, I felt as if I had wings on my feet. The trail into the basin was level for the most part. We moved quickly, leaving Island Lake and climbing up a gentle grade to Pothole Lake. From there, we hiked due north and reached the shores of Lake 10,548, the third lake we had come to that was named for its elevation. There were either too many lakes in the Winds or too little imagination among those who had named them. The three of us swung around the east side of this lake and continued north into the basin, walking fast and taking no breaks. We had agreed on a turnaround time and wanted to get as far into the basin as possible before turning back. We reached the southeast shore of the lower of the two Titcomb Lakes at our scheduled stopping time. There we rested and admired the view. The two lakes spanned nearly the entire width of the basin. Sheer spires rose thousands of feet on either side. Fremont Peak towered directly above us, looking much larger than it had from the opposite shore of Island Lake. The magnificent peaks of the Great Divide stretched away to the north as far as the eye could see. The mountains included Titcomb Needles, Henderson Peak, American Legion Peak, Winifred Peak, Twin Peaks (with

Twins Glacier on its slope), Skyline Peak, The Sphinx, Mount Woodrow Wilson, Babs Tower, Miriam Peak, Dinwoody Peak, Mounts Helen and Sacajawea, and Fremont and Jackson Peaks. This was the most spectacular spot we had seen on our trip. I wished Bobby had come here to see it with us, but he was fishing at Seneca Lake. Or so I thought.

The three of us departed reluctantly and headed south, leaving as fast as we had come. Shortly before we got back to Island Lake, we spotted a curious group resting alongside the trail: two men, a woman, and four goats. Each of the goats was equipped with saddlebags. There was a limit to what each goat could carry, but they seemed more agreeable than the llamas.

We found our packs where we'd hidden them and ate lunch before continuing. I offered to trade my bagels and trail mix for anything Brian and David had. I was ready for something different, anything different. After eating, we continued south toward Seneca Lake. The easy part of our day's hike was over. Not only did we have our packs again, but the path to Seneca Lake had a number of steep climbs and drops. But this was our fifth day on the trail, and we were stronger than when we'd started. We pressed on, reaching the north shore of the lake before four o'clock. We spotted Wilson in the distance fishing from the shoreline but no sign of Blake or Bobby. Brian, David, and I split up to look for them. David spotted a tent among the boulders and yelled that he'd found them. Blake and Bobby, both of whom had skipped Titcomb Basin to go fishing, had neither rigged a rod nor wet a hook. Blake was lying in his tent reading *The Perfect Storm*. Bobby was outside. The temperature was in the forties and the wind was blowing, but the sun was out. Bobby had found a sunny spot protected from the wind. He'd borrowed Wilson's pad and was lying on his back with his eyes closed, his arms folded across his chest. "Better check his pulse," I whispered to David. Bobby smiled, the only sign he was alive. He didn't move or say a word.

Wilson soon returned from the lakeshore. He'd given up. It was too windy to cast and too cold by the lake. His fishing on the trip was over. Eighty-five bucks and not a trout to show for it. As we gathered firewood, the sun disappeared behind gray clouds. Soon it began to snow. I pulled out the last of my whiskey. The Scotch warmed me going down. Blake tried his hand at fishing in the cove below our campsite, but his effort was halfhearted. The snowfall became heavier; the temperature dropped. Blake returned from the lake to the comfort of the fire and declared that there were no fish in Seneca Lake.

Our dinner the last night consisted of pasta primavera, broccoli and rice casserole, and a three-berry cobbler. Maybe we'd just been too long without real food, but we all agreed it was magnificent. By the time we'd cleaned the dishes, the clouds had disappeared, and stars shone overhead. The snow had stopped falling, but the temperature had not. We'd built our fire against a boulder to shelter it, and us, from the wind. But the fire's location had one drawback. There wasn't enough room close to the fire for six, so we jockeyed for position. I sat for half an hour in the prime spot. I needed to relieve myself but didn't want to lose my place. Finally I surrendered to the inevitable and wandered to the edge of the campsite. Away from the light of the fire, the stars were spectacular. As I stared up at the heavens, I noticed that Blake had followed my lead to do the same chore. I saw a shooting star and pointed it out to him. He looked up, but it was too late. Before we could look back down, however, another one flashed across the sky.

Blake and I returned to the campfire. As expected, we'd been replaced on the front row. Brian not only had stolen my spot, he'd also stolen my chair and pushed it closer to the fire. To avoid a repeat of my padless nights in the Cascades, I had brought my repair kit this year. But I wasn't sure it would work and didn't want to have to find out. I also knew I would freeze if I had to sleep with no pad between me and the cold ground. I warned Brian to be careful. He was working on his third bourbon and water and ignored me. Seconds later I felt something hot on my leg. A spark had popped out of the fire, burned a hole in my fleece pants, and was now burning me. Better me than my pad, I thought. Before brushing the spark away, I got Brian's attention: "See what I mean." He nodded as if he understood but didn't retreat an inch. I was left with two pairs of fleece pants with holes burned by sparks, one from our campfire at Phelps Lake in the Tetons and the other from our last night in the Winds. I don't mind the holes; they remind me of my travels with Bobby.

Bobby and David had not pushed to the front when Blake and I had given them a chance. I could tell they were going to call it quits early again. Bobby enjoys time by the campfire as much as I do, but he was suffering.

Before long, he and David said good night and headed off to their tent. I was quiet for a while. Time around a campfire with Bobby is delightful. I had been cheated; all of us, Bobby included, had been cheated.

The first four nights, Wilson had turned in early and had very little to drink. As a result, he still had plenty of whiskey when our last night began. But that changed in a hurry. The four of us huddled close to the fire and swapped stories. As the hour grew late, Wilson's stories made less and less sense. Some of the sounds he made were not words at all. In the firelight, I studied him. He was the picture of contentment, just as when he had admired the Fat Tire beer in Calamity Jane's and the hailstorm from below the brow of Brimstone Peak. I now had two more extremes to add to Wilson's list—soberest and drunkest. Before long, he mumbled something incoherent and stumbled to his tent.

Three of us now remained—Brian, Blake and I, the last three to pack it in every night. We were conflicted. This was our last night, we were having a grand time, and we hated to call it quits. On the other hand, it was now below freezing, and a campfire can only warm you one side at a time. The moon was still not up; the sky was filled with stars. I'd brought my pocket astronomy guide, but it was fifty frigid feet away in my pack. I wasn't that curious. Brian made the short walk to his pack and returned with fuel for the fire: the MREs Bobby had sent him. He'd carried them nearly forty miles through the Winds, hadn't eaten a bite, and was now going to burn them. They proved to be highly flammable. We watched in amazement as the flames grew higher. Each MRE emitted a different color flame. The odor of each was different too, but all were disgusting. As the glow from the last one died away, I sat up straight, saluted, and offered a toast to the American soldiers who have to eat that shit.

At last, we could take the cold no more and retreated to our tents. In spite of the temperature, I had supreme confidence in the combined powers of my Walrus tent and my 20° goose down bag, especially with a leak-free pad between me and the ground. I stripped down to boxers and tee shirt and climbed in. I lay there, rubbing my feet together, waiting to get warm. I didn't. My fleece pants and top were serving as my pillow. I hated to go pillowless, but that was my only choice. I put them on and tightened the drawstring of my sleeping bag. Only my nose was exposed. Soon I was asleep.

* * *

The next morning, the inside of the tent was covered with frost and the outside with snow. David didn't check the temperature until 7:30. By then, it had warmed up to twenty degrees. The low must have been close to ten. Because this was our last morning, Blake had to give it one more try and hiked down to the lakeshore to fish. Even as cold as it was, the surface was ice-free. The lake was too big and the weather too windy. Bobby was bundled up, his toboggan pulled down over his ears. He walked up beside me, and we looked at Blake flailing the water. Bobby shook his head. "Frickin nut, if you ask me." Blake returned in a few minutes, shivering, more convinced than ever the lake was fishless.

After breakfast, we shook the ice and snow from our tents and waited for them to dry. I couldn't decide how to dress. The sun was out, the wind had dropped, and the temperature was climbing fast. It was up to nearly forty, and I assumed it was headed much higher. I decided to think ahead, to dress for the weather to come, and I put on shorts.

The trail led along the western shore of Seneca Lake, then dropped below tree line. It soon became apparent that I had badly misjudged the weather. Clouds rolled in, the temperature dropped instead of rising, and the wind picked up. My legs were cold, but I couldn't bring myself to dig my long pants out of my pack. If I did, the weather would just change again. After several steep climbs and drops, we reached Hobbs Lake, where we passed a lone hiker. He provided an explanation for the helicopter we'd heard earlier in the week. A climber had been crushed to death by a falling boulder on Fremont Peak; the helicopter was retrieving his body. I thought about how precarious it all is, life or death determined by the timing of the roll of a rock.

We spotted a yellow Labrador Retriever on the trail wearing a rebel flag bandana. Then we spotted the dog's owner. He turned out to be a lawyer from Nashville, the one and only Southerner we saw on the trip. He said he and his dog, Scout, had been coming here camping and fishing every September for seven years. We asked him about his fishing on this trip, and he said he'd caught some nice rainbows in Seneca Lake. "That's strange," I said, speaking to him but looking at Blake. "We talked to this one guy who said there weren't any fish in Seneca." Blake smiled and shook his head.

As we pressed on toward the trailhead, snow again began to fall. Nearing civilization, we passed several strings of pack horses and mules and also began to pass more hikers. They stared down at my bluish legs but said nothing. The backpackers heading into the mountains were grim-faced. We were glad to be heading out, and we made great time. From the north end of Seneca Lake to Elkhart Park was just under ten miles. We'd hit the trail at 9:30. With a few rest breaks and a stop for lunch, I'd figured we'd get to the car about 3:30, but we were clearly going to make it sooner than that. Our speed was attributable to a number of factors: The trail was downhill for the most part; we were all in better shape than when we'd started; it was too cold to stop to rest or eat lunch; and, perhaps most important, the rewards of beer and hot showers lay ahead. We stopped together on the trail one last time at a place called Photographers Point, an overlook with sweeping views to the northwest, the direction from which we'd begun our hike five days earlier. Fremont Creek, which we'd hopped across far upstream two days earlier seeking shelter from the rain and lightning, fed the canyon that lay far below. The high terrace on which we'd walked stretched away into the distance. We asked a man who turned out to be from London to take a picture of all of us. On all of our trips, we've met foreigners on the trail, hikers from around the globe who've come here to experience America's beauty. More Americans should see what they're missing.

After our group photo—the only one of all six of us since the waitress took our picture at Calamity Jane's—we sped on toward Elkhart Park. The trail dropped down through a heavy forest of Engelmann spruce and lodgepole pine. I was hiking in front with Brian, but he soon left me in his wake. Moving fast through the forest with long strides, he looked like a yeti. In another half mile, Blake caught and passed me. We split up based on age, just as we had on the climb to Summit Lake. The two young bulls, Brian and Blake, were leading the rest of us back to the barn. Wilson and I were in the middle; Bobby and David trailed. But we were all moving quickly. Just before we reached the parking lot, Wilson stopped along the trail to gather pine cones for his three-year-old son, Gus. I longed for the days when my children would have been happy with pine cones for souvenirs. Wilson and I walked the last hundred yards to the parking lot, where Brian and Blake were waiting. I dropped my pack and checked my watch. It was 1:30. David appeared shortly, followed by Bobby. We loaded into the rental cars and drove the twenty minutes down to Pinedale.

When we got to town, we checked in at the Half Moon Lodge for the second time. The pairings for the rooms were the same as for the tents—Bobby and David, Wilson and Blake, Brian and me. I let Brian go first in the shower so I wouldn't feel guilty about how long I soaked under the water. When it was my turn, the feeling was sublime. I focused all my attention on the shower, basking in the simple pleasure of hot water on my body after six days on the trail. The water that ran off my feet was brown for the first two minutes.

After everybody had cleaned up, the six of us gathered to discuss plans for the day. We had all called home. There were no crises or family disasters. Nobody had been put on ice. We then dispersed into Pinedale. Bobby's goal was a haircut that complied with military specs. He was scheduled to go to the base in Gulfport the day after our return. The rest of us were looking for souvenirs, the price of admission for returning home after a selfish week in the mountains with the guys. Nothing as free as pine cones would do for my family, but I kept things simple. I bought caps and tee shirts. The best souvenir of all, however, was yet to come.

We gathered again at the Half Moon and decided to return to the Corral Bar/Calamity Jane's. Our last night, however, was far more festive than our first. We ordered a pizza at some point during the night, but beer—pitcher after pitcher of Fat Tire—was a much higher priority.

Bobby and I have fantasized about moving to a small town in the mountains. We've often discussed how great it would be to live in a close-knit community in the midst of such beauty. From the descriptions we'd read, it looked like Pinedale might fit the bill. But that was before we saw the clientele in the Corral Bar. I hate cigarettes, and everybody in the Corral Bar smoked. At one point, I counted nine customers on the nine barstools, all with lit cigarettes dangling from their lips. On a scale of one to ten, no woman in the bar exceeded a three, and that was with the lights turned down. It was also with their mouths closed. The town was in dire need of a competent dentist. After we'd finished four or five pitchers, I leaned over to Wilson, opened my mouth, and pointed to my upper right molar. "See this?" I asked. "We're the only people in this bar with this particular tooth in our heads." I had to talk loud to overcome the jukebox, which was playing "Radar Love" by Golden Earring. Wilson pressed his index finger to his lips and looked around to make sure none of the locals had heard me.

* * *

Long after our trip to Wyoming, Bobby called one day to report that he'd experienced yet another of his frequent epiphanies. This was no small matter, he said. He claimed it was on the order of his transcending realization on our trip to Glacier, his discovery that wild bears don't shit in the woods, they shit in the trail. I played along and demanded an explanation.

"Ok, here it is," Bobby said. "This morning when I was brushing my teeth, I realized that the toothbrush was invented in Pinedale. It's true; it's gotta be."

"What are you talking about?" I asked, thinking back to the terrible teeth on display that night at the Corral Bar. "Those people had the worst teeth I've ever seen. There wasn't a full set in the crowd."

"That's just it," Bobby explained. "If the toothbrush had been invented anywhere else," he said, "it would be called a *teeth*brush."

* * *

The pool table was the center of attention in the Corral Bar. Eight ball was the game. A guy named Dave was dispatching all challengers. Dave walked and talked drunk but shot sober. At the end of one game, I saw him make an amazing bank shot on the eight ball and then stumble as he walked over to his victim to shake hands. Dave was wearing a sweatshirt. It featured the face of a grizzly bear, but the bear had antlers sprouting from its forehead. Below the bear in black letters was the word BEER followed by a question mark. We were deep into the evening by now, and it took me a while before I realized that beer is what you get when you cross a bear and a deer. Dave's sweatshirt was old and worn, but I coveted it. I wanted it bad.

First I tried to buy it. I approached Dave and introduced myself, told him I liked his sweatshirt, and offered him twenty bucks for it. I pointed out that both sleeves were frayed, as was the collar. With slurred speech that reminded me of Wilson the night before, Dave said he couldn't sell the shirt; it had too much sentimental value. According to Dave, his former boss had given it to him for two reasons: because Dave always had a beer in his hand and because the bear looked like Dave. I could believe the first reason—after all, Dave had a beer in his hand while he was telling me he always had a beer in his hand—but I was skeptical about the second. I leaned back to get both Dave and the bear in my field of vision. They looked nothing alike. I told Dave I saw no resemblance, hoping he would reconsider. But his allegiance to the sweatshirt remained firm.

There were lots of pool shooters now, and the game changed from singles to doubles. Dave got the pick of the litter for his partner and chose Jed, short for Jedediah. Perhaps Jed was a descendant of Jedediah Smith, but my focus was on the beer and the pool and I didn't ask. I watched their first game. Dave was terrific, but Jed was even better. Wilson drafted me as his partner to challenge them. I'm about a B minus as a pool shooter. Wilson is worse. Before we started, I approached Dave. Another beer had increased my longing for the bear/deer/beer sweatshirt. I proposed a bet: my twenty bucks versus his sweatshirt. Dave had already beaten Wilson and me in singles. He squinted at Wilson, who was chalking his cue. Dave figured this was easy money. We shook on it.

The game was close. Jed was excellent, I was good, Wilson was mediocre, and Dave had finally had one too many beers in his hand. Dave misfired on the last solid and shrugged. I made the last stripe and then had a hard kick shot on the eight ball. I could try a defensive shot, but it was Jed's turn next. I went for the win and made it. The sweatshirt was mine.

Before I could collect my winnings, Bobby called me over to the bar where he was sitting. "I can't believe you're really gonna take Dave's sweatshirt," he said.

"What are you talking about?" I asked. "I won it fair and square."

Bobby wasn't buying it. "Just look at him," he said, "he's gonna wake up in the morning with a raging hangover, freezing his ass off, and not be able to find his sweatshirt."

Now I was feeling guilty. I walked over to Dave and told him I didn't want to take his sweatshirt if it really meant that much to him. He peered down at the antlered bear. Then he raised his head and smiled. "You take it," he said, "it's old." He peeled it off and handed it over. I looked over at

Bobby and shrugged. He shook his head in disgust. A few minutes later, Dave stumbled out into the night with one of the Corral Bar lovelies.

But Dave's departure did not bring an end to the battle for the sweatshirt. Wilson and I successfully defended the table twice, then Jed had another chance to challenge us. He proposed a double or nothing bet: his twenty dollars versus Dave's sweatshirt. He wanted to win his buddy's shirt back for him, and I couldn't refuse. This time Jed was terrific, I was mediocre, Wilson was awful, and Jed's new partner was both good and sober. They beat us easily. I returned the sweatshirt, which I'd owned for less than half an hour. My buddies consoled me—all but Bobby, who said justice had been served.

Our crew, with the exception of Bobby, was now focused on a single goal. The thrill of victory, followed so close by the agony of defeat, had elevated the stature of the sweatshirt. Another empty pitcher of Fat Tire contributed to our obsession. Brian and Blake were up next. They tried to get Jed to play for the sweatshirt again, but he refused. He said he'd won it back for Dave and wasn't going to take another chance. This time it really would have been easy money; Jed and his partner dispatched Brian and Blake in five minutes.

A new pair then took on Jed and his partner. During the game, I noticed that Wilson was chatting with Jed whenever Jed wasn't shooting. Wilson felt guilty about his lousy play and was trying to lay the groundwork for a third sweatshirt bet. I walked over to Wilson and Jed and joined the conversation. As I listened, I noticed that Jed was calling Wilson Will. When Jed walked away to take his next shot, I looked at Wilson and asked: "Will?" He shrugged. "Think that's more manly?" He looked hurt.

Jed and his partner won again, and now it was our turn. Before I proposed another bet, Wilson offered to kick in twenty dollars of his own money, trying to make amends for dragging me down. I approached Jed and suggested the same bet again: twenty bucks versus the sweatshirt. I was holding Wilson's twenty in reserve, to sweeten the deal if Jed balked. But first I tried psychology. I made my pitch, appealing to Jed's sense of fairness as well as his greed. "I played you for the sweatshirt when I had it. It would be bad form for you not to give me the same chance. Plus you and your partner are both better than I am. And Will's awful." (I was going along about the name.)

Jed looked at Wilson chalking his cue. "Will *is* bad," he agreed, "but we could scratch or make the eight ball."

"Anything's possible," I admitted, but Jed knew the odds were stacked in his favor.

After thinking it over, Jed said, "you're on" and immediately walked over to the bar. The bartender reached under the bar, produced a case, and handed it over. Jed opened it and pulled out the two parts. It was his personal pool cue. As he screwed it together, he looked at me and winked.

Jed and his partner were better than we were, but we managed to keep it close. I made a couple of shots, Wilson was much improved, and both of us played good defense. We nevertheless were behind when my turn came late in the game. We had stripes; three remained. There was only one solid, and it lay right in front of one of the side pockets. Jed was on deck; he would surely finish us off if he got another chance.

My first shot was no problem. The second was longer and more difficult, but it went in too. Now I faced an extraordinarily difficult cut shot. The cue ball was on one end of the table, the last remaining stripe on the other, seven feet away. It lay near the end rail and exactly halfway between the two corner pockets. A bank shot was out of the question; there was no way to get the cue ball out of the way. An extreme cut shot was the only hope. To make the shot, I would have to blast the cue ball, barely clip the remaining stripe, and hope it trickled into a corner pocket. I considered a defensive shot, but there was no place to hide. Wilson helped me study the shot. We couldn't decide whether it was even possible to make it, whether the laws of geometry would allow it. After circling the table twice more to get my bearings, I took aim and fired. The cue ball, as planned, barely touched the object ball as it sped past. As the cue ball caromed back and forth down the length of the table, the last remaining stripe rolled at a snail's pace toward the corner pocket. It hesitated briefly, then dropped in. I was ecstatic. Wilson high-fived me, as did Jed, who was the best of sports. I had a relatively easy shot on the eight ball; our crew erupted when it fell in. The sweatshirt, again, was mine. Brian and Blake were as excited as Wilson and I were. Even Bobby was satisfied, now that I'd won it from two sober guys. Jed retrieved the shirt, tossed it to me, and shook my hand. For the first time, I tried it on. The sweatshirt I had so coveted, that had become my obsession, was two sizes too small. But I didn't care.

We got Charlie the waitress, who had served us six nights earlier, to take a final group picture, and then we bade farewell to the Corral Bar. I wasn't about to risk yet another rematch, and the second-hand smoke was about to choke us all. I headed out into the night, my prize clutched in my hands.

When we got to the car, I thought back on a lifetime of participation in sports and games. The highlights were few; from my earliest years, I was slow and short and couldn't jump. I racked my brain. The best I could come up with was the time my first cousin and I won a mixed doubles tennis tournament on the ninth point of a nine-point tiebreaker in the final set. That victory, I decided, was no match for this one. The sweatshirt was old and frayed and didn't fit, but it was better than a tennis trophy any day.

This was our last night, and we weren't ready to call it quits. We went looking for more beer. They don't sell beer in grocery stores in Wyoming, only in liquor stores, but by the time we got to the liquor store in Pinedale, it was already closed. We saw a light on in the back, and a woman's head. Blake and Brian—our two youngest and handsomest—would clearly have the best chance at an after-hours beer buy. Blake volunteered. We watched intently as he spoke to the woman through the barely cracked door. When she walked away, he turned and gave us a thumbs up. She returned momentarily, Blake handed her money, and she handed him two six packs. It was a more successful beer purchase than the one that gave Blake his nickname.

We returned to Bobby's and David's room and sat up telling stories. Before long, Wilson said he needed to call home again and walked across the parking lot to his room. After half an hour, we realized he hadn't reappeared. Blake and I went to investigate and found him tucked into his bed, just about to doze off. We harassed him, but he sure looked comfortable. With cold beer still remaining, we all called it quits and headed to our rooms.

* * *

Bobby and David pulled out early Saturday morning. Their flight home left before ours. The rest of us had time for a big breakfast in Pinedale, after which we squeezed back into the Malibu and headed south on Highway

191, a different route from the way we'd come. But the landscape looked much the same: dry, empty, good for little. We passed a large male antelope on the shoulder. He stood perfectly still as we sped by. We were much quieter than we'd been on the drive up. The only sound was my homemade CDs. As we crossed back into Utah, I told the others we needed to think about future trips. I wanted to know what they would have changed about this one to make it better. Blake had only one suggestion. An eight-day trip, he said, was hard to pull off with three young children at home. For him, shorter would be better.

"What about you?" I asked Wilson. "What would you change?"

Of the six of us, Wilson had been the most inclined to complain, the most likely to bitch and find fault. But you wouldn't know it by his answer. "What would I change?" he repeated. "Nothing. Absolutely nothing. It was perfect." I didn't remind him that he spent eighty-five dollars on fishing gear and didn't catch a fish.

To help me write about this trip, I took a note pad in my backpack on the trail. I spent a few minutes every day writing down what happened, describing the scenery. On the flight from Salt Lake to Dallas, I pulled out the pad to organize my thoughts while they were still fresh, but I didn't have the energy. I was sitting by Blake and sought his help. I asked him to tell me what he thought was most memorable, what was special from his perspective. I sat with my pen poised as he rubbed his chin and thought. "I don't know. Everything, I guess," he said.

My pen stayed poised. "Come on, you can do better than that."

He thought some more. "You know, the mountains and the trout, and that sweatshirt."

I waited, but that was it. I put the cap back on my pen without writing a thing. "You're a regular damn poet, aren't you?" I asked. He smiled and shrugged and returned to the book he was reading. I pulled out a book and did the same.

Jen was waiting for us at the gate in Dallas. This was before 9/11, though just barely, and a non-passenger could still go to the gate. The six of us had promised to exchange emails the next week about how warmly we were greeted when we got home. My money was on Brian. Jen and Brian waited with us in the terminal until we boarded the final leg of our flight. In another hour, we landed in Jackson. As Blake, Wilson, and I walked toward baggage claim, we spotted Wilson's wife and kids. They had balloons. Gus was thrilled to see his daddy. He seemed to have inherited only Wilson's happy side. As we waited for our backpacks, Wilson opened his carry-on bag and pulled out the souvenirs he'd brought home for Gus and Grace, including the Wyoming pine cones. Gus was ecstatic. In the crowded terminal, he yelled, "My daddy, he's the coolest daddy in the world." And Wilson had already said the trip was perfect.

Ann Lowrey and her boyfriend took Blake and me back to our house, where Blake had left his car, and he headed home to Vicksburg. I hauled my pack into the kitchen, then gathered the family around me. I had already decided to give the sweatshirt to Ann Lowrey, who unlike her mother would actually wear it. Before displaying it, however, I told the story, down to the tiniest detail. I spoke at length of the Corral Bar and its clientele, of the music on the jukebox, of the sad state of the locals' teeth. I gave a shot-by-shot description of the pool games, ending with the miracle shot I made to reclaim my prize. When I got to the end and spoke of discovering that the sweatshirt was two sizes too small, Ann Lowrey interrupted. "What are you gonna do with it?"

"I thought I'd give it to you," I said. I opened my pack, pulled it out, and handed it to her. Although she was seventeen, she looked just like Gus did when Wilson handed him the pine cones. The sweatshirt still reeked of cigarette smoke, but that didn't matter. Ann Lowrey immediately put it on. She walked into the hall, studied herself in the mirror, then came back into the kitchen and hugged me. The trip was wonderful, but it was good to be home.

CHAPTER
14

Epilogue

Three days after we flew from west to east across America on our trip home from the Winds, terrorists hijacked four flights headed in the opposite direction and crashed them into the World Trade Center, the Pentagon and, thanks to heroes who intervened, the Pennsylvania countryside. Within a week, Major Robert J. Ariatti had been called up to active duty. When we spoke on the phone, Bobby sounded excited. But his deployment didn't take him far and didn't last long. He was sent to Texas to upgrade the radar system designed to protect George W. on his ranch in Crawford. Within a week, Bobby was back in his windowless office at the shipyard, pondering new schemes to escape.

Shortly after the terrorist attacks, I read an obituary in the Jackson paper. A young man had dropped dead of a heart attack while walking with his wife, who had just found out she was pregnant. The young man, who appeared to be in excellent physical condition, had a congenital heart defect that had gone undiscovered until his autopsy. The obituary reported that he was twenty-six, Brian's age. I read on and discovered that he and Brian had gone to the same high school, graduated the same year, and that he had played football. I tried to call Brian to tell him. Jen answered and said Brian already knew and was en route to Jackson for the funeral. Not long after that funeral, Bobby's secretary called me about another one. Bobby's older sister, his only sibling, had died of cancer.

In the days and weeks following September 11, like millions of Americans, I tried to make sense of things. I tried to draw lessons from the death of innocents at the hands of madmen from halfway round the world, thousands of lives snuffed out in a flash. I thought about the death of Brian's friend, his life ending just as it was beginning, and about the death of Bobby's sister. In the end, the only conclusion I reached is that we should try harder to live life to the fullest. It is all so fragile; it can all be gone so quickly. The lesson is about time. About cherishing the people and places we love. About spending time with special friends in special places. The lesson confirmed something I already knew: I would continue to travel with Bobby.

* * *

Several months after the terrorist attack, the January 2002 issue of *Outside* magazine arrived in the mail. It included an essay by Jack Turner, who spent time in Afghanistan before moving to Jackson Hole. Turner wrote that, in the wake of September 11, he'd found solace in the immutable wonders of the natural world: "I find a measure of relief in the things that haven't changed: the geese that fly south in the autumn, the fir that resists the maul, the winter that has arrived, and the spring to come." Unlike those who reacted to the attacks by deciding against divorce, or starting to attend church again, Turner reported that his response was to go into the wilderness, what Rick Bass has called the church of the wild.

I suppose this was my response as well. Jackson is not Jackson Hole, but I made do. I went for long walks, looking for deer, listening for owls. I built a cabin on a lake thirty minutes north of Jackson. I go there to fish, split firewood, walk in the woods, and watch sunsets. The lake is a grand place for bird watching and listening. Red-tailed hawks glide over the fields north of the lake, searching for movement below. Great blue herons hunt from the shoreline, patiently waiting for unsuspecting fish. Ducks and geese dot the surface of the water. I enjoy seeing them take off and land, hearing them quack and honk. Swans and ospreys have visited the lake, as have two bald eagles. Cedar trees and bodocks, long dead but impervious to rot, remain standing in the center of the lake. In the afternoon, bluebirds and kingfishers flit from one tree to the next. Just before nightfall, they are replaced by egrets, gliding in one by one, lighting on the branches, arranging themselves like Christmas ornaments. I marvel at the flocks of blackbirds, rising and turning and landing in unison. I wonder how they do it, if one of them, the choreographer, somehow tells the others what to do. It's quiet at the lake. When a flock of blackbirds flies over, I can hear their wing beats. The name of the lake is the Sanctuary, and it has become that for me.

* * *

As I've written about my trips with Bobby, friends have asked why I'm doing it. They want to know the story's theme, its purpose, what it's about. I'm not sure I have satisfactory answers. I started writing about my trips with Bobby for a number of reasons. I'd read Bill Bryson's *A Walk in the Woods*. I thought he did an excellent job of describing the difficulties and misery that are part of backpacking, but not the joy and satisfaction. Maybe it's just that my camping trips have been more fun than his walk in the woods. I also thought that some of the things that have happened on our trips—the attacks by a sprinkler in Nevada and a free range cow in Montana, the campsite head suturing in Wyoming—as well as the tales from Bobby's past were worth telling. And third, I enjoy writing. Why else would I come home from days of writing briefs and motions and spend my evenings writing this? I also love to brag about my wonderful daddy, and this gave me another chance to do that.

That is *why* I've written about my travels with Bobby, but *what* I've written is harder to explain. Is this a sort of travelogue, a description of five magnificent places in the American West? That's certainly part of it, but I don't really think of it as that. Is this primarily a story about Bobby, and about our friendship? In the first draft, I put all the stories about Bobby's past up front, before I began describing our trips. I let Brian Drake and one of my law partners read the part about Bobby. They had very different reactions. My partner feared that readers would think Bobby was crazy and have no interest in reading about our trips. He suggested I sprinkle the Bobbyisms throughout the story instead of packing them into the beginning, and I've done that. When Brian read an early draft, he offered the opposite advice. He knows and loves Bobby, and he loved the stories—about Vietnam and Lucky Dog and all the rest. He said I should forget the trips, change the name to *My Buddy Bobby*, and make it a full-fledged biography.

The third explanation for this story, and the one I think is most accurate, is that it's a book of advice, a long, glowing recommendation to hike in the mountains, to do what Bobby and I do, to go where we've gone. Most of my law practice involves defending corporations in lawsuits. I get good results for them more often than not, and I make a good living. But I have no illusions that keeping shareholders' money out of the hands of undeserving plaintiffs is a meaningful contribution to the world. So I like to think of this story as my chance to make a contribution. I hope at least one person will read this and take my advice and decide to go hiking and camping in the mountains.

I am certainly not the first to give this advice, and others have done it better. Along the way, I have quoted the words of a number of wilderness writers. On the subject of this recommendation I have made, let me add the words of Edward Abbey from a speech he gave at an Earth First rally in 1987, two years before his death.

> It is not enough to fight for the land; it is even more important to enjoy it. While you can. While it is still there. So get out there and hunt and fish and mess around with your friends, ramble out yonder and explore the forests, encounter the grizz, climb the mountains, bag the peaks. Run the rivers, breathe deep of that yet sweet and lucid air, sit quietly for a while and contemplate the precious stillness, that lovely, mysterious and awesome space.

So, take this advice. Gather a group of friends, plan a trip, head for the mountains. If you're lucky—real lucky—one of your friends will be like Bobby.

* * *

So now we come to the end. As I write these last words, on a Sunday afternoon in January 2002, Bobby and I have already started talking about the trip we'll take this year. The elimination of options is the hardest part. We're thinking about returning to Glacier. I've been reading about two magnificent backpacking routes in the park: the North Circle and the Great Northern Traverse. Either would allow us to see much more of the park's backcountry than we saw in 1997. We're also considering leaving the country for the first time and going to the Canadian Rockies. Yoho National Park, Banff, and Jasper are spectacular. A third possibility is the Weminuche Wilderness in the San Juan mountains in southwest Colorado, the range where Rick Bass went in search of the lost grizzly. I have read accolades about this wilderness area, but there is one drawback: It's even higher than the Winds, the air even thinner.

We're also talking about doing something entirely different this year. A canoe trip is again under consideration, either to the upper Missouri or the Boundary Waters on the Minnesota/Ontario border. Daddy took his Boy Scouts there in the early 1980s; it's been on my Bucket List ever since. A final option is a backpacking trip to Isle Royale National Park, reached by ferry from the north shore of Lake Superior. Isle Royale is the home of a sizeable herd of moose as well as several wolf packs, which keep the moose population in check. Visitors often hear the wolves but rarely see them.

Right now, as I write this, these are the destinations we're considering. But the list of possibilities for this year will likely grow before it shrinks to one. We want to return to the Sierras and the Cascades someday. I know the Adirondacks are beautiful. We will definitely go to Alaska one of these years. If we really get ambitious, New Zealand, the Alps, and Patagonia are candidates. There are more magnificent places than we can ever hope to see, more wonderful trips than we can ever hope to take. Our options are unlimited. Yours are too, if you take my advice.

Where we will go this year is undecided, but whether we will go is not. We will go this year, and the next, and the year after that. *Travels with Bobby* may be coming to an end, but my travels with Bobby are far from over.

CHAPTER

15

Backpacking Glacier

I know. The epilogue is the end. That's the rule, no exceptions. And the epilogue you just read was supposed to be the end. But time passed, and Bobby and I went on another trip. It was the best yet, and so I wrote about it.

* * *

In early 2002, I emailed the rest of the group from the Winds to see if they were interested in another trip. Bobby was in, of course, but Blake and Brian said they couldn't go, Blake because he'd been invited to go to Alaska on a fishing trip and Brian because he would be graduating from chiropractic school and starting his practice. I didn't hear from David or Wilson, so Bobby and I decided just the two of us would go. I had mixed emotions. I had a great time with all the guys in the Winds, but going camping with one close friend creates a bond that's not possible in a large group.

By late March, Bobby and I had decided to return to Glacier. Our day hikes there in 1997 made us want to backpack to see more of the park's backcountry. Glacier was voted America's best national park for backpacking in part because of a system that limits both the number of backpackers and their impact on the environment. In most of Glacier, backpackers are not free to camp where they please but instead are restricted to established campsites. Each campsite consists of two to six tent sites, a common area for cooking and eating, a pole or cable for hanging food to protect it from bears and other scavengers, and one or two pit toilets. The system is not without drawbacks. Solitude is hard to come by— backpackers have to share meals with other campers they've never met— and campfires are prohibited in most sites. To see more of Glacier, Bobby and I decided we would make a sacrifice we had vowed we would never make. We would do without campfires on most of the nights of our trip.

To plan our route, we searched for the trail guide we'd bought before going to Glacier in 1997. I couldn't find it; neither could Bobby. I blamed him; he blamed me. I ordered the new edition. A few days after placing the order, the missing trail guide arrived, mailed from Jonny Drake in Germany. He'd borrowed it a summer earlier when he was home on leave, and I'd forgotten I'd given it to him. The dead bee stuck on page 120 was still there. Post-mortem, the bee had become a world traveler, flying home from Montana with me in '97, then going back to Glacier, via Texas, on a long road trip with Jonny and an Army buddy, then flying with Jonny to Germany, and then flying back to Jackson in the mail.

As usual, Bobby left most of the planning to me. The route I selected would start at Logan Pass on the Continental Divide at more than 6,500 feet and end at Many Glacier at 5,000 feet. Unlike the previous year, we would start high and end low. With side trips and fishing excursions, we would walk sixty miles.

Access to Glacier's campsites is determined by permits, awarded beginning on April 15. The demand for permits is significant. I fedexed our application to the Park Service on April 15. Even then, we didn't get our first choice. We wanted to go the next to last week in August. A few days after I sent our application, a ranger called and offered us the itinerary and campsites we wanted but for a week later than we had requested. We accepted, booked our flights, and began preparation.

Over the summer, I focused on ways to lighten my load and make the hiking more enjoyable. In an effort to avoid the blisters that plagued me in the Winds, I substituted lightweight hiking shoes for my heavy boots. I replaced my nine-pound Walrus tent with a two-person tent weighing half as much. I bought lighter cooking pots, eliminated unnecessary clothes, and planned a menu that would minimize food weight. I also exercised religiously. From Memorial Day until August 23, when we flew to Montana, I didn't miss a day. I took long walks, lifted weights, and ran. I lost fifteen pounds, winning a weight-loss bet with a friend with no self-discipline. I reached peak condition on the weekend before we left. On Friday night, I walked and ran five miles in a driving thunderstorm, confirming that my new shoes could handle wet conditions. The next day, I ran three and a half miles and lifted weights for an hour. The day after that, I walked fifteen fast miles in the heat of the day. I was ready.

Bobby was not as ready. He was prepared in terms of gear and food; he'd made a list of everything we needed to take months before the trip. He claimed he hadn't been exercising much, but I knew that wasn't true. As always, he was in great shape. The problem was not with Bobby's physical condition but his mental state. As the date of our trip approached, trouble with bears and his wife laid him low.

The bear trouble was caused by Bobby's choice of reading materials. Five years earlier, I had made the mistake of reading Jack Olsen's *Night of the Grizzlies* before our trip to Glacier. Now Bobby was reading a book called *Mark of the Grizzly*, a collection of stories about grizzlies attacking people, including several attacks that occurred in Glacier. This time, bears haunted Bobby's dreams instead of mine. I did everything I could to encourage his bear phobia, reminding him that more grizzlies live in Glacier than anywhere else in the lower forty-eight states. I pointed out that we would be camping our very first night at Granite Park, where a grizzly killed one backpacker and mauled another during the infamous night in 1967 that became the subject of Olsen's book. One night, when I was reviewing the Glacier Backcountry Camping Guide, I found more ammunition for my psychological warfare. The guide contained the most ambiguous of sentences. It said: "There have been cases where pepper spray apparently repelled aggression in attacking bears and accounts where it has not worked as well as expected." I smiled and turned down the corner of the page. The next morning, I took the guide to the office and emailed the sentence to Bobby, highlighting the bad news in the second half. My phone rang seconds later. I smiled again when I saw Bobby's number on caller ID.

"Hello," I answered innocently.

Bobby skipped the hello and got right to business. "What the hell does that mean, it's 'not worked as well as expected'?"

"Beats me," I responded, "I didn't write it. But look on the bright side. If the person was able to report that the pepper spray didn't work, he must have lived."

That seemed to comfort Bobby. Comfort wasn't my goal, however, so I suggested an alternative: "But maybe not. Maybe the person who provided the report climbed a tree, saw his buddy spray the bear, and then saw that it didn't work as well as expected."

"You ain't scaring me," Bobby said, "I can still outrun you."

A day or two later, however, I got an email from Bobby that proved he was still fretting. He wanted to know about my new tent, specifically whether it was a dome tent. Attached to Bobby's email was another one from Mike Kitchen, who'd hiked with us in the Tetons. Mike had just returned from a trip to Yellowstone during which he visited an institute that studies bear behavior. There Mike learned that grizzlies in Glacier had developed an odd fascination with dome tents. According to park rangers, the bears would approach the tents, pick them up, throw them, and watch in wonder as they bounced and rolled. The practice was started by one grizzly and then copied by others. A fad, like bear hula hoop. The report didn't say whether any of the tents that got this treatment were occupied at the time. Mike's email presented another opportunity for me to feed Bobby's bear fear, but I didn't take advantage. I was preoccupied with work and responded without thinking, assuring him my new tent was not a dome tent.

* * *

Unlike Bobby's bear dreams, his problems on the home front were all too real. While we were in the Winds a year earlier, Stephanie had been forced to handle a host of problems alone. The AC in the house stopped working while the temperature was in the nineties, one of the family's cars broke down, and the Ariatti girls fought constantly. When Bobby got home and heard about it, he was overcome with Catholic guilt. Unbeknownst to me, he made a solemn vow that he would never again leave Stephanie alone to go play in the mountains.

After having made this vow, Bobby was understandably reluctant to tell Stephanie he was about to break it. He stalled as long as he could. Finally, ten days before we were about to leave for nine days in Montana, Bobby broke the news. When she learned that Bobby was reneging on his promise, Stephanie did not react well.

I tried to call Bobby at work on Thursday, August 15, eight days before our departure date. His secretary said he wasn't there, that he had taken a day of vacation. He couldn't do that, I pointed out, he was going on vacation with me. She provided no details, saying only that she expected him back the next day. That night, Bobby called me from his car. He sounded tired. He said he was on his way home. When I asked where he'd been all day, Bobby told a tale of woe:

"The Pecan Grove landfill," he answered.

"And what exactly have you been doing at the landfill?"

"Looking for my camping gear."

"Do what?"

"Yeah, I've been out there all day looking for my camping stuff."

"How in God's name did your camping stuff wind up at the dump?"

"It got put out with the garbage. We were cleaning out the storage room this weekend, and my camping gear wound up getting thrown out too. I don't think Stephanie did it on purpose, but she's sure not happy about our trip."

"Do what?"

"But whatever happened, it all got thrown out. Tent, sleeping bag, two backpacks, stove, water filter, clothes, boots, the works."

"You're shittin' me."

"I wish I was."

"Did you find it?" I could see our trip going up in smoke.

"Yeah, almost everything. I might have lost a few little things, but I got everything I need. These two guys who work at the landfill spent hours helping me look. Great guys. Most all my stuff was in plastic containers with blue tops; that made it a lot easier to find. Plus it kept the stuff from having that garbage dump smell."

"That's a good thing. That smell would draw bears like flies."

"Yeah." Bobby managed a laugh. "Like chicken ranchero."

"Why now?" I asked. "Did something happen?"

262

"Well, I never quite got around to telling Stephanie about our trip. I finally told her day before yesterday."

"You're shittin' me."

"I meant to, but I just kept putting it off."

"I told my wife in April. That was like telling her we were going in ten years. She's had four months to get used to it."

"You're right. I'll try that next year. If there is a next year. Anyway, when I got home yesterday, everything was gone. I asked her what happened. She said it must have gotten thrown out with the trash."

I couldn't believe it. "That's the worst thing I've ever heard. She knows how much you love camping."

Bobby managed another laugh. "The guys at the dump felt the same way. They were a big help. After we got through, I went and bought us a six pack. While we were drinking it, one of them asked how all my camping stuff wound up in their dump. When I told them I thought my wife threw it away, one of the guys got this real serious look on his face. He looked me in the eye and put his hand on my shoulder. He said, 'Listen, buddy, you bring her body out here, they'll never find it.'"

The next morning, I called Bobby at the office. I was still shocked at what Stephanie had done, but he defended her and said it must have been an accident. I said he had Stockholm Syndrome and asked how on earth he could justify what she did. Bobby then told me the rest of the story, which he had obviously not shared with the guys at the landfill. First he told me of the solemn vow he'd made the previous year, his promise that he would never again leave Stephanie for a week to go hiking in the mountains.

"So?" I was unimpressed. "That still didn't give her the right to throw your stuff away."

"Well, it kinda did. I wanted her to think I really meant it so I told her if I ever tried to go again, she could throw my camping gear away."

"You're shittin' me," I said. This was becoming my standard response. "I guess it's no damn wonder she threw your stuff away. I would have thrown it away too."

"This is definitely gonna be my last trip. I just can't go off and leave her with the kids like this. It's just not fair to her."

* * *

That was Bobby's low point. He was soon himself again, and he has never again suggested that any trip would be our last trip. On Monday, four days before we would fly to Montana, Bobby emailed me with a question about some detail he would need to know, he wrote, if he didn't have to back out. I took the bait and called immediately. Bobby laughed when he heard my voice. "I knew that would make you call. Don't worry. I'm going. All my gear is hidden in a safe place."

So the trip was on and Bobby was in, but he wasn't the only one. At the last minute, David declared himself in need of a wilderness fix and decided to join us. I told Bobby that my family was relieved; they liked the idea that an ER doc would be going. Bobby laughed. "What do they think, that David's gonna save your ass from a grizzly with an Ace bandage?" Bobby was still reading *Mark of the Grizzly*.

David booked flights arriving in and departing from Montana with us, but he said he didn't want to spend the entire week backpacking. We questioned him about what he planned to do instead, but he remained vague. He mentioned the possibility of staying at least one night at some place called the Izaak Walton Inn on the southwest border of the park. He also said he could probably pick Bobby and me up at Many Glacier when we hiked out at the end of the week. Other than those scant details, David's plans remained a mystery, at least to Bobby and me.

When our day of departure finally came, I flew from Jackson to Memphis, where I met Bobby and David, who'd flown up from Gulfport. We continued north to Minneapolis and west to Kalispell, landing at two o'clock p.m. The three of us collected our gear and walked into the bright sunshine. It felt great. We had shed twenty degrees of temperature and fifty percentage points of humidity. Across the valley to the east, we could see the mountains of Glacier rising to the Continental Divide. An airport shuttle took us into town, where we picked up an '86 Dodge Aries wagon touted by Rent-A-Wreck as the Glacier backpacking special. We then headed straight for the park to pick up our backcountry permit. Along the way, David disclosed more details about his strange plans. He would hike in with Bobby and me for three days and camp with us for three nights. Then he would leave us, returning the way we came and hiking and camping the next three days and two nights by himself. This would allow him to return to civilization a day before we did, spend one night at the Izaak Walton Inn, and pick us up at Many Glacier when we hiked out.

The next time Bobby and I were alone, we tried to fathom David's thinking: "What's the deal with this Izaak Walton place?" I asked. "He's gonna hike three days by himself in grizzly country. Even if he doesn't see a bear, a sprained ankle and he's a dead man. And he's gonna miss some of the most spectacular scenery in the whole world. There's only one thing I can think of that's powerful enough to make him do it."

"Can't be a woman," Bobby responded. "David's happily married, and he said the room he reserved was big enough for us if we changed our minds. I think it's something else. He came out here with some girl in the seventies. I think they must have stayed there. He wants to go back for old times' sake." But that wasn't it either. Later I asked David if he'd ever been to the Izaak Walton. He said no. We never did figure it out.

We picked up our permit at the ranger station. David lucked out and was able to get an extra permit for the two nights he would camp by himself. A bulletin board listed recent grizzly sightings. Spots along our entire route were prominently mentioned. I studied Bobby as he studied the list. He didn't look happy. Like all backpackers, we were required to watch a video about bear encounters. If a grizzly charges, the video instructed, the proper response depends on whether the charge is "aggressive," on the one hand, or "reactive/defensive" on the other. If the former, according to the video, the bear probably regards you as prey, you have nothing to lose, and you should respond aggressively. But in the latter case, you should lie face down, protect your face and abdomen, and the bear will probably leave you alone. As we walked back to the Aries, I heard Bobby muttering to himself. "Aggressive, reactive, defensive, what am I supposed to do, ask the frickin bear?"

We left the park, checked into the Super 8 in Columbia Falls, and hauled our gear and backpacks upstairs to our room. The airline had put a warning label on Bobby's oversize duffel bag that said "Heavy—Get Help to Lift." Not a good sign. For the next two hours, however, we eliminated duplication and luxuries. Several freeze-dried desserts were cast aside. We got rid of extra clothes. I decided to leave my compass behind. I chose my new ultralight headlamp over a flashlight. When Bobby compared my tiny headlamp to his, which was older, larger, and heavier, he said he felt like Loretta Lynn's old man. But Bobby shucked extra gear too. When he'd finished loading his pack, his duffel was still half full. In the end, however, Bobby refused to part with one item. Smiling, he held up his package of wet wipes and offered sound advice for all backpackers: "You can go a week without a shower, but you gotta wash your ass."

At the end of the gear-shedding process, we divvied up the team gear, loaded our backpacks, and lifted them. Our efforts had paid off. Our packs weighed at least ten pounds less than last year. Bobby had brought his dad's old fisherman's scales to Montana just so we could weigh our loaded backpacks. Bobby tied the scales to a luggage rack, and we took turns weighing. All three packs were less than 45 pounds. Even with a few items that some might regard as non-essential—fly rod, book, and quart of Famous Grouse Scotch, for example—mine weighed only 42.

Earlier in the week, I had gone to Chattanooga on business with two of my partners. On the flight home, one of them was flipping through an article about restaurants in the most recent issue of *Bon Appetit*. One of the featured restaurants was the Tupelo Grille in Whitefish, Montana, ten miles from Columbia Falls. I decided that we should go, thinking how pleased the staff of the Tupelo Grille would be to have a customer who grew up in Tupelo. After weighing our backpacks, we made the short drive to Whitefish. To establish my authenticity, I wore my souvenir tee shirt from Troop 12's 600th campout, which identified Tupelo as the home of the troop.

The food at the Tupelo Grille was excellent and the waitresses beautiful, but nobody gave a tinker's damn that I was from Tupelo. After we arrived, the first thing I did was confirm that the restaurant was named for my hometown, not Van Morrison's song. This was easy; the menu said "Tupelo—First TVA City" on the front cover. Tupelo was in fact the first city served by the Tennessee Valley Authority. With a measure of pride, I pointed out to the hostess that I grew up in Tupelo. She hardly looked up. As we had a Moose Drool beer while waiting for a table, I tried again, this time with the bartender. He didn't even raise an eyebrow. I was ready to give up, but Bobby pressed the issue with our waitress, pointing to my tee shirt to corroborate my connection to Tupelo. Surely, or so it seemed, at least our waitress would be interested. We hadn't paid yet, so she had a direct economic incentive to act like she cared. But she didn't care and didn't act and, unlike the waitress in Leavenworth, she didn't flirt.

The next morning, we ate a big breakfast—our last indoor meal for a week—and made our final purchases. We stopped at a liquor store so David could buy Tequila. Bobby had brought a fifth of Black Bush Irish whiskey from home. I tried to get him to buy another half pint so his quantity of Black Bush would equal my quart of Famous Grouse, but he declined. All three of us bought pepper spray at the Army-Navy store in Columbia Falls. The decision to buy it was not an easy one. Each canister cost forty bucks, and we already were on notice of "accounts where it has not worked as well as expected." I suggested another downside. I have never kept a gun at home because I've always figured one of the Easons would be more likely to get shot by accident than an intruder would be to get shot on purpose. The same was probably true of bear spray, I said.

* * *

After we got back from Glacier, the legitimacy of my concern about a self-inflicted pepper spray wound was confirmed when Rick Bass came to Jackson for a book reading. I called Bobby to see if he would come. He was at home; the shipyard had closed for the day because of Hurricane Isidore. Bobby said he was sitting on his back porch, smoking a cigar, watching the Wolf River rise. Their electricity was off, so Bobby had boiled water for coffee on his camp stove. This, Bobby said, had really pissed Stephanie off. I asked if he had not made coffee for her. "Not that," he explained. "It was just the sight of camping equipment." Bobby said he would try to come to Jackson to see Rick Bass, but he didn't make it. I went to the reading by myself.

Bass read a story about spraying himself accidentally with pepper spray. Believe it or not, he'd done it more than once. The first incident occurred many years ago, when Bass was young and single and foolish. He was in a bar in Utah with an attractive young woman. When she excused herself to go to the ladies room, Bass spotted what he thought was breath spray in her purse. Imagining a night of romance, Bass opened his mouth, aimed, and fired. His plans for the evening were immediately derailed. The blast knocked him off his bar stool. A short period of retching and writhing on the barroom floor was followed by a longer period of recovery and repair in the men's room. After Bass had made himself as presentable as possible, he returned to the bar, only to have salt rubbed into his self-inflicted wound. The young lady whose pepper spray he'd mistaken for breath spray had disappeared into the night.

Many years later, Bass had another accident while hiking with his young daughters in the Yaak Valley west of Glacier. When they spotted large, fresh grizzly tracks, Bass unlocked the safety on his pepper spray in anticipation. The safety was there for a reason. Bass promptly misfired, soaking himself and his overalls. They were hiking along a stream, and he sought refuge there. He was able to get the spray off his skin, but had less luck with his clothes. He scrubbed hard, but he couldn't rid them of the irritating spray. Rather than hike out naked, Bass created a barrier between his skin and clothes by stuffing his overalls with moss and black, stringy lichens. His daughters looked on in wonder as he packed his clothes full, swelling in size. On the drive home, Bass stopped at a store to buy snacks. By then, he'd forgotten about his stuffing. While he was paying, the store clerk pointed out that Bass's fly was open. Bass looked down. Not only was his fly open, but stringy, hair-like lichen was protruding. Without considering the impact on the clerk, Bass plucked the stray lichen from his fly and tossed it into the garbage. The clerk, like the girls, looked on in wonder.

* * *

After our shopping was completed, Bobby, David, and I returned to the park and headed east on Going to the Sun Road. We drove past Avalanche Creek, where we'd hiked in the rain with Brian on the first day of our trip five years earlier, and McDonald Creek, where we'd picnicked on the last day of that trip. Our hike would start at Logan Pass on the Continental Divide. David was going to hike out later in the week to a trailhead at a switchback in the road called the Loop, where we'd planned to hike the first day five years earlier. At the end of his hike, he figured he'd be able to hitchhike from there up to Logan Pass to retrieve the Aries. Our first day this year would be an easy one—eight level miles—so I suggested he go ahead and get the hitchhiking out of the way now. He would also probably have better luck hitching a ride now because he looked and smelled much better than he would in six days. We unloaded at Logan Pass, and David drove back down to the Loop and left the Aries there.

He caught a ride back up with a woman in her late forties who lived in New England. The woman told David she'd grown up near Glacier and was working in the park on the night of *The Night of the Grizzlies* in 1967. Panicked campers had rushed into her cabin to report the fatal attack on a backpacker at Trout Lake. I took the opportunity to remind Bobby that we would camp this night at the site of the other fatal attack that occurred that same night. I also told him it happened in August, the same month it was now. There was no end to the coincidences.

Before shouldering our packs, we ate peanut butter and jelly burritos I'd made in Jackson. The smell attracted a pair of ground squirrels, which exhibited the characteristic fearlessness of national park animals. One tried to run up my leg.

The first few miles of the Highline Trail to Granite Park provided grand views. The Garden Wall, which forms the Great Divide, towered above us to the east. This knife-edged ridge, called an arête, was formed when glaciers carved away both sides of what was then a mountain mass. Five years earlier, we had viewed the other side of the Garden Wall as we descended from Piegan Pass, following a grizzly's tracks in the snow without knowing what they were. We were here a month earlier this time, and the ground was covered with wildflowers instead of snow. In the distance to our west, the peaks surrounding the McDonald Creek drainage stretched away into the distance. Bird Woman Falls dropped hundreds of feet to the valley below.

The scenery was beautiful, but we had not yet escaped from civilization. We could see Going to the Sun Road far below us, crowded with cars. The trail was crowded too. We were still within range of day hikers on the Highline Trail. After a couple of hours, however, the trail wound around the east side of Haystack Butte, and the road disappeared from view. We left civilization behind, as well as the crowds of day hikers.

About halfway to Granite Park, we came upon three more members of the roving cast of national park animals. They were bighorn sheep; two were mature rams. We spotted them grazing just above the trail. As we approached within thirty yards, we tiptoed and spoke in whispers. Our caution proved unnecessary. The sheep were neither scared nor interested. I walked to within twelve feet without spooking them. I spoke, trying to provoke some reaction. The two big rams looked up briefly, but they were as unimpressed with me as the staff at the Tupelo Grille was. After a few minutes of posing, they sauntered away, having done their national park duty.

Long before reaching the campsite, we spotted Granite Park Chalet atop a ridge in the distance. The chalet, one of two in the park, offers hikers a chance to spend a night or two in the backcountry without carrying a heavy pack or sleeping in a tent. The stone and timber chalet was built in 1913, three years after Glacier became a national park.

The campground at Granite Park is three-quarters of a mile beyond and below the chalet. When I got to the chalet, I was fifteen minutes ahead of Bobby and David and hiking by myself. A thunderstorm was threatening, so I pressed on to the campsite instead of stopping for a tour. Thinking about *The Night of the Grizzlies* and the warning at the ranger station, I sang a John Prine medley. I was pleased to find the campground empty—no bears and no people—but the site itself was a disappointment. The tent sites were too close together, and trees obscured the view of the peaks to the west. The trail guide written by Erik Molvar—the same one we'd used in 1997—overrated this campsite, giving it the highest possible grade and declaring it a scenic attraction in itself. Maybe the trees had grown since he wrote it. Later in the week, we learned that Molvar had made mistakes both ways, underrating campsites as well as overrating them.

Bobby and David arrived shortly, and we put up our tents and hung our food from the bear pole near the eating area. My friend Bob Smith had been here with his daughter two weeks before us. He told me he'd left a business card for us to find under a rock near the bear pole. Bobby and I made a halfhearted search, flipping over eight or ten rocks, all the while figuring that Bob had lied to me. When Bob called me after his trip but before ours, he told me he'd met some young backpackers here and recounted the story of the fatal grizzly attack described in Olsen's book. They, too, thought he was lying. One laughed and asked if there was a sequel called *Night of the Mountain Lions*.

The storm had missed us, passing to the north. In the late afternoon quiet, laughter drifted down the ridgeline from the chalet. We decided to walk back up to investigate. A raucous group of men and women, loud from wine, sat on the front porch. One of the men announced, "We can have multiple orgasms too. It just takes us a week." We toured the old structure and surveyed the bear photos on the wall. I leafed through a paperback on fishing in Glacier, trying to commit it to memory for later in the week. Bobby, David, and I sat on the front porch and enjoyed a luxury—cold drinks purchased from the chalet's refrigerator. The view from up here was spectacular, much better than from the campsite on the slope below.

We walked back down to our tents and heated water for our freeze-dried spaghetti. Even though it was Saturday night in the peak of the backpacking season, we still had the campground to ourselves. Just before dark, however, we heard voices approaching on the trail. We were joined by three young hikers from San Francisco, Eric and Melissa Roza and Chris Turner. They turned out to be the best of camping companions. No campfires were allowed at Granite Park, but the six of us sat in a circle in the cooking area as if we had one. Chris prepared a fancy meal that included couscous. They reported that they'd started the day at Many Glacier, where we would end six days from now, and made the steep climb over Swiftcurrent Pass. The thunderstorm that had narrowly missed us had soaked them. When I asked how they'd come to be in Glacier, Eric pointed to Chris. Chris was the Eagle Scout, Eric said. He'd planned the whole trip. I used the opportunity to do one of my favorite things: bragging on Daddy and his Eagle Scouts and his campouts.

Chris told us a story of camping by himself in Canyonlands National Park in the Utah desert. Far from civilization, he had a flat tire in his rental car and discovered to his great dismay that there was no lug wrench. He figured it was a three-day hike out the way he'd come, but he had only a two-day supply of water. He plotted a cross-country shortcut and made it to a ranger station just before he ran dry.

* * *

Our second day would take us twelve more miles north on the Highline Trail to Fifty Mountain campground. We didn't break camp until ten o'clock, but Eric, Melissa, and Chris, who were also headed for Fifty Mountain, were clearly going to be much later than that. When we hiked out, their tents were still up, and they were just starting breakfast. At the rate they were going, we wondered if they would make it before dark.

As we left the campground, I spotted a mountain goat on the steep slope far above. Bobby wondered if there had ever been a mountain goat with acrophobia. Animals aren't afraid of heights, I declared. Bobby disagreed, citing the black flies of the Cascades that we escaped by climbing.

The first five miles of the day were an ideal walk: a level trail and magnificent scenery. We paralleled the Continental Divide, which towered above us to the east. The peaks of the Livingston Range rose to the west, across the valley through which McDonald Creek flows. From south to north, we could see Heavens Peak, Longfellow Peak, Anaconda Peak, Mount Geduhn, and Trapper Peak. It was a beautiful day, and the walking was easy. My summer of exercise had paid off.

After several miles, the trail swung to the east and crossed a snowdrift. I hiked across and then held my breath as Bobby, top-heavy as always, followed. He'd invested in high-tech walking sticks before the trip and had no problem. The trail continued through the rocky basin beyond the snowdrift, past picture-perfect streams running down the slope. My pack and shoes were comfortable, and the altitude—below 7,000 feet—was not an issue. I made good time and again left Bobby and David behind. I stopped for lunch at another narrow stream, Ahern Creek. I pulled out my raisinets and Bartlett Brothers beef jerky, which I had ordered after *Backpacker* magazine ranked it as the best there is. Bobby and David were slow in arriving, and I asked what had kept them. They said they'd seen three mountain goats above the trail and stopped to watch. Before they left, several marmots appeared, and they watched them too. After lunch, I pulled out the pages I'd copied from Molvar's book about this section of the trail. He wrote, with accuracy: "The rocky basin beyond the snowdrift is prime habitat for mountain goats and marmots, who graze together in the meadows below the cliff walls." This was too much of a coincidence. I decided the goats and marmots Bobby and David had seen were just more props in the great national park show.

From Ahern Creek, the trail wound down for the next two miles through firs and wildflower fields to its lowest point, where it crossed Cattle Queen Creek. The creek was covered by a broad snow bridge left over from the previous winter. Park service employees performing trail maintenance near the creek warned us to hike around the snow bridge rather than over it. The risk of breaking through the snow was too great.

The trail guide added weight to their words, declaring that slipping or falling through spelled certain injury and could even be fatal. Bobby and I chose to hike down the creek bank to a safe crossing and then ascend the other side. David decided to go up first, cross upstream, and then come down. Bobby and I wound up having to bushwhack through dense bush up a steep slope to reach the trail on the other side. David arrived ahead of us and was resting when we rejoined him. He clearly made the better choice, but he didn't make the best one. Several other hikers we spoke to later, none of whom had the benefit of the trail workers' warning, walked across the snow bridge without mishap.

From Cattle Queen Creek, the trail climbed 1,500 feet over the next three miles. As we passed above tree line, another afternoon thunderstorm threatened. Lightning struck to the north as we climbed a scree slope. Marmots and ground squirrels capered among the rock gardens and wildflowers above us. David pointed out a square block of stone near the trail and observed that it looked just like a gravestone. I studied the exposed landscape; it would be winter here soon. I said it wouldn't take long to die if we stayed here. Bobby, who was tired from the long climb near the end of a twelve-mile day, said it would take him about twenty minutes.

The trail continued north, but the Continental Divide, which had been on our right for twenty miles, took a hard left and turned due west. On top of a rocky saddle, as the storm gathered, the trail and divide intersected, and we crossed over to the other side. Raindrops from the coming storm would land close together but wind up far apart. Those falling behind us would run down the slope to McDonald Creek and on to the Pacific. Those falling ahead of us would make their way to the Waterton River and ultimately to Hudson Bay.

From the saddle, we wound down another mile through a beautiful wildflower meadow to Fifty Mountain campground. Among the evergreens in the campsite were a number that were killed by the Flattop Mountain Fire in 1998. As the rain started to fall, we rushed to put up our tents and hang our food. We made it just in time. We climbed into our tents—Bobby and I into mine, David into his—just as the bottom fell out. It was 5:30. The wind whipped the tent flaps, and lightning lit up the sky. The rain fell in sheets. Bobby and I worried about Eric, Melissa, and Chris behind us on the trail, but there was nothing we could do. Bobby took a nap, and I read Hemingway's *To Have and Have Not*. At one point, Bobby came to and asked about the book. I told him it was about rum-running between Cuba and the Keys, that the main character was named Harry Morgan. "Wasn't he in MASH?" Bobby wanted to know. Different Harry Morgan, I explained. Satisfied, Bobby went back to sleep.

After seven o'clock, the rain broke, and we crawled out of our tents. I spotted Eric and Melissa and Chris coming down the trail, soaked to the bone. They'd been caught in the rain both days, while we'd stayed dry. They managed tepid waves. We decided not to cook a full meal but to make do with instant tomato soup. In the cooking area, we met four more backpackers, two brothers from Philadelphia and Boston and a pair of young men in the Navy, one from Montana and the other from Thibodeaux, Louisiana. I asked the one from Montana how the flatlander was doing in the mountains. He demurred, telling me his friend from Louisiana was an Eagle Scout and the stronger hiker of the two. This was the second Eagle Scout I'd met in two days. We are all products of our pasts. The sailor from Louisiana, Chris Turner, and I were all here because we'd learned to love camping when we were Boy Scouts.

* * *

In Chapter 8, I bragged about the performance of my leak-free Walrus tent during our trip to the Tetons in 1998. Three years later, beside Island Lake in the Winds, my Walrus tent leaked. In Chapter 10, when I described the relative merits of hiking in the East versus hiking in the West, I declared that "afternoon thunderstorms are common in the mountains of the West, but a full day of unremitting rain is rare." This, too, proved to be wrong. The rain that began the second afternoon of our trip stayed with us, almost without remission, for two full days.

It rained throughout the night at Fifty Mountain. At least it was raining every time I woke up. Just after daybreak, however, it stopped. We were able to cook breakfast—I had my standard two packs of instant oatmeal and two cups of coffee—and break camp during the short break. We'd taken pains to follow proper bear precautions both nights, hanging our food promptly. When I was loading my backpack at Fifty Mountain, however, I discovered my jerky and raisinets were still in my pack, four feet from the front flap of our tent. But we survived the mistake; the rain kept the bears at bay.

The trio from San Francisco had learned their lesson the day before about lollygagging in camp. They were nearly ready to hit the trail when we were. We were headed in the same direction and for the same ultimate destination, Many Glacier, but we weren't scheduled to stay in the same campsite again. In all likelihood, we would never see each other again. Before leaving, we said goodbye and wished them well.

I studied the sky, searching for a patch of blue, but the weather got worse instead of better. Five minutes after we left camp, the rain began to fall again, and it continued non-stop for the next eight miles. As I sloshed along, I tried to remember the exact words I'd used in the earlier chapter about how it never rains all day in the mountains. Who was I, I asked myself, to issue pronouncements about the weather in the West? I don't live there.

After rising briefly to a saddle at nearly 7,000 feet, the trail descended steeply, dropping almost 2,500 feet in three miles. The downpour was unrelenting. I talked myself into believing that hiking in the rain wasn't so bad—it sure beat making or breaking camp in the rain—but it wasn't so great either. My legs and feet were soaked, and the views were hidden by low clouds. I was out front, hiking by myself and making great time. In the pouring rain, there was no reason to stop or even slow down, and my low center of gravity helped me avoid slipping on the steep, slippery grade. I caught and passed the brothers from Boston and Philadelphia just after reaching the Waterton River. They'd sought shelter under a massive spruce alongside the trail and were eating lunch. They should have gone just a little farther. In another ten minutes, I reached a patrol cabin with a covered porch, where I ate lunch with a young couple from Chicago who were headed for Fifty Mountain. The woman was short and plump—her center of gravity even lower than mine—and I wondered how she'd do on the steep climb ahead of them.

Bobby and David arrived at the hut in an hour. After they took a short break, the three of us pressed on together in the pouring rain. We crossed a footbridge, left the Highline Trail, and turned east on the trail to Stoney Indian Lake and the pass beyond. Over the next three miles, the route regained 2,000 feet as it ascended through an evergreen forest. At four o'clock, the rain finally stopped, but the views behind us to the west were still obscured by clouds. We hiked along Pass Creek, fed by the lake in the cirque above. I spotted a narrow snow bridge spanning the creek and flung rocks, trying to break it. But wearing a backpack ruined my aim, and I gave up after a half dozen attempts.

At last, the trail leveled, and we reached our destination for the night, the campsite at the foot of Stoney Indian Lake. The setting was spectacular. The lake was surrounded on three sides by towering cliffs. Along the north shore was a wildflower meadow in full bloom. The spot reminded both Bobby and me of Blue Lake in the Cascades, but this time we weren't alone. The other tent sites were already taken. We set up our tents in the last remaining spots, which were muddy from the heavy rain. Three hours of daylight remained, and I considered pulling out my fly rod for the first time. The brothers we'd met were already fishing. Before going to the trouble to rig my rod, I checked their progress. They'd had no luck and seen no trout. I watched them cast without success for fifteen minutes and walked around the lake, peering into the crystal-clear water. I saw no movement, no fish. I noted this additional similarity to Blue Lake and left my rod in its case.

The clouds broke up, and we enjoyed a gorgeous sunset. The lousy weather appeared to be over. For dinner, we had Mountain House pasta primavera, which had been such a hit in the Winds. For the third night in a row, we were in a spot where campfires are prohibited. After we cleaned up and the sky grew dark, there was little to do. David turned in first. After Bobby and I finished our after-dinner drinks and cigars, we followed. I put on my ultralight headlamp and read more about Harry Morgan's troubles.

* * *

We woke in the morning to trouble of our own. It was raining again, raining hard. This was getting old. Bobby and I were to be in the mountains for four more days and three more nights. Even if we decided to make a forced march out, we were two days from civilization. There was no good solution. I looked over at Bobby.

"Bobby, please go make me a cup of coffee."

"Sure, honey. You want cream and sugar?"

"Yes, please. And if it's not too much trouble, I'll have French toast and bacon too."

"No problem. I'll be right back."

From time to time, as the morning wore on, the rain stopped, or at least seemed to stop. Each time it happened, I sat up and began to dress. Each time I began to dress, the rain started again. The first and second times, it was funny. The third and fourth, it was not. There was nothing to do but read. By 10:30, Harry Morgan had met his end, we were still in the tent, and it was still raining.

Bobby teases me about my camping constipation, but now his clock-like regularity was working against him. By mid-morning, nature was calling. The downpour continued; Bobby refused to answer the call. As a bear precaution, Bobby had brought an empty plastic big-mouth Miller Lite beer bottle, one of the beers he'd drunk with his new friends at the garbage dump. The bottle was to have one use on the trip. If Bobby needed to pee in the middle of the night, he could use the bottle instead of stumbling out of the tent into the jaws of a grizzly. But nature was calling on Bobby to do more than pee now. He eyed the empty Miller Lite bottle. He picked it up, focusing particular attention on the mouth of the bottle, studying its diameter. Soon he had a plan designed to relieve his discomfort yet keep him dry. But he couldn't do it all by himself. The plan required an accomplice.

"You're my friend, aren't you?" Bobby wanted something; the only question was what.

"Of course I am, Bobby." Agreeing that I was his friend was safe enough.

"Will you do me a favor?" This was predictable.

"Depends. What is it?" I wasn't committing, not without details.

"Hold this beer bottle and let me take a dump in it." I had not predicted this.

I propped myself up on my elbow. I thought of all the times Bobby had made fun of me when I *couldn't* go. This was frontier justice, it seemed to me.

"You really have to go?"

"Big time."

"I'd like to help, I really would, but I don't think so."

"I'll pay you." Nature was no longer calling; now it was screaming.

"Five thousand dollars," I proposed. And for five grand, I would have done it.

"Okay, I'll pay you when we get back." Just like he promised Stephanie he'd never go camping again.

"Nope. Cash on the barrelhead. Now." This was a sure deal killer. He had sixty bucks, and it was in his pack outside in the rain.

"I thought you were my friend." Sure. Friends do this sort of thing all the time.

Bobby pulled on his boots and headed for the pit toilet.

* * *

It was time for us to part ways with David. His hike on this day would be longer and harder than ours, and he was in more of a hurry to get started. We heard him outside, taking down his tent in the rain. Before leaving, he tapped on our tent and wished us well. We did the same. We wouldn't see him again until Friday afternoon, three and a half days later. When he was safely out of earshot, I again tried to figure out his plan.

"What the hell is he thinking? We're just getting to the most spectacular part of the trail. And he's turning around and heading back the way we came. Making that same crappy hike we hiked yesterday the opposite way. The hard way. There's gotta be more to it than the Izaak Walton Inn."

Bobby defended the indefensible, just as he'd defended Stephanie. "I don't know. He said he would probably go all the way to the car tomorrow. He'll be in a dry bed tomorrow night. Doesn't sound too bad to me."

The weather didn't justify it, I insisted. "You know what's going to happen. All things must pass. This rain ain't gonna last forever. David's gonna make it out of the mountains right when the weather gets good."

Bobby capitulated. "You're right. He's a dumbass, all right." We were pleased that it was finally someone else's turn.

We kept waiting for the rain to stop, but we finally gave up. We crawled out of the tent and into the rain at 11:30. All of our fellow campers were long gone. Bobby and I had a miserable breakfast, my oatmeal thinned by the rainwater dripping off the hood of my rain jacket into my bowl. We took down and rolled up my wet tent. It was ultralight no more. Wet clothes also added to the weight of our packs. I pulled my squishing shoes on over my soggy socks. There was no point in sacrificing a dry pair. We broke camp just after noon, hiked around the lake, and began climbing a series of switchbacks up the east face of the cirque. A strong wind blew the rain nearly horizontal. Even with my hood pulled down, I couldn't keep my glasses dry. In good weather, the climb up from this lake would have been as spectacular as the climb up from Blue Lake. But in the driving, blowing rain, what should have been a high point was the low point of our trip. The rain was this year's black flies.

We'd climbed up from Blue Lake on the fourth day of our trip to the Cascades. This was also the fourth day of this trip. As was the case in Washington, having three days under our belts made the ascent up the steep slope easier than we thought it would be. Within half an hour, we reached Stoney Indian Pass and crossed over into the Mokowanis River drainage. The trail guide promised that we would enjoy fantastic views on all sides below the pass, but the author did not account for the weather. The canyon was filled with dense clouds. We heard many waterfalls, the decibel level raised by the rain, but we saw few. Soon, however, we descended into a gorgeous parkland filled with close-up beauty. The park was strewn with flowers and rock gardens and bisected by the river. The beauty far exceeded anything a high-priced landscape architect could conceive. Bobby and I stopped to study a moss-covered ledge with a stream flowing over it. It was lovelier than any man-made fountain. An occasional break in the clouds revealed towering spires on both sides of the valley. Cascades dropped hundreds of feet from the peaks to the valley floor. The falls here all bear Indian names—Paiota, Atsina, and Raven Quiver. The Stoney Indians, who lived here, were cousins of the Assiniboine.

The trail descended into a forest of spruce and fir. The rain continued, and we slogged on. Our itinerary called for us to stay at Upper Glenns Lake, which I'd chosen in part because fires are permitted. This was to be our first night with a campfire. But when we arrived at the campsite at 3:00, the promise of a campfire was a cruel joke. The downpour showed no sign of slowing, and every stick of wood in the forest was waterlogged. We were too.

Bobby and I took a break and caucused. We could stop here as planned, hoping the weather would break and we could build a fire. Or we could press on for another seven miles, gambling that we could find an open spot at Gable Creek, the campground where we were scheduled to stay the next night. We debated the alternatives. The solid gray curtain across the sky made us want to get closer to civilization, to seek an escape route. David's plan wasn't looking so bad after all. If the weather didn't improve, we were ready to make the fifteen-mile march from Gable Creek to Many Glacier the next day. We also figured that backpackers would be fleeing in droves in search of a dry place to sit, eat, and sleep. John Muir had left San Francisco in search of anyplace wild. The search today was for anyplace dry. Surely, we convinced ourselves, there would be an open tent site at Gable Creek. To raise our spirits, I told Bobby the rain was going to stop by four o'clock, as it had the day before. By dark, I declared, we would be sitting by a roaring blaze at Gable Creek. We would be toasting each other with Famous Grouse and Black Bush. The rain would be gone for good. With this fantasy to guide us, and with no good alternative, we kept walking.

And the fantasy, at least the first part of it, came true. At exactly four o'clock, the rain stopped. The clouds began to break up. Near the campsite at Lower Glenns Lake, we met a handsome couple with two handsome children, blondes all. We compared notes and itineraries. I asked if they would be returning to the trailhead by hiking up to Ptarmigan Tunnel and then down to Many Glacier. When the father said they would, I expressed admiration for the children and their ability to make such a tough hike. He said they were seasoned hikers by now, that they'd just spent five weeks in the Bob Marshall Wilderness before coming to Glacier. As we continued down the trail, Bobby and I decided the parents must be school teachers or professors. The children were more fortunate than they knew. All children should get to spend a summer hiking in Montana.

Just before five o'clock, we reached the campground at Cosley Lake. We'd covered more than ten miles in less than five hours. Bobby suggested we stop to investigate, which turned out to be a grand idea. We found a lakeside campsite that was both magnificent and empty. We caucused again. We had no permit for either Cosley Lake or Gable Creek. We'd crossed the permit Rubicon four miles back at Upper Glenns Lake and would be outlaws wherever we stayed. The weather was improving by the minute. An early departure from the mountains no longer seemed likely, getting close to civilization no longer a priority. It was nearly three more miles to Gable Creek, and the campground there might be full. We decided to stay put.

We pitched our tent, changed into dry clothes, and spread our wet clothes and gear on the rocky shore to dry. With no more cloud cover, the view from the shore was something to behold. Waterfalls, freshened by the rain, dropped from the peaks across the lake to the south. Slopes on either side at the west end of the lake framed the mountains beyond. More waterfalls cascaded over the ledges of those peaks. The mountains were so perfect, and framed so perfectly, that they looked artificial, like a backdrop in an old Western. We took pictures, but the pictures didn't do this magnificent place justice. They never do. Bobby and I agreed it was one of the most beautiful places we'd ever seen. Molvar's trail guide got it wrong again. He gave the campground only an average rating, describing it as a site of only moderate scenic value. As we stood on the shore taking it in, Bobby's look changed from awe to a broad grin. "I was just thinking what Brian would say," he said. I knew what he would say. This was definitely the shit.

I studied the breathtaking scene at length, trying to burn it into my memory. Bobby and I reveled in the non-rain. As I watched, rising trout dimpled the surface of the lake. I decided to try my hand, assembled my four-piece backpacking rod, and tied on a fly. I fished for nearly an hour. I didn't raise a fish, but that was fine with me. The combination of the scenery and the rhythm of casting a fly was enough. Trout live in the best places.

As I worked my way down the lake toward the eating area, I spotted movement to my left. Four mule deer—two does and two fawns—came walking toward me along the shore. They, too, or at least the does, were national park veterans. They showed no fear and approached much closer than would any wild deer that has to live in the real world. About thirty feet before they reached me, they angled inland, but not to avoid me. The deer headed straight for the cooking area to look for leftovers. These were no rookies.

After the deer were gone, I spotted another animal moving along the opposite shore of the lake. I summoned Bobby to help identify it. It was a black bear, our first bear of the trip, the first non-car bear of any of our trips. The bear moved slowly among the vegetation, feeding on berries, fattening. Grizzly bears sometimes eat black bears, but this bear ambled along with the nonchalance of a creature secure in its position atop the food chain.

I gave up on fishing, and Bobby and I mixed drinks before dinner. I toasted him for suggesting we stop here. It was 7:30, and we still had the place to ourselves. The day had improved immeasurably. We watched the colors change on the mountains west of the lake. Bobby picked beef stroganoff for dinner. Just as we were finishing, we heard voices. Bobby and I sat quietly, hoping for the best. We were trespassers; we had no right to be here, no permit. The first figure that came into sight looked familiar. It was Chris, our San Francisco friend. Eric and Melissa were right behind him. Bobby and I were delighted but surprised to see them. We had compared itineraries three days earlier, and I was sure they were scheduled to be somewhere else tonight. Chris said they were supposed to have stopped at Mokowanis Junction, four and a half miles up the valley. They had done just what we had, passing by their appointed campground. We were all here by happenstance. We weren't supposed to be here, they weren't supposed to be here, and nobody who was supposed to be here was here. It was perfect. They had walked much farther than we had, covering more than fifteen miles, including the long climb from the Belly River to Stoney Indian Pass. And their packs were much heavier than ours. I looked at Melissa, with a brace on one knee. Like John Colter, she was a badass.

We compared notes on our experiences since we'd last seen each other. They had camped at Kootenai Lake and seen several moose. We were mooseless so far and would remain so for the rest of the trip. Their lowest point during the steady rain of the last two days had occurred at exactly the same site as ours. Three hours after we broke camp in the driving rain at Stoney Indian Lake, they had eaten a late, miserable lunch in the same spot, choking down stale bagels. Eric also reported a most unsatisfactory experience atop the exposed pit toilet there. Bobby chimed in, empathetic. He'd had the same experience, in the same spot, after I refused to hold the beer bottle.

We told them about the black bear we'd seen. I looked across the lake; the bear was still there, still unconcerned. Melissa was especially excited. Eric said she really wanted to see a bear, that their trip was now complete.

But soon we saw another. Chris spotted a huge dark bear on our side of the lake in the meadow about a hundred yards away. The bear was so big that I thought it might be a very dark grizzly. Determining the species of bears based on color can be difficult. Some black bears are brown, some grizzlies nearly black. Thanks to Famous Grouse, my courage was up, my judgment down. I decided to get a closer look. I stalked the bear, approaching to thirty or forty yards. From the lack of a hump between its shoulders, I decided that it was a big black bear instead of a dark grizzly. While I was watching, the bear moved down into the trees between the meadow and the lakeshore and disappeared. Losing sight of the bear sapped my courage, and I retreated to the campsite. Minutes later, in the fading light, we spotted the bear walking away from us along the shore of the lake. This bear, like the one across the lake, was the master of its domain, unconcerned about anything but the search for food.

We returned to the cooking area and watched as Chris prepared another fancy meal. At nine o'clock, we heard more voices approaching in the darkness. The voices took shape, joined us, and introduced themselves: Jake from Utah and Megan from Alberta. After we exchanged pleasantries, I told them there was a huge black bear right below the trail east of us, from where they had just come. I sure wouldn't want to be hiking at night in Glacier, I said. Jake felt the need to explain. He said they had decided to shed the shackles of civilization and had taken off their watches at the trailhead. I thought of John Muir's aversion to clocks, almanacs, orders, and duties. Jake explained that they'd obviously spent way too long in the tent in the rain at Elizabeth Lake before heading this way. They exchanged knowing glances. They had obviously spent a more enjoyable morning than Bobby and I had. I love camping with Bobby, but there's one creature comfort he can't provide, at least not to me. When they finally broke camp, Jake said, it was obviously later than they thought. Then they'd stopped to fish on the Belly River between there and here. The trout were biting, and they had a hard time quitting. All of a sudden, it was dark. He said they'd made a lot of noise during the last hour of their hike.

By now, Chris, Eric, and Melissa were through with dinner. Eric left us briefly and returned with a surprise, a backpacking guitar. This was their fourth night on the trail but his first night to play. He'd carried it more than forty miles without unpacking it. It had been his Marley's chains, at least until now. Eric handed it to me. I'd heard of backpacking guitars but had never seen one. It weighed next to nothing. Eric asked if we had any requests. I was delighted to have music and didn't want to suggest something he didn't know. Jake jokingly requested "Free Bird," Eric played it, and we all sang along.

Eric asked for more requests. Bobby and I were still reluctant to tell him what to play, and he turned to Melissa. She suggested he play something by Steve Earle. Bobby and I looked at each other and grinned. Steve Earle has been one of my favorites for many years. Eric sang several of his songs—"Hardcore Troubadour," "Someday," and one of his best, "My Old Friend the Blues"—and Bobby and I sang along. Ten hours earlier, we had been climbing the switchbacks above Stoney Indian Lake in a driving rain. The day had gone from miserable to perfect. Eric then sang Dylan's "Tangled Up in Blue." He forgot the lyrics halfway through, but Bobby rescued him and led him through the verse about working as a cook in the great north woods. Next was "The Weight" by the Band, one of the great songs of all time. We all took a load off Fannie. We could probably be heard for miles.

If it had been up to me, we would have stayed up the rest of the night singing. Eric was game, as was Bobby, but it had grown cold. With no campfire, we had grown cold too. Bobby and I were willing to suffer, but not Melissa. She'd walked fifteen miles in a knee brace, and Eric's singing was nothing new to her. At midnight, she told him it was time to call it quits. With a campfire, we might have gone all night. The combination of a magnificent setting, great music, great company, and dry weather might have carried us till dawn. Bobby and I thanked Eric for his concert before heading to the tent. When we turned in, Bobby summarized the day: "It started out as a shit sandwich but ended up as filet mignon."

I woke at 7:30 and stuck my head out of the tent. Sunlight and shadows, no clouds and no rain. It was beautiful. Because we'd overshot Upper Glenns by four miles, we had less than three miles to cover today to get to Gable Creek. There was no reason we couldn't dawdle, and it was a perfect day to dawdle.

Before heading to the cooking area for breakfast, Bobby and I walked out to the lakeshore. The sun was rising above the east end of the lake, illuminating the mountains to the west. Both of us took more pictures. My

284

wet clothes had dried by sundown the evening before, but I'd left them out all night. They were now soaking wet from a heavy dew. They had to dry all over again. There was not a ripple on the surface of the lake, and the shore was covered with smooth, flat rocks. It was a rock-skipping paradise. I picked up a rock and started to throw it. Before I let it fly, however, I summoned Bobby and proposed a bet. If I skipped my first rock of the day more than ten times, Bobby had to buy the first round of beers on Friday night. Ten or fewer, I was on the hook. Bobby agreed. I dropped my rock and looked for another one, for the perfect skipping rock. Soon I found it—three inches in diameter, perfectly round, flat but not too thin and not too light. I loosened my shoulder and let fly. We lost count when it reached twenty skips. It was going to be another good day.

Bobby and I walked east along the shoreline. A big mule deer buck came toward us, his antlers covered in velvet. When he spotted us, he turned away from the lake and trotted into the woods. We sat in the cooking area long after we finished breakfast, enjoying the company of our new friends from San Francisco. I spotted a small miracle of nature—a dew-covered spider web illuminated by the morning sun. Chris got out his camera and captured the shining web from several angles.

Chris told us they had initially planned to camp another night, but then realized they couldn't make it out in time to catch their flights on Thursday afternoon if they did. Eric and Melissa were flying south to Jackson Hole for a wedding, Chris home to San Francisco. They had another fifteen-mile day in store today, all the way to Many Glacier, but they seemed in no hurry to get started.

The talk of the Jackson Hole wedding led to the subject of marriages, some good and some not so good. This led inevitably to a discussion of Bobby and Stephanie and the near tragedy involving Bobby's camping gear. While Bobby was down at the lake rinsing his bowl, I told the entire ugly story. Even with a balanced presentation, including Bobby's promise a year ago that Stephanie could throw his gear away if he ever tried to go again, Eric and Melissa stared in disbelief.

We also talked about college. Eric had gone to Michigan and then to Stanford for graduate school. I told them about Ole Miss, claiming it had the greatest concentration of beautiful women in the world. Chris said that's what he thought at first about his school, Santa Clara University. When he visited during the summer, the place was brimming with gorgeous girls. He decided this was for him; he couldn't wait. But when the school year began, the babes were gone, replaced by non-babes. Chris found an upperclassman and questioned him. The older student asked when Chris had visited. He smiled knowingly at Chris's answer. "You were here when they were having high school cheerleader camp."

Over breakfast, I had told the San Francisco trio that I was writing about my travels with Bobby. Eric told me Chris had a story I should include about an evening spent in Nebraska with a pair of gay rednecks and a fashion-challenged amnesiac who went by the name of T-Bone. I was intrigued by the cast of characters. Chris was beside the lake, spreading wet clothes to dry. I walked up the lakeshore and interviewed him about his night in Nebraska. The tale he told follows.

* * *

Chris was en route to the Badlands in South Dakota for a solo camping trip when a hailstorm hit. The radio announcer said the hailstones were the size of golf balls and warned all on the road to seek shelter. Chris headed for Chadron, a small town in northwest Nebraska, found covered parking for his Dodge Neon rental, and checked into a motel. He chose a restaurant downtown, where he ate dinner by himself. It was still early when he finished, and he wasn't ready to turn in. A poolroom adjoined the restaurant. Chris climbed onto a bar stool and bought a beer. Soon he had company.

The company was a man in his early fifties. He said his name was Bill, that he was a college professor visiting from Amarillo. When Chris said he was from San Francisco, Bill's eyes lit up. Just the sound of those two magic words gave Bill reason to hope. Emboldened, he confessed he'd been watching through the window as Chris dined alone in the restaurant next door. "Yep," Bill said, "I saw you eating dinner and I said to myself, 'there's a mighty attractive feller.'"

Well, what do you say in response to that? Chris couldn't think of a thing. After an awkward silence, Bill continued. "Where are you staying?" Chris said he had a hotel room but wisely provided no details. Bill was more specific. "Me too. I'm staying in the Best Western. Room 219. Yep. Room 219." Chris, again, didn't know what to say.

But then Chris was rescued. An odd-looking man walked into the bar. Like St. Nick, he was dressed all in red from his head to his feet, but, unlike St. Nick, he had a thing for Nike. From top down, he wore a red Nike cap, red Nike tee shirt, red jogging shorts pulled up high, and red high-top Nike tennis shoes. He cut a striking figure. All present fell silent. The young man introduced himself to Chris and Professor Bill. He said his name was T-Bone; he asked if either was interested in a game of pool. Chris saw a chance to escape from Bill and accepted the challenge. T-Bone suggested a friendly wager. Chris watched as T-Bone opened his case and screwed his two-piece pool cue together. Chris declined T-Bone's suggestion. When T-Bone proposed stakes of one dollar, however, Chris relented. It's not like they were playing for an old sweatshirt.

T-Bone's fancy cue turned out to be no indicator of ability. He was all cue and no game, all hat and no cattle. Chris won the first game easily. T-Bone coughed up a dollar and asked for a rematch. As T-Bone was leaning over the table for a difficult shot, Chris noted that Professor Bill was studying T-Bone's long legs and short shorts. Bill offered a compliment. "You must be a runner. You sure got nice calves."

All the elements of the scene hurt Chris's game. He shot poorly. T-Bone looked on, leaning on the adjacent pool table. The surly female bartender spotted T-Bone and took umbrage. "Don't sit on the damn pool table." T-Bone tried to protest, but she would have none of it. She was foul-humored and uncompromising. Chris could not concentrate. Moments later, he lost game two and returned T-Bone's dollar. The bitchy bartender saw the money change hands and again took umbrage. "That's it. You're out of here, the both of you. Betting's illegal in this town. We could lose our license." It was now T-Bone's turn to take umbrage. He demanded to see the manager. This was a mistake. "Manager? I'm the *owner*," the bartender said. "Get the fuck out." T-Bone and Chris gave up. They walked out into the night, Professor Bill in tow.

The professor now decided to take his leave. He looked intently at Chris. T-Bone's calves notwithstanding, Chris was still the one. "Maybe I'll see you later. I'm staying in Room 219 at the Best Western, room 219."

Chris wasn't so shocked this time and managed an ambiguous response: "Perhaps our paths will cross again."

Professor Bill left, but the night was still young. Chris and T-Bone headed for the other pool hall in town. This one was more crowded, the bartender more hospitable. But the clientele was not. When they saw T-Bone, they turned away, avoiding eye contact. T-Bone knew a number of them and called them by name. Several turned reluctantly to face him, addressing him as Tommy when they spoke. This was the first time Chris had heard his real name. T-Bone didn't like it a bit. He was T-Bone, he insisted. He demanded to be called T-Bone. A guy at the end of the bar rolled his eyes. "T-Bone. Sure. Whatever."

Another of the patrons walked over and introduced himself to Chris. Like the professor, his name was Bill. When Chris disclosed that he was from San Francisco, the new Bill reacted just as the old one had. His eyes lit up, brimming with optimism. The two Bills had more in common than their names.

When T-Bone went to the men's room, Chris asked the new Bill, "What's the deal with T-Bone?" Bill told the sad tale. Tommy had been the most popular guy in town. He was handsome, a good athlete, smart and funny. He got all the girls. Then one night he was driving home and crossed the railroad tracks. The right of way was overgrown, and the warning lights didn't work. Tommy never saw the train coming. It hit him broadside, T-Boning him. Thus Tommy's new name of choice. Tommy was in a coma for months. When he finally woke up, he couldn't remember a thing. Tommy's whole life before the wreck was a blank. Not only that, but now Tommy was, well, different. At this point in the story, Tommy a/k/a T-Bone was coming out of the men's room. Bill tipped his beer bottle toward T-Bone and his monochromatic outfit to emphasize the point.

When T-Bone rejoined them, Chris offered to buy a round of beers. Both Bill and T-Bone seemed touched. T-Bone said he could only have an O'Doul's because of the medication. When Chris returned from the bar, Bill changed the subject to himself. He felt a certain closeness to Chris, just as the other Bill had. He confided that he was frustrated with Chadron. People here just didn't understand him; he didn't fit in. Plus there was the matter of a job. He'd tried ranching and farming, but neither was for him. His true calling, he told Chris, lay in interior design. Chris looked around at the poolroom clientele and thought of what he'd seen of Chadron so far. He then offered some obvious advice: if Bill wanted to be an interior designer, he might have to go someplace else. Bill nodded appreciatively and said he might just do that.

At closing time, Chris offered to give both Bill and T-Bone a ride home. When T-Bone saw the rented Neon, he became ecstatic. He rubbed the hood. He wanted to know what kind of car this was, how fast it would go. He asked Chris if he could drive. Chris said sure. When Chris told me about his night in Chadron, he didn't say how many beers he'd drunk in the two bars. His decision to let T-Bone drive suggests that it was more than a few.

Once behind the wheel, T-Bone became even more excited. He was dying to fire the Neon up, to see what this baby would do. Chris wouldn't hand over the keys until T-Bone promised he wouldn't go over thirty. T-Bone objected, declaring that he knew all the cops and wouldn't get a ticket. Chris was less worried about a ticket than a train. T-Bone finally agreed and drove home slowly, without incident, sulking all the way. Chris then drove Bill the rest of the way to his house. Bill had been pondering Chris's advice to venture out, to leave Chadron. Before saying goodnight, he told Chris he might just head west and check out San Francisco. Chris said he knew of some spots in the city Bill would probably just love. They shook hands, and Chris drove back to his hotel. Before he got out of the car, Chris sat for a minute and considered the evening. He smiled and shook his head, marveling at the absurdity of it all.

When Chris got through telling the story, I asked him, "Did you ever get the feeling they were all actors—T-Bone, both Bills, the bitchy bartender?"

"Maybe so," Chris said. He looked up and smiled. "Maybe so."

* * *

T-Bone's two-piece pool cue reminded me of my exploits at the Corral Bar in Pinedale. Consistent with the principle that it's okay to brag if you don't have to change the subject, I told Chris the story of my bear/deer/beer sweatshirt conquest at the end of our trip to the Winds. He pronounced it a great story. I said that the characters in his were more interesting.

I walked back along the shoreline. Melissa was busy packing, but not Eric. The freest spirit of the three, he had his guitar out and was singing to the day. When I got close enough, I recognized the tune—"And It Stoned Me" by Van Morrison, another of my favorites. I sang along again. At the end, like the night before, Melissa told Eric it was time to stop. "Just one more," he said. They both laughed. Eric said this was always the way. It would be time to stop, time to leave. Melissa would say so. And Eric would always respond the same way: just one more.

They were finally ready to leave. Before Eric put his pack on, I picked it up. It weighed at least fifteen pounds more than mine. They had noticed, with some envy, that our packs were smaller and lighter than theirs and asked how we did it. Bobby and I explained the process and offered advice. We'd come a long way as backpackers in two short years. In August of 2000, Bobby had struggled up the trail in the Cascades with an overloaded pack, gear swinging from side to side on the outside and a full bottle of Williams Lectric Shave on the inside, and now he was giving advice.

We exchanged email addresses, and I promised to send them this chapter when I finished it. When I did, and Eric read it, he responded that he found it amusing that I thought he was a free spirit. He said he was a total Type A, focused and intense. Maybe, I suggested, the mountains make free spirits of us all. John Muir got it right. In Glacier, Eric's cares had "dropped off like autumn leaves."

After they headed up the trail, I looked at my watch. It was noon; they would be lucky to get to Many Glacier before dark. Bobby and I talked about the San Francisco crew as we ate lunch. We had both been hesitant about returning to Glacier because we wouldn't be able to camp alone. Solitude—time away from the madding crowds—is one of the reasons we go camping, and we hadn't wanted to share our campsites. But Bobby and I agreed that our time with Eric, Melissa, and Chris had been one of the highlights of our trip.

Since the trip to Glacier, we have kept in touch with these new friends. I had dinner with all three while on business in San Francisco, camped with Chris in Colorado, and spent a football weekend at Ole Miss with Eric and Melissa, who had moved from San Francisco to Franklin, Tennessee, just south of Nashville. When they moved to Boulder, my wife Carrie and I spent a weekend with them there. Funny how little things in life turn into big things. Had we not all wound up at Cosley Lake, had we not all camped there as outlaws, we would never have seen each other again. When we camped together at Glacier, the Rozas had no children and I had no grandchildren. Now they have four, and I have four.

* * *

Like us, Jake and Megan had a short day ahead. Also like us, they were in no hurry to leave Cosley Lake. I walked past them as they sat on the shoreline soaking it all in—the lake, the mountains, the waterfalls. I remembered that they were watchless. When they looked up at me, I looked down at my watch.

"Hard to believe it's already 4:15," I said casually. It was really 1:20.

Jake wasn't buying. "It's not 4:15." He laughed, a sort of forced laugh. Then he looked over his shoulder at me. "Is it really 4:15?"

I looked down at my watch again. I started to answer, but then caught myself. "I'd tell you, but you said you didn't want to know. Remember?" Jake looked away. He studied the angle of the sun. He didn't know me, and he wasn't sure.

A few minutes later, it was my turn not to be sure. Near the cooking area, Jake pointed to two berry-laden bushes. The berries on one were white, on the other blue. Jake said two of the white berries would kill a grown man, but the blue berries were tasty and harmless. He picked two blue ones and offered them to me. Jake seemed like a good guy—surely he wouldn't kill me just because I lied about what time it was—so I took the blue berries and ate them. They were good, and they had no ill effects. Jake was more trustworthy than I was.

After some more unsuccessful fishing, Bobby and I walked back up the shore to our tent and began packing. We looked down the lake, and Jake and Megan had ventured into the deep water and were skinny dipping. Megan watched us watching her and gave us a big wave. She was young and attractive, and Bobby and I were on our fifth day in the mountains. We considered walking back down the shoreline to block her exit. We could trap her. Eventually she would have to come out; we would get a closer look. But we thought better of the plan. It would be poor manners, and Jake was a big guy.

Bobby and I decided a little lake water and hygiene wouldn't hurt us either. We walked up the lake, where a curve in the shoreline took us out of Jake's and Megan's sight. Bobby stripped down, walked out, and dived in. I was more cautious. I left my clothes on the bank and walked out to thigh depth, but that was as far as I would go. I bent over and washed my hair and face and armpits, but I wouldn't go all the way under. It was just like at Island Lake in the Winds. There was a limit to what I would do to be clean. As I rinsed my hair, I looked down the lake and realized that I'd walked out too far; the curve of the shoreline was no longer protecting me from Jake and Megan. I was now in plain view. The water was ice cold. I thought of the Seinfeld show about George Costanza and shrinkage. We returned to shore, dressed, and rejoined Jake and Megan. She asked about our swim. I told her I couldn't bring myself to walk out to the magic depth. Megan laughed; she knew just what I meant. I wondered if women have a magic depth.

Finally we broke camp, wished Jake and Megan well, and began the short hike to Gable Creek. Not far from camp, above the meadow where we'd last seen the big black bear, the trail wound through a dense berry patch. The bushes were high; our view was obstructed.

"Look at all these berries," I observed. "You know what likes berries, don't you, Bobby?"

"Squirrels and chipmunks?" Bobby was playing dumb.

"That's not all, Bobby. What else? What else likes to eat wild berries?"

"Euell Gibbons? He eats berries, doesn't he?"

"Euell Gibbons died years ago, Bobby. What else?"

But we made plenty of noise, and the bears, if there were any, left us alone. On the Mokowanis River, below the outlet of Cosley Lake, we came to Gros Ventre Falls. We left our packs unattended, leaning them against the sign that warned not to leave packs unattended, and walked down to the riverside to get a closer look. The river spilled over a steep rock ledge at the head of a deep pool. It looked like it ought to be full of trout. We considered fishing, but we had left our rods with our packs. We climbed back up to the trail and soon reached a swinging bridge over the Belly River, flowing north en route to Hudson Bay. A sign said only one hiker at a time was allowed on the bridge. This time, we obeyed. First Bobby, then I, studied the river from the bridge, looking for fish. We saw none but were not discouraged. We decided to return to the river with our rods after making camp.

Just east of the river, we crossed Gable Creek and reached our campsite for the night. It was nice but too civilized. There were handsome views of the surrounding peaks, but we were within a hundred yards of a horse paddock and two hundred yards of the Belly River Ranger Station. Molvar had given this campground a higher rating than Cosley Lake, but it wasn't even close.

The company wasn't even close either. In the end, however, our new campmates proved to be highly entertaining. One of our fellow campers was a young man from Sand Point, Idaho. He was backpacking by himself because his friends had bailed out on him at the last minute. He was intelligent and normal. The other two hikers at Gable Creek were neither. They provided the entertainment.

The two were from Minnesota. Both had long, scraggly ponytails. From the minute we arrived, the younger one, who looked to be in his forties, launched into a tirade about the travails they had endured hiking and camping in the rain. The older one was the silent type. He had gray hair and a handsome handlebar mustache. He was also adorned with tattoos and festooned with jewelry. One tattoo in particular caught my eye: a faded bighorn ram on his right wrist. I studied it, comparing it to the real thing we'd seen on the Highline Trail four days earlier. The tattoo looked older. Four huge turquoise rings complemented the array of tattoos. The centerpiece of the display was a huge silver and turquoise talisman hanging from his neck. The poor guy must have been toting five pounds even before he picked up his pack, and he could ill afford the extra weight. He was not much over five feet tall and was wearing size thirty Levi's. I figured him for 125 pounds, dripping wet and bejeweled.

And dripping wet is what they had been. Bobby and I listened as the younger one complained about the hardships they had suffered during the two days of rain. A day earlier, their clothes and sleeping bags soaking wet, they had retreated to this point, coming the eight miles down the valley from Mokowanis Lake. Their quest, like that of the protagonist in Jack London's short story, was to build a fire. They had succeeded in achieving little more than a smolder, but at least they didn't freeze to death. They had spent all day today drying their gear and eating their food, preparing for the uphill hike to the trailhead. The young one said they'd been eating non-stop to cut down on the weight they would have to carry out. They'd sat by the smoky fire, gobbling granola bars and home-made beef jerky. Unless their digestive system worked faster than mine, they weren't accomplishing a thing. They were just shifting weight from their backpacks to their bellies. Either way, they would have to pack it out.

As the younger one spoke, I noted their attire. They were wearing jeans and cotton flannel shirts, both absorbent and slow to dry. I also surveyed the vast array of gear spread around them. From the bear cable hung two large food bags. Both were suspended from thick ropes nearly an inch in diameter. Below the cable were two heavy, insulated water bottles. Whether the insulation was to keep the water hot or keep it cold, I couldn't decide. An empty carton of Marlboros lay on the ground beside three pint bottles of Jack Daniels. The thick glass bottles themselves must have weighed more than a pound. Not surprisingly, they were empty too. On a nearby log was a portable cassette player. Let me repeat—*a portable cassette player*. It had to weigh five pounds and was as big as my sleeping bag. But it wasn't as big as theirs. Out of the corner of my eye, I spotted an oversize, quilted sleeping bag spread on some bushes to dry. It was a ten-pound cotton bag, green on the outside, with pheasants depicted on the flannel lining. It was the kind that's suitable only for car camping and sleepovers, the kind that's as big as a beer keg when you roll it up, the kind that only the clueless would dream of taking on a backpacking trip.

That was just it: These guys were clueless. As Bobby and I searched for an open tent site, we spotted their tent. It was one of those ten by ten family tents, big enough to stand up and walk around in. Compared to my tent, it was a circus tent. My tent weighed less than five pounds. The Minnesotans' tent, with its complex system of inch-thick aluminum poles, must have weighed at least twenty. Bobby and I stopped on the trail and stared in amazement. Bobby summed it up: "These guys are car camping without the car."

Before our trip, I had never spent any time in Minnesota or any time with Minnesotans. As a result of my ignorance, I was guilty of overgeneralizing, of stereotyping. I lumped all Minnesotans together, viewing them as sophisticated, intelligent, and politically liberal. I would have considered "Minnesota redneck" an oxymoron. I should have known better. After all, what other state has ever elected a pro wrestler as governor? But I didn't know better, at least not until now. The conclusion was undeniable; these guys were rednecks. When we were out of earshot, Bobby gave them nicknames. The young, talkative one he named Yahoo. Not *the* yahoo, not *a* yahoo, just Yahoo. The older, bejeweled one was Little Yahoo. Collectively they were Yahoos.

After putting up our tent, we returned to the cooking area to hang our bear bag. The cable was higher than in other campgrounds, and it took me six or seven tries before I was able to throw our twine over the top. Yahoo found me amusing, which seemed only fair, as amusing as I found him. Bobby and I borrowed their ax, chopped wood to contribute to the night's campfire, and then walked back to the Belly River to fish.

We climbed down the slope and waded into the current. Bobby had only a spinning rod. It was of little use in the swift water, so he decided to sit on the bank and watch. And I put on a show, but not by catching fish. I worked my way downstream, fishing the riffles and pools with no luck. As I headed back up, I stepped on an especially slippery rock. I teetered and started to fall. I struggled to gain purchase, just as Bobby had on the snowy trail in the Tetons. Like Bobby, I failed. I, too, landed face down, but at least I had the water to break my fall. I climbed back to my feet and performed a self-assessment. At first I thought the only casualty was my disposable Kodak camera. I pulled it from my pocket; water dripped out. But then I realized my pill bottle full of dry flies was missing. I looked around, but it was long gone, headed downstream to Canada. We had other flies, however, and Bobby had a camera, so the fallout from my fall was still insignificant. But then I realized that one of my toes was hurting. It was the one next to my little toe on my right foot. My ring toe, if there is such a thing. I tried to wiggle it; the pain increased. I waded to the bank, where Bobby and I examined it. It was already purple and swollen. Bobby was as sympathetic as I had been when he split his head open in the Tetons. His comment made clear that he thought turnabout was fair play: "I guess I'm not the dumbass this time. David either."

I had asked Sam Morris, an old and dear friend who lives in Bailey, Colorado, to go with us to Glacier. He and Bobby don't know each other, but they are kindred spirits. I wanted to introduce them, then sit back and enjoy. Sam loves to camp, but he had to decline. He responded by email that he would love to go to Glacier with Bobby and me more than life itself, but he was too old, too fat, and too arthritic. He might keep up for a day, he wrote, but then Flight for Life would have to fly him back to civilization. As Bobby and I studied my toe, I told him of Sam's response. "I don't guess they send Flight for Life for a broken toe," I concluded. I limped slowly back to camp. In less than twenty-four hours, I'd gone from singing with Eric beside Cosley Lake to camping with Yahoos with a broken toe. On our roller coaster of a trip, I was down to rock bottom again.

This was our only night of the trip with a campfire, but the wood was still wet, and there was more smoke than flame. As we cooked dinner, we learned more about the lives of Yahoo and Little Yahoo. We were surprised to learn that they both owned tepees: large, expensive replicas of the real things. They traveled to fairs and trade shows, where they set up the tepees and performed demonstrations. They told us about the key tepee features that let smoke from campfires out but keep rain from getting in and that keep the tepee standing in hundred-mile-an-hour winds. It was interesting, but I couldn't see the point in Yahoos' tepee hobby, which sounded neither lucrative nor enjoyable. I suppose it gave them a chance to meet other tepee owners. Maybe there are even tepee groupies.

The talk turned from tepees to the mountain men and fur trappers of the 1800s. Yahoos fancied themselves mountain men, but no real mountain man ever had a cassette player. Bobby and Yahoo discussed a movie about the old West starring Brian Keith and Charlton Heston. When Bobby quoted from memory one of Brian Keith's lines—"I've never been lost in the mountains; disoriented for a month or two maybe, but never lost"— Yahoo grew visibly excited. He remembered the line too. When I told the John Colter stories that are included in the chapter about our trip to the Tetons, Yahoo hung on every word. Then it was his turn. He told us about a book he owned that was his pride and joy. The book was about mountain men; it dated from 1852. He said it even had fancy pictures on fancy paper. In describing the book, Yahoo got so worked up that he reached a point of resolution. He announced that he had made an important decision. "I'll tell you what I'm gonna do," he vowed. "When I get home, this is what I'm gonna do. I'm gonna take that book out, and I'm gonna *read* it." What we have here, I thought to myself, is truly a man of letters.

I had made Bobby promise not to tell Yahoos about my toe. I was afraid they would want to examine it and try to set it or something. Bobby betrayed me. After dinner, looking at me to gauge my reaction, he revealed that I'd fallen in the river and broken my toe. Neither Yahoo stirred. Despite their interest in tepees, neither, apparently, was a medicine man. A few minutes later, they said goodnight and headed for their cavernous tent. I felt sorry for them. They'd driven twenty hours non-stop from Minneapolis, hitting a deer along the way and damaging Little Yahoo's new pickup. Their time in the mountains had been undone by weather and bloated packs. But I had to give them credit. Before turning in, they were talking about where they would go camping next year. Yahoo said they were considering Sequoia National Park in California. I asked if they'd ever seen a giant sequoia. They said no, and Yahoo became excited again when Bobby and I told them about the big trees. After they retired to their tent, we stayed by the fire with the young backpacker from Idaho. He was good company, but he couldn't compete with Yahoos for entertainment value. We said goodnight at ten and turned in.

The next morning, Yahoos spread all their gear in the cooking area to pack. It looked like a multi-family garage sale. Even rolled up tight, Little Yahoo's sleeping bag was five times as big as mine. While Bobby and Little Yahoo were down at the creek filtering water, Yahoo studied the scene in disgust. He nudged the cassette player with his toe. He picked up a first aid kit, which they'd undoubtedly bought just for the trip. He opened the kit and studied it; something caught his eye. He removed the offending object and held it up for me to see. "A tongue depressor. A fucking tongue depressor. Why in God's name would we need a fucking tongue depressor?" I couldn't say, but the tongue depressor was the least of their worries. It weighed next to nothing in comparison to a cassette player.

Shortly after breakfast, a park ranger named Ezra came into camp. He walked back to the tent sites to make sure we had our permits properly displayed and then returned to the cooking area, looking confused. Our permit was for three, David included, but we had only my tiny two-person tent. Either somebody was missing, or the three of us were extremely close. I told him David had gone back a different way, and he asked why. When Bobby told him that David had split off so he could get back a day early

297

and spend a night at the Izaak Walton, the ranger looked confused again. He couldn't understand either.

Ezra was pleased to see that our food was hanging from the bear cable. He said they had to have strict, clear rules, that if they didn't, some backpackers would inevitably do something stupid. Yahoo agreed. He offered a pearl of wisdom: "You gotta have strict rules. Cause it's just like I always say, some people are just smarter than others."

Well, who could argue with that? I had but to look around the campsite to see the clear and undeniable truth of Yahoo's words. We were surrounded by evidence—compelling evidence—that some people are definitely smarter than others. Before saying anything, I surveyed the evidence: the keg-size sleeping bags, the cassette player, the thick Jack Daniels bottles, the circus tent. I sneaked a peek at Bobby; he looked away to keep from laughing.

After composing himself, Bobby offered a suggestion to the ranger. It sure would be nice if the Park Service provided some kind of trading post for backpackers. Hikers coming off the trail could turn in unused fuel and pepper spray and uneaten food. Other backpackers could then make use of the leftovers. "Take pepper spray," Bobby said. "A canister costs forty bucks, and they won't let you take it on a plane. So we'll just have to throw ours away. And this is the next to last day of our trip. Chances are, we won't be using it."

"Speak for yourself," I interrupted. "I'm gonna blast me a couple of ground squirrels."

Yahoo cut his eyes at me and laughed. "I forgot. You're from Mississippi." Bobby and I looked at each other. He winked. We were thinking the same thing: Yahoo thinks *we're* the rednecks.

We needed to break camp to make the short hike to Elizabeth Lake, where we hoped that good fishing awaited. But I wasn't eager to try out my broken toe, and Bobby and I couldn't tear ourselves away from the spectacle of Yahoos' packing. Trying to lighten their loads, they repeatedly offered us food, but we weren't taking. They somehow squeezed everything in. Their enormous packs were filled to the brim, the seams stretching. When everything was loaded, they stood back and admired their handiwork. I was about to congratulate them when Yahoo looked at Little Yahoo and said, "Okay, let's go get that fucking tent." Their tent was behind me; I thought they'd already packed it. It was a bigger problem than the tongue depressor, but they somehow strapped it on. Fully loaded, Yahoos' packs were gargantuan. They looked like those Sherpa packs on Mount Everest documentaries. They made Bobby's pack in the Cascades look like a knapsack. A backpacking rule of thumb is that your pack should not exceed one-third of your body weight. Little Yahoo's load, not counting the jewelry and the extra food he ate, had to weigh as much as he did.

Before they left, Yahoo said they were looking forward to their next trip. They'd learned a lot this year, he added. They asked us a few questions, which we answered, but we didn't volunteer much. Bobby and I figured that they may have been dumb, but they weren't blind. Yahoos and the hiker from Idaho were headed for the same destination: the trailhead at Chief Mountain Customs on the Canadian border. The young man left first. As he studied Yahoos' enormous packs, he said he had a cooler of beer waiting for him in his car. He promised to hide a couple in the wheel well of Yahoos' new pickup. Sympathy beers and proof that backpackers are kind to one another.

Bobby said later that Yahoos reminded him of another movie about mountain men, *Jeremiah Johnson*. Jeremiah, played by Robert Redford, met up with elderly mountain man Bear Claw Chris Lapp, played by Will Geer. Bear Claw no longer trapped, but he still hunted grizzly bears for their teeth. With Bear Claw's help, Jeremiah later became a real mountain man, but this was early in the movie and he was still green. After observing Jeremiah's lack of skills and concluding that he wouldn't last long in the wilderness, Bear Claw told him, "Whatever you learned down in the flat will do you no good up here. You've got some work to do." And so it was with Yahoos.

* * *

The trail from Gable Creek to the foot of Elizabeth Lake was little more than three miles long and nearly level. We had planned a short hike this day to give us plenty of time to fish. Molvar's trail guide gave Elizabeth Lake top ratings as a fishery for both rainbow trout and grayling. Bobby was skeptical. "He got the campsites bassackwards. I bet there ain't a frickin fish in the whole lake." But I wasn't ready to give up on Molvar. He

299

had written that the Belly River was generally considered poor for fishing. As I gingerly pulled on my right shoe, I was thinking how right he was.

It was another beautiful day, and hiking with a bad toe wasn't nearly as painful as I had feared, not nearly as bad as the blisters in the Winds. We walked through a forest of lodgepole pines and then descended to another suspension-bridge crossing of the Belly River. One at a time, as the sign directed, we crossed to the west side. We took turns standing on the bridge looking and listening, enjoying the sights and sounds of a mountain stream in the morning sunlight. We soon arrived at a short spur trail that dropped to the base of Dawn Mist Falls, fed by a creek coming down the slopes west of the river. The waterfall cascaded over the rock of the Lewis Overthrust sill. Beautiful yellow wildflowers dotted the opposite shore of the creek below the falls. The flowers loved shade and moisture, and they had plenty of both.

Shortly before reaching our campsite at the foot of Elizabeth Lake, we came to a fresh pile of berry-filled scat in the trail. The scat was enormous, as thick as my forearm. I started in on the same medley I'd sung on our first trip to Glacier.

When we got to the campsite, Bobby and I discovered that grizzlies weren't the only hazard. The food-hanging area had not only a cable but also a half dozen five-gallon plastic buckets with lids. The danger here was such that hanging food fifteen feet off the ground was not enough; it also had to be secured in one of the buckets. The reason, a sign explained, was to protect the food from flying squirrels.

We ate lunch—I was sick of beef jerky by now but never got tired of my raisinets—and then hung our food in one of the squirrel-proof buckets. After picking a site and pitching our tent, we began the two-and-a-half-mile hike to the head of the lake. Hikers had told us the fishing was best where the Belly River flowed into the lake. The trail along the west shore of the lake provided spectacular views. Natoas Peak and Mount Merritt towered above us to the west, Gable and Seward Mountains across the lake to the east. Ahead of us to the southwest was Ahern Peak. Snowmelt from Ahern Glacier, which nestles against the Continental Divide, is the source of the runoff that forms the Belly River. To the southwest, we thought we could see the trail rising along Ptarmigan Wall and then disappearing into the tunnel, the same tunnel we'd hiked through from the other side with Brian and David five years earlier. We met a group of four men on their way to Helen Lake, another three miles to the south. They asked us to be on the lookout for eight guys from Cleveland with whom they were to rendezvous the next day.

At the south end of the lake, I changed into my Tevas and waded out into the icy water alongside the inlet stream. Bobby and I could see fish rising. I dropped my dry fly into the water and let the current take it into deep water. After half a dozen attempts, a nice fish rose and inhaled my fly. I set the hook, and the fight was on. Rainbows are jumpers. This fish didn't jump, so I decided it was a grayling. The fish tired after two or three minutes, and I slid it toward me. When the fish spotted me, however, it summoned its last energy and flopped violently. The fly came flying; the fish swam back to safety. It was just as well. Fresh fish would have been great after five straight dehydrated dinners, but Bobby and I had already decided we would release anything we caught. After seeing the elephant-size bear scat on the trail, neither of us was willing to hike back to camp at dusk carrying fresh fish. Even Yahoos weren't that dumb, Bobby observed.

Soon I hooked another fish. This one was smaller than the first one—the big ones always get away—but this time I landed it. I held it aloft as Bobby photographed it with our remaining camera. I forgot to use the old fisherman's trick—thrusting the fish toward the camera to make it look bigger than it really is. From its large dorsal fin, I identified the fish as a grayling, my first ever. It was maybe fourteen inches long. After Bobby snapped the picture, I released it.

Bobby was casting from the shore, avoiding the frigid water. A few minutes later he caught a grayling himself, a little smaller than mine. Then the clouds rolled in, the wind picked up, and the fish quit biting. At about 4:30, we began to see lightning in the sky to the west. Bobby called it quits and headed back to camp. My feet were completely numb—at least my toe didn't hurt—but I was still reluctant to give it up. This was our last shot at fishing, and one was not enough. I kept at it for thirty more minutes, but neither the weather nor the fishing got any better. I packed up my fly rod, dried my feet, and changed back into my hiking shoes. I hurried back along the lake, singing Eric's Steve Earle medley to scare away the source of the scat Bobby and I had found on the trail.

The eightsome from Cleveland we were told to be looking for had arrived at the campsite shortly before Bobby made it back. They turned out to be great guys, but only after making a terrible first impression. When I made it to the north end of the lake, Bobby was waiting. He was pissed.

"You're not gonna believe what those bastards have done."

"What?" I was surprised. The other four members of their group seemed like good guys.

Bobby decided to show me. "Come look."

We walked to our tent site. Two more tents now crowded the same spot. This would never do. This was our last night in the mountains. The invasion of our privacy was intolerable. I studied the guys who had put up the tents. They were all our age or older. At least one of them would snore all night and keep us awake; there was no doubt about it. I didn't want to demand that they move—after all, we had to share the same cooking area—but we had to do something. I approached the subject gingerly. "Are all the other tent sites full?" One of them looked up and gave a tired nod. Bobby and I decided to see for ourselves. He went one way; I went the other. We returned minutes later, both shaking our heads. Three of the tent sites were still empty. Figuring out what had happened was easy. This was their first day. They had started at Many Glacier, climbed 2,500 feet to Ptarmigan Tunnel, and then descended more than that to the lake. They didn't mean any harm, but when they got here, they were just too tired to look. I offered this explanation to Bobby, but he thought it was lame: "There's a map at the eating area that shows all the tent sites. These guys must be dumber than Yahoos."

I reported to the invaders that there were several open sites. They didn't stir. Bobby and I were willing to flip a coin to decide who would move. We even considered taking down our tent and moving it without saying another word. This would hardly be fair, but surely they would feel guilty. That would give us at least some satisfaction. Before we could do anything, however, another member of the eightsome—one of the younger ones—intervened. Bobby overheard him telling the guys in our site they needed to move, that we surely didn't come all the way to Glacier to camp with a bunch of people we'd never met. The four finally stirred from their lethargy and began moving their gear. Bobby and I pitched in and helped.

We now had our tent site back to ourselves, and the threatening weather had passed us by. Bobby and I had rationed our whiskey so we would have plenty left for our last night. I mixed a Famous Grouse and water. He poured himself a straight Black Bush and called me a candy-ass for diluting mine. I rigged up my chair kit, and we walked down to the lakeshore for happy hour. The slopes west of the lake were growing dark, but the sun still lit the peaks to the east. The surface of the lake was perfectly slick. Fish occasionally rose to the surface, but they were too far out to tempt us. When the ripples cleared, the reflections of the surrounding peaks returned. Bobby and I sat in silence for a minute or two. Then I lifted my cup and offered a toast. "To you and me and the great outdoors."

Bobby then offered one of his own. "To the Almighty, for making all this."

I have written about my skepticism of those who claim to have it all figured out. I have little patience for those who are perfectly willing to condemn to eternal damnation anyone who doesn't believe as they do. But it really is hard to go to places like Cosley Lake and Elizabeth Lake, places so magnificent you just shake your head, and not believe there's a guiding hand. I suppose it could all be the result of happenstance, but it doesn't seem possible.

I thought about David. "Wonder what David's doing. I guess he's at the Izaak Walton."

"I can't believe he did that," Bobby answered. "Yahoo was right. Some people really are smarter than others."

As we sat and sipped our drinks, one of the Cleveland crew called out from down the shoreline and invited us to join them in the cooking area for wine and cheese. After our bad start, Bobby didn't want to, but I told him we should give it a try. It turned out that our first impression had been wrong. The eight men from Cleveland turned out to be more great camping companions. They ranged in age from 41 to 72; the oldest was Jim, the youngest Chris. They said that a few of them had started going on an annual camping trip fifteen years earlier. The group had grown steadily since then. Chris said this was only his second trip and his very first time to hike in the mountains of the West. He was thrilled with his first day in Glacier.

They tried to get us to drink their wine, but we already had drinks of our own. They also offered cheese and pepperoni. Bobby took them up on it, but not me. I had already diluted my drink with water. I didn't want to dilute it further with food, at least not yet. They were good hosts and kept handing the plate of cheese and crackers and sausage my way, urging me to reconsider. I didn't want to appear to be an ungrateful guest, so I explained. "This is the last night of our trip. We're gonna eat later, but first we're gonna get a little bit drunk." This they understood.

Bobby was impressed that Jim and the other older members of the group had come from Many Glacier and climbed to Ptarmigan Tunnel. Chris said it had been a tough day. The guys who were in better shape had been forced to carry some of the others' gear. They had taken nine hours to cover the ten miles.

After I'd mixed a second drink, still undiluted by food, they asked about our trip so far. Bobby tends to clam up in big groups, but not me, especially not when I'm a little bit drunk. I described our roller coaster of a trip and told them about our two days of rain. One of them asked if it had rained hard. I answered without hesitation: "Like a cow pissing on a flat rock." I picked up this expression years ago from a redneck named Tommy with whom I built swimming pools one summer during high school. The guys from Cleveland loved it. I also recounted the day the weather and our trip changed for the better, starting with rain at Stoney Indian Lake and ending with music at Cosley Lake. I quoted Bobby, telling them the day began as a shit sandwich and wound up as filet mignon. They loved that one too.

The Cleveland crew had several different backpacking stoves, but all required complicated assembly, pumping, and priming. More than ten minutes elapsed from the time they pulled out the stoves until they were cooking. When Bobby and I were ready to cook, he got his ultralight GAZ canister stove, screwed it to the top of the canister, and fired it up. The process took all of thirty seconds. Several of the guys from Cleveland picked up Bobby's stove and admired it. They had also noticed that our packs were smaller and lighter than theirs, even though they were camping for only three nights compared to our six. They asked how we did it, and we again offered advice. As it turned out, our packs were lighter—or at least looked lighter—than any others we saw during our seven days on the trail.

After everyone had eaten and cleaned up, the Cleveland guys made toddies of apple cider and 151 proof rum and passed them around. Someone suggested we move the party to the lakeshore. We lined up facing the lake, spotted shooting stars, and picked out constellations. The moon had not yet risen. I shied away from the fire-water toddies, but not Bobby. The rum helped him overcome his shyness in large groups, and he told a story.

* * *

Several years earlier, Bobby began, his daughter Allison, who was then four, asked him one night if she could paint his toenails. It wasn't real polish, just the play stuff that washes off with water, so he said sure. Allison chose hot pink with silver sparkles and did a commendable job for one so young. As his toenails dried, Bobby dozed off. He wound up sleeping on the couch, just as he had before coming to Montana.

Bobby woke early the next morning, dressed in the dark, and headed for the Navy Seabee base to work out. Covered by shoes and socks, his pink toenails were out of sight and out of mind. After working out, he undressed to take a shower, never looking down. Several other men were already in the large communal shower. Bobby was soaping himself up, chattering away, when he noticed the pink polish. In a panic, he rubbed his toes with his feet, but the washable polish didn't wash off. He tried covering one foot with the other, but the top foot remained exposed. He looked around to see if the others had noticed. If so, they weren't saying. But he outranked them all, which may have explained their silence. Bobby started to mutter an explanation, but then thought better of it. He decided to keep his mouth shut and hide his toes as well as he could. After he dried off, he dressed in a hurry, socks first.

I second-guessed Bobby's judgment. "You should have told them the whole story."

"Why?"

"Because you had an innocent explanation, a funny explanation."

"But they didn't act like they'd noticed. Nobody said anything."

"You're a major, Bobby. What were they going to say? 'Major, your toenails are hot pink, sir.' 'Major, I know we have this don't ask/don't tell deal, but you're coming pretty close to telling there, sir.' Yeah, you definitely should have told them."

"Maybe you're right."

"Well, maybe not. Maybe they didn't notice. But if they did, I'm guessing they didn't keep it a secret."

"Shit."

* * *

At about 11:30, the party on the lakeshore started to break up. Our whiskey was gone, but Bobby and I didn't want to leave. This was our last night; we wanted to suck out the marrow. Soon there were only three: Bobby, Chris, and me. As a result of his exuberance, Chris had drunk to excess. He was shit-faced and getting more so by the minute. He offered to share his drink. I took a sniff before I took a sip. It was the 151 proof rum, this time with no mixer. I barely touched it to my lips; it burned going down. Bobby took a bigger sip. He shook his head, like a punch-drunk boxer sniffing smelling salts. Bobby handed the drink back to Chris, and Chris took a gulp.

Chris had been good company throughout the evening. It was fun being around someone for whom all this was brand new. He loved being here, and he loved his buddies from Cleveland. But as time passed and Chris kept sipping, his skills as a conversationalist waned. He made less and less sense and, finally, no sense at all. I was reminded of a line from Blazing Saddles. Chris spoke in authentic frontier gibberish. But—and this is what's remarkable—he knew it. At the end of a long, incoherent monologue in which Chris mixed words and non-words with equal facility, it suddenly dawned on him. He turned and looked at Bobby and me and slurred an announcement: "I'm too drunk to talk."

Well, who could argue with that? For the second time in the same day, a fellow backpacker had spoken the absolute, unvarnished truth. Just as Yahoo was right about some people being smarter than others, Chris was right as rain; he *was* too drunk to talk. Chris stumbled off to his tent. Bobby and I followed to make sure he found the right one. By now, the night had grown cold, the moon had risen. We took one last look at the lake and headed for our own tent. Before falling asleep, I asked Bobby a question.

"Amazing. Reckon how Chris knew he was too drunk to talk?"

Bobby was no help. "I dunno. I'm pretty drunk myself."

The next morning, Bobby and I gathered in the cooking area for breakfast with the early risers from the Cleveland crew. I noticed that one of them was wearing a Boy Scout cap. He said his son was a Boy Scout and he was an assistant leader. This gave me another chance to tell the story of Daddy and his years as a Scout leader, the streak of monthly campouts and all the Eagle Scouts. When more of their group made their way to the cooking area, one of the early birds made me tell them about Daddy again. I loved doing it; I always will.

Chris appeared before long. He was moving slowly, but he was in much better shape than he deserved to be. I told his friends how Chris had ended our night by the lake, and I congratulated him on his powers of observation. I couldn't have done it, I said. I've never known I was too drunk to talk when I was too drunk to talk. Chris accepted my compliment and offered us some cheesy bread. The last bread Bobby and I had eaten was French toast six mornings ago in Columbia Falls. After cleaning up, I walked on the trail toward our tent site. Two of the guys from Cleveland were in the site next to ours and didn't see me. As I walked past, I heard one ask the other, "What was it he said pissed on that flat rock?" I started to answer but decided to let them pick their own pisser.

This was our last day, and we had a tough hike ahead of us. We had only ten miles to cover, but the halfway point, Ptarmigan Tunnel, was half a mile higher than we were. We needed to get going to meet David at Many Glacier by 3:30, our appointed time. But we didn't want to leave. We were acting just like Eric, Melissa, and Chris at Cosley Lake. And the guys from Cleveland were acting just like we had. They would be in the mountains two more nights and had an easy day ahead. They were lounging on the lakeshore, in no hurry to go anywhere or do anything. Bobby wanted to stay with them. They had more than overcome their bad first impression. As we were packing, Bobby was slipping into his standard end-of-the-trip funk.

"It's not fair. The weather's great; these guys are great. But we have to leave, and they get to stay. It's not fair."

"But this is our seventh day, Bobby. It's only their second. And we're out of whiskey."

"They'd share their whiskey with us, you know they would."

"We've gotta go, Bobby."

"I know. I know."

By this point, the Cleveland crew had invited us to join them on their next annual trip, though both the date and destination were unknown. Bobby used the invitation to console himself. "But I tell you what, we ought to go with them next year. They're some great guys."

We put on our packs and walked out to the lakeshore to say goodbye, exchanged email addresses, shook hands, and headed up the trail. Just below the lake, we crossed a suspension bridge over the Belly River for the third and final time. Just as Bobby made it across, we heard a voice behind us on the trail, yelling for us to stop. It was Chris with his camera. Bobby and I posed at the end of the bridge, and we said goodbye again. Chris turned and headed back to the lake; we turned and headed up the trail toward Ptarmigan Tunnel. It was 10:30.

The trail climbed steadily through the forest east of Elizabeth Lake. On one of the switchbacks, we passed through an avalanche chute. It looked fresh; it must have been created the previous winter. The chute bore testimony to the extraordinary power of avalanches, the force generated by a wall of snow and debris speeding down a steep slope. Trees a foot thick had been snapped like matchsticks.

Our ascent continued, but we were strong at the end of a week in the mountains, and my toe was only a minor distraction. Bobby and I agreed the hiking was much easier this year than last. A number of factors contributed, but it was impossible to know what mattered most. The lower altitude obviously made a difference, as did our lighter packs.

"It's been neat," Bobby said, "having people ask our advice about packing, what to take and what to leave behind."

"Yeah. We've come a long way. Nobody was asking you for advice in the Cascades, that's for damn sure."

We stopped at another avalanche chute and looked down at the lake, which made me think of fish.

"Our packs would be even lighter if we didn't have these damn fishing rods."

"You got that right."

"How many fish did you catch this year, Bobby?"

"You know good and damn well how many fish I caught. One frickin fish, just like last year. How many fish did you catch this year, dipshit?"

"One, but mine was bigger than yours. And last year I caught more than you did."

"But nobody's asked you for any fishing advice."

On a curve in the trail, we crossed a beautiful stream only a few feet wide. A water ouzel popped up from under the surface, spotted us, and flew away. We were now even with the south end of the lake, where we had fished the afternoon before. From our perch six hundred feet above the lake, we spotted two fishermen, probably two of our new friends from Cleveland, fishing where we'd fished. We watched for a minute or two to see if they were doing any better than we did. Bobby then spotted something moving in the cove just east of the fishermen. It was huge and hulking; its color was light brown. It waded in the cove with the nonchalance of a creature that is the master of its domain. It could only have been a grizzly, the first one Bobby and I had seen on any of our trips. We looked at the fishermen; they had no idea a grizzly bear was fifty yards from them. A curve in the lakeshore obscured their view. The bear appeared to have no idea either. Only Bobby and I could see the whole thing, but there was nothing we could do. We yelled, but the wind carried our voices away. We watched as the drama played out. The fishermen were lucky. The bear waded in the opposite direction, reached the southeast shore, and disappeared into the woods.

For some reason, I started thinking about the last days of our other trips. I remembered singing on the Pacific Crest Trail in the Cascades. I sang the same song again: "You Never Even Called Me By My Name" by David Allen Coe. When I finished, Bobby and I got into an argument about who wrote the song. Bobby said Steve Goodman wrote it and sent it to Coe, claiming it was the perfect country song, but Coe disputed the claim, pointing out there was nothing in the song about Mama, or trains, or trucks, or prisons, or getting drunk. Goodman answered the critique by writing another verse. I had the roles reversed, with Coe the writer and Goodman the critic. I wasn't sure, but I still proposed a bet, for the second round of beers. It was a no-lose proposition for me. As a result of my rock-skipping, Bobby was already on the hook for the first round. I figured I'd be buying the second no matter what. As it turned out, Bobby and I forgot about both bets by the time we made it back to civilization, and we didn't check to find out who wrote the song. I looked it up later; Bobby was right.

When I stopped on the trail to eat the last of my raisinets, Bobby did the unprecedented; he passed me. For the rest of the steep climb to the tunnel, he stayed in front, making good time. Maybe half a mile before the tunnel, we reached familiar territory. We passed the spot where we'd eaten lunch and turned around when we'd hiked up from Many Glacier five years earlier. As we continued the climb, we came to the first day hikers we'd seen in six days. We were within a few hours of civilization, five or six miles from a restaurant and hotel. We were now among tourists. I came to a realization: The last time we were here, we *were* tourists. But no longer. Now we were backpackers. And we were already snobs about it. We looked down our noses at our former selves.

Underscoring the fact that we were returning to civilization, I recognized someone from having seen him on television when we walked through the tunnel to the south side. It was PGA golfer Stewart Cink, hiking with two women. We exchanged greetings, but I decided to respect his privacy and not tell him I knew who he was. I figured he wasn't here to shake hands with strangers or talk about golf. Bobby and I assumed one of the women was his wife, but we had no idea which one. One was a tall brunette, the other short and blonde. We heard them discussing a plan to go off trail and slide down the snow field above Ptarmigan Lake. The taller one invited me to join them in their adventure. She was gorgeous and had a Southern accent. I was tempted, but the snow field looked steep and dangerous and, unlike them, I had a backpack. I asked her if she would carry my pack. She declined, so I declined. Bobby and I stopped on one of the switchbacks below the tunnel to watch the threesome slide down the snow field. I wondered what Cink's agent would have thought if he were here, watching his client take the risk. But they slid slowly, stopping often, and made it to the bottom without incident. A month after our trip, I learned that the tall brunette was Cink's wife when they appeared together on a commercial during the Ryder Cup.

We were now going downhill, and I returned to my accustomed spot in front. Bobby had been bragging on his walking sticks throughout the trip, and he let me try them. I didn't like them or need them—I'm not built like a stork—and I soon gave them back. We were making great time and considered a side trip when we got to the junction with the trail to Iceberg Lake. We had considered the same side trip when we reached this spot five years earlier with Brian and David. We decided against it again because the four extra miles would make us late getting to Many Glacier. The trail was crowded with day hikers now. At Ptarmigan Creek, a man heard our accents, studied our beards, and asked where we were from and where we'd been. When we told him, he summoned another member of his group, a woman who had moved to Whitefish from Tupelo and knew of Daddy. I told her about our evening at the Tupelo Grille, that nobody there cared that I was from Tupelo. She wasn't surprised; she said it was a restaurant for tourists. We shouldn't have gone, I thought; we're backpackers, not tourists.

We sped on toward the trailhead, passing hikers who didn't have the burden of a pack. We hiked along a south-facing slope that was covered with berry bushes. This looked like prime grizzly habitat, Bobby said. This was where I'd sung in 1997 to ward off the bears. I agreed with Bobby, but I thought surely the bears would be in their day beds during the heat of the afternoon. I later found out I was wrong. Just before getting to the end of the trail, Bobby and I took a water break and talked about coming to the end of our trip. Two years before, we'd hiked out through a horde of black flies. In the Winds, it had been cold and snowing. But this year, we had no incentive to want the trip to end. It was a beautiful, fly-free day. And even after seven days, we didn't want to leave the trail. Part of it was because we felt strong. Our bodies were used to the rhythm of walking. We felt we could go forever. As we descended the last steep slope, I asked Bobby if he thought we could turn around and hike back up to Ptarmigan Tunnel and back down to Elizabeth Lake. "Piece of cake," he answered. We reached the end of the trail at 3:30, exactly when we told David we'd get there. Our friends from Cleveland had taken nine hours to walk this route in the opposite direction the day before. We had covered the same distance in five hours.

We had last seen David three and a half days earlier, when we parted ways in the rain at Stoney Indian Lake. Bobby and I talked about what we would do if he wasn't here to meet us. A hundred things could have happened—a grizzly bear, injury, lightning strike, car trouble—but none of them did. When we walked around to the front of the Swiftcurrent Inn, David was waiting for us in a rocking chair. And, God bless him, he had a six pack of beer on ice waiting with him. The first sip was indescribable.

Before we loaded up and headed out, David told us of a bear experience that far surpassed any of ours. When he arrived at Many Glacier an hour earlier, he decided to hike up the trail a ways, lie in wait, and photograph Bobby and me as we returned to civilization. He walked up from the trailhead a couple of hundred yards, found a good hiding place in the berry bushes, and pulled out his camera. The light wasn't quite right, however, so he moved up the trail thirty feet and found a better spot. Just as he was getting situated, he heard a noise on the trail behind him. He looked back just in time to see a huge grizzly come out of the bushes and cross the trail at the precise point where he'd been hiding two minutes earlier. If he'd still been there, the bear would have tripped over him.

David reacted calmly, he said. He knew better than to run. He raised his camera to shoot. The bear was so big and so close, it more than filled the viewfinder. David had to pull his telephoto lens in to get the whole bear in the picture. After the trip, David emailed the photo to Bobby and me. The picture was a little fuzzy, as if the photographer hadn't been perfectly still. I wouldn't have been either. But the bear was oblivious, in a berry-feeding frenzy. David spotted two nearby hikers armed with pepper spray and took refuge between them. The three watched as the bear moved down the slope, stripping berries as it went. When the grizzly was out of sight, David returned to the Swiftcurrent Inn and the comfort of his rocking chair. Hiding in the bushes to take our picture no longer seemed like such a good idea.

Bobby and I found pay phones and called home to check in. When we both hung up, I asked how things were at his house. He said Stephanie claimed their daughters had behaved perfectly while he was gone, much better than they ever did when he was there. If that were the case, I observed, she should want him to go camping with me. He grinned and said, "Give me a pen so I can write that down."

We loaded the Aries and retraced our route from five years earlier, heading east to Babb, then south to St. Mary, then west on Going to the Sun Road. After two beers, Bobby fell asleep. David was driving and had only one. That left three for me and, by the time we reached Logan Pass, they were gone. We drove past where we'd set out seven days earlier, passing eight or nine mountain goats posing for the tourists. They looked as comfortable and lazy as housecats. We dropped down from the Divide, continued west along McDonald Creek, and left the park at West Glacier. After another half hour, we checked into the Super 8 in Whitefish. I let Bobby go first in the shower. When it was my turn, I had to soap up my legs three times before the water ran clear.

After dressing, we headed for Main Street, which had been lively seven nights earlier. It looked quiet tonight. We picked an Italian place for dinner. This was our last night. It was time to get rowdy, but none of us had the energy. We ate well but drank moderately. After dinner, we walked down the street to the pool hall we'd spotted a week earlier. I was imagining another sweatshirt souvenir. But the bar, which had been full of life when we'd last seen it, was now dead. We were pretty much dead too. With little debate, we decided to head back to the Super 8. In less than five minutes, David later reported, Bobby and I were snoring in unison.

The next morning, we returned to Main Street, had a big breakfast of huckleberry pancakes, and then split up for souvenir shopping. When we reunited, Bobby and I found that we'd noticed the same thing about Whitefish. I was the first to mention it.

"Boy, the women here sure look better than they did in Pinedale."

"Yeah, more teeth too," Bobby added.

Bobby decided we should mail our pepper spray home to ourselves instead of just throwing it away. I couldn't figure out why it was okay for bear spray to fly on a mail flight but not a commercial flight, but evidently it was. While we stood in the post office parking lot and packed the spray and addressed the label, Bobby and I quizzed David about the Izaak Walton. We wanted to know about the mystical place. At first, David was coy. "Interesting" was his one-word description. We pressed the issue. He said the inn formerly served as barracks for railroad workers. When he said it was right by the tracks, Bobby detected an opening.

"Were there trains?"

"Yeah, there were trains."

"At night?"

"Sure."

"Did they wake you up?"

"I don't think so. A few times during the night when I was awake I heard them—there was a switching station or something—but I don't think they woke me up."

When David went in to mail the package, Bobby and I looked at each other.

"Poor guy," I said. "We were sleeping beside Elizabeth Lake while he was not sleeping beside a train station."

Bobby shook his head. "It's just like I always say"—I joined in, and we finished together—"some people are just smarter than others."

We thought back on everything David had missed, all so he could spend the night with the trains: the beauty of the Mokowanis River valley, the magnificence of Cosley Lake, the reunion with the trio from San Francisco, Eric's lakeshore concert, the amusing night with Yahoos, the splendor of Elizabeth Lake, and the evening with our new friends from Cleveland. He'd missed it all. We had told David some of what he'd missed, but the telling, like the pictures, didn't do it justice.

As we were pulling out of the post office parking lot, I decided to remind Bobby of his pre-trip promise to Stephanie. "I don't understand why you're mailing the pepper spray home, Bobby."

"What are you talking about?"

"This is your last trip. You're never going again. You promised, remember?"

"Yeah, that's what I said last year too."

The afternoon before, while we drank our beer at Many Glacier, I'd told David about my toe. He'd seemed unconcerned; his brush with the grizzly undoubtedly seemed more important. Later, at the Super 8, I'd tried to show him my toe. He'd glanced at it nonchalantly and said it was probably broken. When I'd questioned him about whether I should do anything for my probably broken toe, David was equally casual. "Nah. Leave it alone. It'll heal." After we dropped off the Aries and were waiting to board our flight to Kalispell, I looked down at my purple toe. I was wearing my Tevas, the least painful footwear I had. I decided to harass David for his lack of concern. "Yeah, my family was comforted when they found out we were going to have a doctor with us—an ER doc, in fact—and I go and break my toe, and what good is he? He doesn't look at it, he doesn't set it, he doesn't do a damn thing."

David shrugged. "You get what you pay for, I guess. I'll wiggle it for you if you want me to."

Bobby had an idea. "Here's what you should have done. You should have taken Yahoos' tongue depressor, broken it in two, used some of Yahoos' adhesive tape, and made yourself a toe splint. It wouldn't have helped your toe, but it sure would have made Yahoos feel better about bringing all that useless crap."

Bobby and David upgraded to first class for the first leg of our flight home. I was stuck in the back. It was just as well. I borrowed David's legal pad and started writing, wanting to record the details while my memory was fresh. By the time we landed in Minneapolis, I had written about the first half of our trip and Bobby was drunk on the free first-class liquor. We had time for one Sam Adams before we boarded the flight to Memphis. As soon as I took my seat, I started writing again. Thirty minutes before we landed, I got to the end of our trip. My final words were about Bobby's suggestion for the tongue depressor toe splint. I had fifteen pages of single-spaced notes on legal-size paper. My hand ached more than my toe did.

* * *

After getting off the plane, I said goodbye to Bobby and David, and we parted ways. The gate for my flight to Jackson was in one direction, the gate for theirs to Gulfport in the other. I walked along the concourse by myself, thinking about the highlights of the trip. When I thought about Yahoos, I laughed out loud. A woman saw me and stared at me like I was crazy. Maybe I am crazy, I thought, but at least I'm smarter than some people. After all, I didn't carry a cassette player in my backpack, and I didn't skip Cosley and Elizabeth Lakes only to be kept awake by trains. But as I walked along, I thought back on our trips and remembered all the times when I had not been so smart. I didn't carry a cassette player or sleep with trains, but I hauled a fly rod nearly two hundred miles to catch a handful of trout, I pitched a tent right beside a sprinkler head, I pumped gallons of water through a filterless filter, and I broke my toe because I couldn't stand up. I had no business throwing stones at anyone—not at David, not even at Yahoos.

I was about to decide that Yahoo was wrong, that some people aren't smarter than others. Or at least that I'm not. But as I settled into my seat for the flight to Jackson, something dawned on me that restored my self-esteem: I may have done some dumb things on our trips, but taking the trips was anything but dumb. Our second trip to Glacier had proven the point again. My decision to travel with Bobby, made on the spur of the moment six years earlier, was one of the wisest decisions I'd ever made.

About the Author

Brooks Eason grew up in Tupelo, Mississippi, where he learned to love camping and hiking from his father, Paul Eason, an extraordinary man who served as a Boy Scout leader for sixty years and whose troop has gone camping every month since August 1951.

When Brooks met Bobby Ariatti in 1993, neither of them had ever taken a hiking trip to the mountains of the American West. They took their first trip—to Yosemite National Park—in September 1996, and they have explored the mountains together on annual trips since then. *Travels with Bobby* is the story of their first six trips.

Brooks is a lawyer in Jackson, Mississippi, where he's teaching his grandchildren to love camping and the outdoors. His wife Carrie enjoys being outside but prefers to sleep inside.